Rabbi Jesus

Rabbi Jesus

AN INTIMATE BIOGRAPHY

Bruce Chilton

IMAGE BOOKS
DOUBLEDAY
A PEEKAMOOSE BOOK
New York London Toronto Sydney Auckland

AN IMAGE BOOK
PUBLISHED BY DOUBLEDAY
a division of Random House, Inc.
1540 Broadway, New York, New York 10036

IMAGE, DOUBLEDAY, and the portrayal of a deer drinking from a stream
are trademarks of Doubleday, a division of Random House, Inc.

Book design by Jennifer Ann Daddio

The Library of Congress has cataloged the hardcover edition as follows:

Chilton, Bruce.
Rabbi Jesus: an intimate biography / by Bruce Chilton.—1st ed.
p.   cm.
Includes bibliographical references and index.
1. Jesus Christ—Jewishness. I. Title.
BT590.J8.C45 2000
232.9'01—dc21
[B]   00-031548

ISBN 0-385-49793-8

PRINTED IN THE UNITED STATES OF AMERICA

First Image Books Edition: April 2002
12   14   16   18   20   19   17   15   13   11

To My Teachers

Contents

List of Illustrations

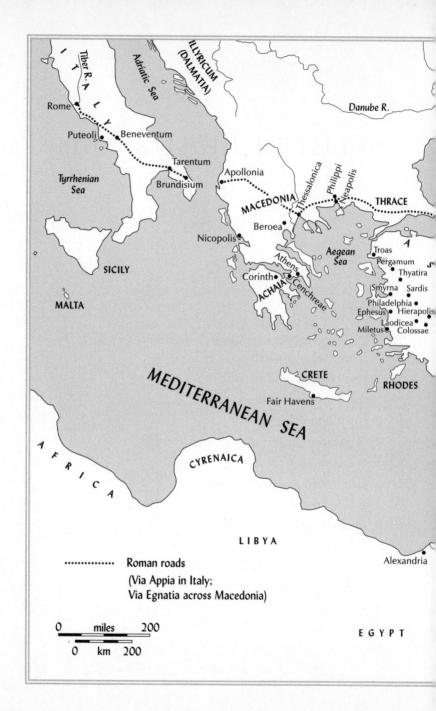

THE MEDITERRANEAN BASIN IN THE

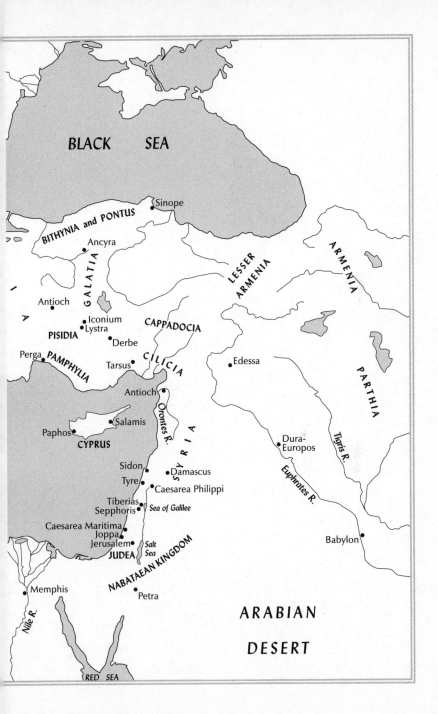

FIRST CENTURY, FROM ITALY TO PARTHIA

Timeline

Timeline

323	Following Alexander's death, Israel falls under the control of the Ptolemies, his dynastic successors in Egypt
200	The Seleucids, the Mesopotamian competitors of the Ptolemies, exercise hegemony over Israel
167	"The abomination of desolation:" the Seleucid king Antiochus IV, devotes worship to Zeus in the Temple and commands swine to be offered on the altar
164	Judas Maccabeus restores the cult of Yahweh in the Temple and establishes the most successful dynasty in the history of Israel since the destruction of the Temple, nationally allied with the Romans in 161
134–104	John Hyrcanus, both ruler and high priest, conquers the largest territory ever governed by an Israelite monarch
63	In the midst of internecine strife among the Maccabees, Pompey claims Jerusalem for Rome and personally enters the Temple
47	Julius Caesar arranges for the governance of what becomes Syria Palaestina, the Philistine coast of Syria, including Israel, prior to his death in 44
40–4	The reign of Herod the Great as a client king of Rome
31	The empire of Augustus becomes secure (although Octavian did not accept the title "Augustus" until 16 January 27)
4	The death of Herod results in the division of his kingdom: his son Archelaus takes Judea, Herod Antipas inherits Galilee and Perea; Herod Philip rules Trachonitis

Timeline

62	The death of James by stoning in Jerusalem, at the instigation of the high priest
64	The death of Paul and Peter in Rome
70–73	The burning of the Temple by the Roman troops under Titus; the composition of Mark's Gospel in Rome; the end of the revolt against Rome in Palestine
75	Josephus publishes his *Jewish War*
80	The composition of Matthew's Gospel, in Damascus
90	The composition of Luke's Gospel, in Antioch
93	Josephus publishes his *Antiquities of the Jews*
100	The composition of John's Gospel, in Ephesus

These datings fall well within the parameters of scholarly discussion. They inevitably involve estimation. Ancient chronologies dated events by the reigns of rulers, and coordinating these different schemes is problematic. Calendars did not even agree on the season when a new year began. So we can think of important, public events as being "circa" a given date. When we attempt to place figures whom ancient historians considered marginal—such as John the Baptist and Jesus—the degree of inference rises.

Foreword

This book completes a journey that began in 1967 when I was just shy of eighteen years old and traveling in the former Yugoslavia. One oppressively hot day, wandering around the seaside town of Dubrovnik, I ducked into the dark confines of a medieval church. It was cool inside and very still. I'm not sure why, but I knew I was completely alone. I smelled the faint residue of incense, the musty aroma of damp stone. My steps echoed as I walked down the aisle between worn wooden pews, drawn to a frieze behind the altar depicting Christ on the cross. It was a typically medieval portrait; none of the gory details had been spared. The figure's head in bluish stone was askew, lolling. Spikes were driven through palms and blood ran down the wrists and arms. The feet had been turned sideways and nailed through the ankles. The bent knees were contorted and looked particularly vulnerable, helpless. The figure was slumped, the body twisted and broken. I had a momentary but searing impression of agony; I was moved by the figure's fragility in the face of a vast and violent universe, and I felt the crushing pain of our common mortality. But paradoxically, deep inside myself, I also felt the answering reverberations of something beyond pain, beyond despair. I turned and walked slowly out of the church and into the sunlight on cobbled streets.

I was a kid, and the illumination was fleeting. I had better things to do than dwell on suffering and death. I bought a bottle of beer from a vendor near the harbor and sat drinking it, looking out over the blue Adriatic. Then I took a swim. My spiritual quest to that point had involved halfhearted attempts at Buddhist meditation. But the frieze and what it invoked germinated inside me. I couldn't shake it, and the Dubrovnik experience eventually led me to seek ordination.

Later I entered seminary and began to learn the techniques of biblical criticism. I was especially excited by how the study of ancient languages could yield insights into the original meanings of the texts, and I was drawn to academic research when I found that few scholars had examined the ancient literature of Judaism in Aramaic, the common language of the Jewish people in the first century that Jesus spoke. The Targums, paraphrases of the Hebrew Bible rendered in Aramaic, especially fascinated me. The Targums were part of the "Torah on the lips," the oral version of Scripture that Jesus worked from, and they were different in important ways from the Hebrew texts. I sensed they were key to understanding what Jesus believed and taught. I knew that the priesthood would be a futile pursuit for me unless it was based upon the best possible knowledge about Jesus and the origins of the Christian faith. How could the Church fail to pursue the cultural and social background of Jesus? How could we as priests fail to ask what Jesus' life had been like and how he had come to develop his extraordinary vision of God?

So alongside the priesthood I pursued a career as a scholar and teacher, learning Greek, Hebrew, and Latin (the stock in trade of New Testament scholarship), Aramaic to study the Targums, Coptic to study Gnostic texts, and Syriac—a language closely related to Aramaic—to explore early Christian sources like the Old Syriac Gospels. Instructed by these ancient literatures and no longer limited to what the Greek Gospels said, I began to understand Jesus on his own terms rather than in the categories of conventional scholarship and theology. I was stunned to discover that not only the inspiration behind Jesus' teachings, but also its actual content—point by point—was drawn directly from Jewish sources. A portrait of Jesus as an inspired rabbi with an exclusively Jewish agenda began to emerge. I started to see a completely new meaning in baptism, anointing the sick, the Lord's Prayer, the Eucharist, and resurrection. It became clear to me that everything Jesus did was as a Jew, for Jews, and about Jews.

I became part of the reevaluation of Jesus and Judaism. The basic fact that Jesus was Jewish is now fairly well established within scholarship and popular writing. The previous work of W. D. Davies, Asher Finkel, and Samuel Sandmel is a highly regarded part of the critical canon. By placing Jesus in his Jewish context they helped to overturn the once fashionable notion that the New Testament illuminated the contours of early Christian faith in Jesus, but taught us nothing important about the man himself.

Thanks to these and other penetrating studies, and a wealth of literary and archeological evidence that has accumulated since World War II, Jesus has emerged today as a truly historical figure. New evidence ranges from the discovery of the Dead Sea Scrolls and fourth-century Gnostic gospels to the excavations of the Temple of Jerusalem, the tomb of the high priest Caiaphas, the city of Sepphoris, and a number of Galilean settlements, including Nazareth and Capernaum. These discoveries have added startling detail and depth to our understanding of religious culture at the dawn of the Common Era and shed bold new light on the life and character of Jesus.

A portrait of Jesus has emerged both in scholarship and popular literature from the discussion these finds have ignited. He becomes a witty philosopher, a Mediterranean peasant-savant descended from Greco-Roman heritage whose Judaism is an incidental fact of his ethnic background. This Jesus is fashionably separated from the traditional forms of religions against which intellectuals are perennially on their guard. The portrayal that has frequently emerged from "The Jesus Seminar" is a case in point: it has explored intriguing possibilities and sparked much useful controversy and debate, yet it fails to grapple with the complex issue of Jesus' own religious orientation as a Jew. In that regard, the "historical"

Jesus who has emerged in recent years is as flawed as the venerated images of Christ from Renaissance art or glowing hagiographies by sectarian theologians.

For the past decade, I have felt that my colleagues in scholarship were isolating and analyzing the pieces of Jesus' life, but that no one was putting them together into a coherent whole. That is what I attempt to do in this book.

Rabbi Jesus offers the first comprehensive, critical biography of Jesus to date. I have been wrestling with fundamental questions about Jesus still largely unanswered, even while a growing consensus of scholarship has demolished the secularist myth that Jesus was a figment of faith. Why do the Gospels persistently refer to him as a rabbi? What did it mean to be a rabbi in the Judaism of the first century C.E.? Was Jesus typical of the rabbis of his time, or a maverick? Where did he get his ideas? How did he develop his teachings? How much can we unravel of his motives, the decisions he made, the choices he faced?

Recent excavations in Nazareth, Bethlehem, and Gush Halav give us a clear picture of the Galilean environment in which Jesus was born and raised. Jewish peasants vigilantly shielded themselves from the incursions of Hellenistic culture; they were a beleaguered people under the thumb of Rome who cherished their rich Judaic customs and traditions. For the most part, like Jesus, they were illiterate, and oral traditions such as the Targums represent were the foundation of their faith. These folk traditions illuminate Jesus' Judaic orientation and the vocabulary in which his teachings were framed. When we come to grips with the kind of Jew Jesus was, the arc of his life comes into focus for the first time.

The Jesus of scholarship has been doggedly two-dimensional; attention in book after book has been limited to the last three years of his public ministry, after his religious ideas had fully matured. This is because the Synoptic Gospels (Matthew, Mark, and Luke), the primary sources of New Testament scholarship, compressed the events of Jesus' life into a short period of time in order to make the story easy for new converts to assimilate. Even the best scholarship has hopelessly confused the abbreviated structure of the Gospels with the actual chronology of Jesus' life. Moreover, the Gospels pin the death of Jesus in their dramatic presentation for Greco-Romans on "the Jews," not the Roman government. That is historically inaccurate, but the popular acceptance of that error has fueled the fallacious belief that Jesus rejected Judaism and wanted to found a new religion. Nothing could be further from the truth.

Jesus' biography continues to be shrouded in mystery because the huge body of New Testament scholarship has been largely deaf to Judaism, while Jewish scholars regard Jesus as a forbidden topic, and with few exceptions refuse to examine him. As a non-Jew—and a priest, at that—I will doubtless make both Jews and Christians apprehensive with *Rabbi Jesus*. So inculcated are the taboos of our culture, so visceral the abyss between Judaism and Christianity, that I sometimes feel as if I am cross-dressing: transgressing basic categories that define who we are and how we differentiate ourselves in the world. But my hope is that *Rabbi Jesus* can point the way across the gulf of artificial ideologies and misguided animus that has long divided Jews and Christians (and different sects within Christianity) from one another.

Inference and logical reconstruction are, of course, necessary in order to explain Jesus' development and imagine how his life unfolded. Surmise is a stern taskmaster. I do not take any source that refers to Jesus, in the New Testament or elsewhere, at face value. I persist in asking: how did Jesus act, what did he say, to produce the results he did within the Judaism of his time? I do not read *from* the texts, I read *behind* them, and that means (for reasons that are explained as we move through Jesus' life) that the order of the Gospels as well as what they say often has to be contradicted, sometimes radically. Each position I take is a conscious choice among scholarly options, each the result of years of discussion with my students, and the rich debate I have enjoyed with hundreds of scholars, theologians, and lay people in different parts of the world interested in the fields of New Testament and ancient Judaism.

This book synthesizes my work as researcher and priest, a scholar who has pursued objective evidence with an eye on faith. I hope that by reconstructing Rabbi Jesus' life, I can help change our culture's perception of itself, because Jesus is a point of reference as we define who we are: Jew or Christian, believer or skeptic, scholar or seeker. My own study has been vastly enriched by the work of my predecessors and my contemporaries in scholarship; for each chapter, readers interested in digging deeper will find notes to guide them at the close of the book. Yet however much I have disagreed with the arguments of critics and the conventions of belief, my purpose in *Rabbi Jesus* is not to offend anyone, but to search through the complexities of evidence and arguments in order to find the core from which Christian faith was generated. The scenes that unfold in this book are set in the environment of Galilee and Judea and in the world of Judaism. Archaeology and scholarship have illuminated those contexts in ways that were scarcely conceivable a generation ago. Some readers have had problems with my speaking of specific deeds, words, thoughts, and emotions in those settings. Of course, no source gives us a literal record: what Jesus did and said at any particular time will always be a matter of inference. But scholarship is clear on issues such as how he dressed, what he would have eaten, heard, seen, and smelled as he traveled through Galilee and Judea. That impulse has guided my life both as a scholar and a believer who has been shaped by the vision of God that Jesus conveyed.

Rabbi Jesus

ONE

———— ✿ ————

A *Mamzer*
from Nazareth

Jesus' life in Judaism opened with his *berith,* the ritual of circumcision mandated by the Torah for every male child of Israel.[1] As required in the book of Genesis (17:9–14), he was eight days old when the foreskin of his penis was cut. In the small, poor village where Jesus was born, communal rituals often occurred in the open village center, near the wine press, olive vats, and pottery kiln. Circumcision, however, especially during cold weather, required shelter to help ward off the infant's shock, which is why I think Jesus' *berith* would have taken place in his family's courtyard.

Guests gathered for the ceremony, probably in the early morning, when blood clots more easily. *"Shelama!"* they greeted each other. *Shelama* is the Aramaic equivalent of *shalom,* "peace," in Hebrew. Aramaic, not Hebrew, was the language most commonly used by the Jews of Galilee, Judea, and Syria at the dawn of the Common Era. Standing in relation to Hebrew something like Italian does to French, Aramaic is a Semitic tongue, one of

---

1. Circumcision was originally called "cutting off" (*mulah*; Exodus 4:26) and later "covenant of cutting off." The link to the covenant (the *berith* with Abraham in Genesis 17:9–14) lies at the foundation of the rite, so the designation *berith* (or *beris* in the pronunciation of Eastern Europe) best conveys its meaning.

the world's oldest continuously spoken languages. Once as widespread in the Near East as Arabic is today, it is now nearly extinct,[2] except as kept alive by a few native speakers in Iran, Iraq, Syria, Turkey, and Azerbaijan.

The *shelama* greeting in the Galileans' own tongue celebrated Jewish survival in a land under foreign dominance by reminding Jews of God's enduring covenant with Abraham—the very covenant put into practice in Jesus' circumcision. Even his name in Aramaic, *Yeshua*, conjured up the memory of Joshua, the heroic successor of Moses. Those gathered in the little village must have been keenly aware that they were a tiny, powerless group in an occupied province of the Roman Empire whose Jewish identity was under siege.

Galilean Jews were indentured but not defeated. They burned with pride in a living memory of themselves as the people called Israel, descended from the patriarch Jacob, grandson of Abraham. They had tilled this soil and called this land theirs for more than a thousand years, fighting war after war, enduring defeat, genocide, and exile at the hands of foreigners, later suffering the prejudice and dominance of the wealthier Jews of Judea to the south. Their identity as Jews was bound up in the land and the covenant that made the land theirs. The covenant was their last defense against Rome, a cultural fortress that stood long after the political and military institutions of Israel had failed.

Their understanding of the covenant came not from the written Torah and Prophets in Hebrew, which few could read, but from their oral *targum* (Aramaic for "translation"). A *targum* was more than a verbatim translation of the Hebrew text: whole paragraphs were added and long sections loosely paraphrased by the *meturgeman*, a "translator" who handed on the local tradition of rendering Scripture. (Just as a local rabbi designed ethical norms for living the Torah, a *meturgeman* memorized and recited the

---

2. Out of historical interest, and because Aramaic is likely to cease to be spoken soon, a project sponsored by the National Endowment for the Humanities to produce a *Comprehensive Aramaic Lexicon* has been organized since 1985 out of Hebrew Union College and Johns Hopkins University. I have been a member of that project since its inception, and prepared and analyzed the Aramaic text of the Targum of Isaiah for its database.

oral Scripture). These renderings vivified the Torah and the Prophets in a visionary language detailing Israel's coming supremacy over other nations and emphasizing the promises God had made to an oppressed, indentured people. One day, these Scriptural renderings promised, God's Kingdom (*Malkhuta*) would supersede every other form of rule. That was the fervent hope of the Galilean Jews who filled the courtyard to witness Jesus' circumcision; the cutting of the infant's foreskin brought them one small step closer to the Kingdom where God would rule, not Rome. God himself would reestablish the glory of Israel and vindicate the chosen people.

Mary and Joseph were seeking their own vindication as they held the infant ready to have the covenant with Israel marked in his flesh. Jesus had been conceived before they were married, and doubts about his paternity were the result: "His mother Miriam was contracted in marriage to Yosef; before they were together she was found pregnant from holy spirit" (Matthew 1:18, in my own translation). His parents must have hoped the circumcision would reduce the stigma of his birth.

Controversy about whether God, Joseph, or some other man impregnated Mary has been intense and long-standing. Churches have viewed departure from established doctrine in these matters as heresy, and the penalties for such heresy have sometimes been extreme and violent. Even today, there are instances of Catholic and Protestant clergy being silenced or excommunicated for denying Mary's virginity, even in the Anglican church of which I am a priest. Perhaps that is why scholarship has shied away from resolving crucial questions of fact about the nativity.[3] Al-

---

3. Raymond E. Brown, a noted Catholic authority, produced a massive study on the stories of Jesus' nativity, weighing and assessing scholarly opinion. But he came to no conclusion concerning the actual events. See *The Birth of the Messiah. A Commentary on the Infancy Narratives in the Gospels of Matthew and Luke* (New York: Doubleday, 1993). Brown concludes that "the *scientifically controllable* biblical evidence leaves the question of the historicity of the virginal conception unresolved" (p. 527). Because we are not in a position to verify any of the biological facts, I do not see how it is reasonable to expect that kind of certainty. The issue is rather: What about Jesus' birth generated the divergent understandings of it in Christian and Jewish literature?

though we can never recover all the details of Jesus' birth, I do think it is possible to construct a credible overall picture.

The charge that he was illicitly conceived plagued Jesus all his life. Even far from his home, during disputes in Jerusalem after he had become a famous teacher, Jesus was mocked for being born as the result of "fornication" (John 8:41). The people of his own village called him "Mary's son," not Joseph's (Mark 6:3). Scholarship should explain both why Jesus was insulted for his allegedly irregular birth *and* why the legend developed that he was born of a virgin. By examining the ancient Jewish commitment to the maintenance of family lineage—which was the cultural context of Jesus' birth—we can explain the charge of illicit conception and discover one of the most profound influences on Jesus' personal development.

Miriam, Mary as we now know her, was some thirteen years old—the age Jewish maidens of that time married—when Jesus' father, the widower Joseph, came to her village of Nazareth, in all likelihood to repair the house of her parents. Joseph was a journeyman from nearby Bethlehem, a roofer, stonemason, and rough carpenter.[4] It makes sense that he met Mary in the early spring. Although heavy rains made travel difficult then, he could ply his trade before he was needed at home to tend his fields of wheat and barley. Legend—bowing to the imperial Roman feast of *Sol Invictus*, the invincible sun, which was widely celebrated during the third century C.E.—has Jesus born on December 25. But reckoned from his parents' likely time of meeting, his birth was earlier, probably in the late autumn.

The attraction between Joseph and Mary must have been immediate; they broke with custom and slept together soon after meeting and

4. Joseph's trade as a journeyman (a *tekton*, not a carpenter) is attested in the New Testament, because Jesus himself became known as a journeyman (see Matthew 13:55; Mark 6:3). Joseph's first marriage has been recognized from the fourth century, by a theologian and historian named Epiphanius; see Richard Bauckham, "The Brothers and Sisters of Jesus: An Epiphanian Response to John P. Meier," *Catholic Biblical Quarterly* 56 (1994) 686–700.

well before their marriage was publicly recognized. Mary's family had agreed to a contract of marriage with Joseph, but the couple was not yet living together when her pregnancy became obvious. The wording of the New Testament itself, although written many years after the events and richly laced with legends concerning Jesus' birth, attests to this simple fact in Matthew 1:18: before they resided together Mary was obviously pregnant.

That precise statement in Matthew's Gospel explains why, over time, Jesus was considered to be born of fornication by some and the product of a miraculous birth by others. The early pregnancy touched off vicious rumors in Mary's village of Nazareth: perhaps Joseph was not really the child's father. So, for the birth, Joseph had brought Mary to Bethlehem of Galilee, where he had lived with his first wife, to shield her from Nazareth's wagging tongues.

Christmas cards, of course, make Bethlehem of Judea (near Jerusalem) the place of Jesus' birth, instead of the far more logical Bethlehem of Galilee. That is because Matthew's Gospel (2:1–6), written around the year 80 C.E. in Syrian Damascus, relates the nativity to a prediction in the book of the prophet Micah (5:2) regarding the coming of the Messiah from Judean Bethlehem. Matthew fills in details of Jesus' birth by declaring that the events "fulfilled" texts from the Scriptures of Israel. Another example of Messianic fulfillment is the biblical text "Look, a maiden shall conceive," culled from the book of Isaiah (7:14) and applied by Matthew to Mary's conception of Jesus before she was actually living with Joseph (Matthew 1:22–23).

Christians later used Matthew to support their claim that Mary was a biological virgin at the time of Jesus' birth. In one influential text, the Protoevangelium of James (19–20), an assisting midwife, Salome, reaches into Mary's vagina after Jesus' birth and feels Mary's intact hymen. Generations of scholars have been frustrated by the way such legends have clouded how their students and the general public read the New Testament. (A recent study published by the Scripps Howard News Service and the E. W. Scripps School of Journalism at Ohio University found that

7

a staggering 62 percent of Americans believe in the virgin birth.) In their frustration, many professors have dismissed Matthew's version of the nativity as mere legend, and have rejected its historical value.

I can understand my colleagues' frustration—but Matthew's Gospel is not to blame for the embellishments that came after it. The famous text in Greek, "a maiden *(parthenos)* shall conceive," became "a *virgin* shall conceive" when Matthew was translated into Latin during the second century, and the change of a word fed the development of the legend of Jesus' miraculous birth. Both *almah* in Isaiah's Hebrew and *parthenos* in Matthew's Greek (and come to that, even the Latin *virgo*) refer to a "maiden" rather than a biological "virgin."

Matthew accurately presented some details of Jesus' birth, although they have been clouded by polemics. Two persistent strands emerged from Matthew in ancient scholarship: Mary was either Christianity's immaculate virgin or the Talmud's common whore who had slept with a Roman soldier (in the Babylonian Talmud, see Sanhedrin 67a). Rather than take sides in this stark controversy, modern scholarship has left the circumstances of Jesus' birth in a haze of doubt. In addition, because they have distrusted Matthew's nativity, many scholars have ruled out Bethlehem as Jesus' birthplace. Recent discoveries show that is a mistake.

Bethlehem in Hebrew means "house of bread," a common name for settlements with mills capable of producing fine flour, rather than the coarse grade most Israelites used for their daily needs. In 1975, amid the musty, damp, and badly lit back shelves of the University Library in Cambridge, I first learned of a Galilean Bethlehem, near Nazareth, from an obscure study of the Talmud published during the nineteenth century. I was surprised at the dearth of discussion of this place in New Testament studies as the possible site of Jesus' birth, especially since a northern Bethlehem is mentioned in the Hebrew Bible (Joshua 19:15).

Conscious of how easily a new idea can be rejected, I was intrigued but wary. The Talmud was composed centuries after Jesus lived and the book of Joshua centuries beforehand, so one cannot assume they accurately reflect Galilee's geography in his time. I appended my findings to my Ph.D. thesis (although some of my professors were bemused that I used the Talmud to understand the Gospels) and let the matter rest. Now, however, archeological excavations show that Bethlehem in Galilee is a first-century site just seven miles from Nazareth, so my former reserve can be put aside. There is good reason to surmise that the Bethlehem to which Matthew refers was in Galilee.

We can envisage Jesus' *berith* on the basis of the excavations of Bethlehem and Nazareth, together with historical information from ancient sources such as the Mishnah (composed during the second century C.E., but incorporating earlier oral sources). The weather at that time of year in Galilee was probably cool and clear, and guests wore rough woolen cloaks over their basic flax tunics against the chill. The landscape around Bethlehem was similar to Nazareth's, although somewhat rockier. Terraced fields climbed up the hillsides. There were orchards of almonds, pomegranates, and dates, and trellised vineyards of red grapes that made a ruddy new wine at harvest time—a sweet, heady drink that would have been mixed with oil to dress Jesus' wound, dribbled into his mouth to cut his pain, and served to guests after the ceremony.

Mary handed her firstborn to Joseph. The ritual performance of *berith* was a male preserve. The couple shared one of the two or three small mud and stone houses, with dirt floors and low wooden beds, that surrounded a large, central courtyard. Joseph carried Jesus into the courtyard, reenacting Abraham's willingness to circumcise Isaac on the eighth day and even, if necessary, to sacrifice his son (see Genesis 21:4; 22:1–18).

A village dignitary would have pulled Jesus' flesh tight and cut quickly, then carried the unclean foreskin away on a broken pottery shard and disposed of it in an abandoned spot outside the village. Circumcision was performed by a respected and physically competent elder. He had to cut accurately, tear the foreskin, suck the wound clean (as the Mishnah prescribes in Shabbath 19:2), and apply a dressing of wine and olive oil with balm (tapped from a terebinth tree) and cumin. The procedure had not yet been assigned to a professional *mohel,* or circumciser, as in later Rabbinic tradition.

The privilege of circumcising made the elder who touched the foreskin unclean. (Foreskin was a source of contagious impurity for the various peoples, Semitic and not, who practiced circumcision.) Rather than join the celebration after the cutting, the dignitary ritually bathed to wash away the uncleanness, and removed himself temporarily from the community.

Blood of childbirth, blood of *berith,* blood of animal sacrifice, blood of the ancestral convenant made a Jew a Jew. Blood was the most holy thing in Israel's system of purity. It was life itself, coursing in their veins as alive, mysterious, and potent as the streams that flowed from the mountains of Galilee or the wind that rushed over the fields and villages at night. Galilean Jews were not only connected to the divine in their minds, they were bound by blood to God. The ritual bleeding of an animal prior to con-suming it, ritually causing a male infant to bleed at his *berith,* the ritual of secluding women after childbirth and menstruation—all reflect the root wisdom that blood belongs to God alone (see Leviticus 17:10–11).

Moses had commanded Israel in God's name to eat no animal's blood; blood was either to be sacrificed to God in the Temple in Jerusalem or poured into the ground (Deuteronomy 12:23–27). Blood was forbidden to Israelites because it was *too* holy, not because it was inherently impure in the way a foreskin was. In ancient Judaism, blood and the parts of beasts to be offered in sacrifice are forbidden because they belong to the divine alone, not to human beings. But other things, impure beasts and carcasses, are not fit for consumption or contact (as in the case of fore-skins), whether human (Israelite) or divine. The laws of cleanness in Leviticus (chapters 11–26) were Israel's means of producing sacrifices that were acceptable to God, apart from which the land itself could not be retained. Leviticus warns that the former inhabitants of the land had failed to keep the rules of purity and *for that reason* were expelled; Israel might suffer the same fate (Leviticus 18:24–30). The land, in Leviticus, is not for Israel; Israel is for the service of God in his land.

The elders who joined in the ceremony must have been inspired by their conviction that such rituals were necessary for the survival and prosperity of Israel. Jesus' circumcision represented the endurance of the people of God. Each elder had a role in this perpetuation, but only one of them, descended from the tribe of Levi, was authorized by Scripture to give the infant the priestly blessing (Numbers 6:24–26): "The Lord bless you and keep you, the Lord make his face shine upon you and be gracious to you, the Lord lift up his face to you, and give you peace."

Generous feasts followed major family and community celebrations such as the *berith*. Guests at Jesus' feast would have brought their own cups of wood, clay, or carved limestone. There were no plates, forks, or dinner knives. Excavations of dwellings in rural Galilee indicate that households lived minimally, in a cooperative fashion. Jesus' followers in Jerusalem carried on this communal ethos after the resurrection, when they vigorously—sometimes violently—insisted that all their wealth had to be collective (see Acts 4:32–5:11).

Lamb or goat butchered for the feast was sliced on a spit and served by hand on round, flat bread. The lamb's slaughter the previous morning had perhaps been performed with the same sacrificial flint that was used for the circumcision. The bread had been baked from coarse flour ground in the mill that stood in one corner of the courtyard, near the cistern for catching rainwater and the stone and pottery vessels for carrying water for drinking, cooking, and ritual washing. Leeks, lentils, and onions were boiled in rough ceramic cooking pots that sat in the coals of the fire pit. Children were served a stew of small pieces of meat and vegetables. Those over forty, their teeth no longer reliable and, in many cases, absent, ate from that pot, too. A full set of teeth was considered a mark of beauty, even at a young age (see Song of Songs 4:2; 6:6); the study of skeletal remains, many of them toothless, shows why. Except for the ceremonial cutting of slices of meat for respected elders, the heart of the meal was sharing this rich stew, which was ladled up and served on bread.

Mary herself did not cook and was forbidden to serve her guests. Leviticus provided that for forty days after delivering a male child, the mother was freed from household work. For daughters, the term of a mother's seclusion was eighty days, since the female child was herself a potential bearer of children and, therefore, a bearer of blood (Leviticus 12:1–5). Each woman in her childbirth and in her periodic bleeding bore what was holy within her; and women bore this blood by their very identity, not by choice. The seclusion of women in ancient Judaism was not a punishment or a devaluation of who they were: it was rather recognition that they were the only human source of divinely bestowed life.

This seclusion due to the impurity of giving birth provided Mary with the greatest luxury she would ever know. Not since her early childhood had she enjoyed so much leisure. Blood made her unsuitable for contact with others in Israel and exempted her from working in the fields and the ceaseless round of chores that filled her days: cooking, milling grain, cleaning house, oiling vessels of wood and stone and metal to clean and preserve them, mending and washing garments, caring for children.

The moment when the flint cut Jesus' foreskin must have been particularly poignant to Mary. She probably knew her son would always be considered a *mamzer,* an Israelite of suspect paternity. Such men and women lived in a caste apart, unable to marry within the established bloodlines of Israel, and so were often excluded from the mainstream of religious life. Although Mary may have been teased and shunned because of her promiscuity, she knew that Jesus' circumcision assured him a place in Israel: the bond of blood united all Jews, even those of the *mamzer* caste.[5]

It is vitally important for us to understand the distinction between a *mamzer* and a "bastard" or "mongrel," which is how the term is usually

---

5. At a later time, and in the idiom of song and heavenly vision, Luke's Gospel portrays the angel Gabriel coming to Mary, and assuring her that what was conceived in her was to be called "God's son" (Luke 1:35). The many twists and turns in Jesus' life and Mary's demonstrate that her assurance was not anything like as complete or categorical as Luke suggests (see the entire psalm attributed to Mary in Luke 1:46–55). That is not surprising, since that Gospel is written the better part of ninety years after these events and for a different culture with a different language. But Mary's feeling at the *berith* of her own first-born son was for her as dramatic as Gabriel's visitation is in Luke. It was as if God were vindicating Jesus, whatever the circumstances of his birth.

translated by scholars. Jesus was not illegitimate in the modern sense of the word (i.e., a child born out of wedlock). The term *mamzer* refers specifically to a child born of a prohibited sexual union, such as incest (see Mishnah Yebamot 4:13). The fundamental issue was not sex before marriage (which was broadly tolerated) but sex with the wrong person. An unmarried woman impregnated by a man outside her own community was in an invidious position, suspected of illicit intercourse.

Unless she could bring witnesses to show she had been in the company of a licit father, it was assumed she had been made pregnant by a *mamzer* or another prohibited person, so that her child was a *mamzer* (Mishnah Ketubot 1:8–9). Mary's sexual relations with Joseph had not been prohibited, but given that Joseph had lived in Bethlehem and she in Nazareth when she became pregnant, it was virtually impossible for her to prove that he was the father. In the absence of proof, Jesus was considered a *mamzer*, what the Mishnah at a slightly later period calls a *shetuqi*, or "silenced one" (Qiddushin 4:1–2; see also Qiddushin 70a in the Talmud), without a voice in the public congregations that regulated the social, political, and religious life of Israel (Deuteronomy 23:2).

Scholars have overlooked the fact that the conditions of Jesus' conception as Matthew refers to them made him a *mamzer*, no matter what his actual paternity was. Western cultural preoccupation with sex before marriage has caused scholarship to convert the issue of Jesus' status in Israel into the anachronistic question of his "legitimacy," and thus to ignore one of the most powerful influences on his development. On any theory of his birth, he belonged to the caste of the *mamzer* or "silenced one." From the beginning of his life Jesus negotiated the treacherous terrain between belonging to the people of God and ostracism in his own community.

The feast celebrating Jesus' *berith* would have gone on until well past sundown, but gradually the guests left, and the family retired into the house. Before the winter rains came, Joseph would have returned his Bethlehem holdings to his first wife's parents: the land outside the village

and the courtyard complex that had been her dowry. In ancient rural Israel (indeed, in the Middle East as a whole), husband and wife married
by exchanging the resources of their two families. The woman brought
her house, domestic skills, and family fields. The man brought his farm-
ing skills and sometimes a trade, as well as his descent as an Israelite.[6]
The return of land upon remarriage was customary, as we see from ancient manuscripts that were found near Qumran, at a place called
Murabbaat.

A Galilean Jew had scant personal possessions. Joseph collected his
clothing and tools and left the fields he had tilled and the orchards and
vineyards he had tended. He walked from Bethlehem to Nazareth with
his children from his first marriage, James and Joses. The newborn son
rode comfortably against his fourteen-year-old mother's breast, swaddled
and tied in a wide sling around her neck. Joseph must have felt reluctant
to return to Nazareth, where embarrassing rumors about Jesus' paternity
were rife. But there was no practical alternative.

It is hard to exaggerate the isolation and unease the boy would have
felt growing up as a *mamzer* in Nazareth. *Berith* or no *berith*, he would always be considered a child of doubtful fatherhood—just what occupied
Israel could not abide. Few in Nazareth could read, but everyone knew
what Scripture said in their local *targum:* "No *mamzer* shall enter the
congregation of the Lord" (Deuteronomy 23:3). A *mamzer* was, in effect,
an untouchable—a status that continued for ten generations, as that
same passage goes on to say. Uncertain ethnic paternity was intolerable

---

6. The wealthier the families involved in a marriage, the greater the probability—especially in an urban environment—that the woman would join her husband in *his* house,
and bring a dowry of movable riches or money. But in situations in which wealth was
what you lived in, a man would indeed "leave his father and his mother and cleave to his
wife" (see Genesis 2:24). During the second century and subsequently, Jews were de-
prived of lands on a large scale, and that disrupted the custom of exchanging land and
heritage in marriage. Military actions and pogroms over time also separated married couples and made the whole question of establishing paternity fraught. Under those conditions, the practice of reckoning Jewish descent through the mother became prevalent (in
the Babylonian Talmud, see Qiddushin 68b).

in northern Israel at the time of Jesus' birth, for by then, the Israelite identity of Galilee had been under siege for centuries. The Assyrians had annexed the region and turned it into their own imperial province during the eighth century B.C.E., shredding the ancient ideal of the territorial integrity of Israel. During the Assyrian exile, and under the conquering empires that followed (Babylonian, Persian, Greek, and Roman), the northern Israelites who remained in the Galilee maintained their ethnic identity in the face of overwhelming military force by tracing their lineage back to ancient Israel.

Judea to the south faced the loss of its ethic identity when the Babylonian king Nebuchadnzezzar ordered the burning of Jerusalem and its Temple in 587 B.C.E. His army had looted the city and put the Temple priests to death. Zedekiah, king of Judea, was forced to watch his sons killed, and then had his eyes gouged out (2 Kings 25). That was only the beginning. The Babylonians deported what remained of the royal family, along with the wealthiest and most powerful of Jerusalem's Jews.

Under the Persians, the Temple was restored, and the Judeans enjoyed some limited political autonomy that kept their identity intact. But the Galileans did not enjoy the same autonomy. Their confidence in their status as Israel could be threatened by sexual conduct such as Mary's that resulted in a child of doubtful ethnic paternity: they felt imperiled by a *mamzer* at a level that was both visceral and communal.

As a *mamzer*, Jesus was ostracized by the elders of Nazareth. Although Joseph had always openly acknowledged his paternity, and did not shun his son, Jesus did not accompany him to the gathering of elders called the synagogue, which met in the central area in the village near the wine press and kiln. His fellow villagers kept him from the elders' gathering, while his brother James (Joseph's eldest son from his first marriage) emerged as an authority in the congregation. James could claim that he was descended from King David through his father, while Jesus' claim to that birthright was always challenged. Davidic birthright gave James a special place within Israel. Like David, he came to be viewed in the later church as uniquely qualified by God to guide Israel by interpreting the divine will. Within the caste system of Israel, wisdom (especially the wisdom to heal), as well as power, were prerogatives of the house of David. James is portrayed as giving advice concerning divine wisdom and healing in the New Testament epistle attributed to him (James 1:16–27; 5:13–18). In the book of Acts he expertly cites Scripture (Acts 15:13–21) and establishes policy for the entire community of Christians[7] after Jesus' death in Israel, Syria, the Near East, Asia Minor and, perhaps, even as far as India. James acted with exactly the kind of easy, recognized, literate authority that Jesus never possessed. He must have been one of the few children in Nazareth who could read, as a result of Joseph's efforts and James' own acceptance within the synagogue. But Jesus was forced by the circumstances of his birth to look outside the provincial establishment for an understanding of who he was and what it meant to be an Israelite.

Insults such as exclusion from the synagogue were a regular part of Jesus' childhood. In later life, Rabbi Jesus spoke of children's persistent squabbling, not of their generosity or innocence (Luke 7:31–33):

> To what shall I liken the humanity of this generation: and what are they like? They are like children in market sitting and shouting to one another, that say, We fluted for you, and you did not dance, We wailed and you did not weep!

Behind these words I see a small child, standing apart from other children, wishing to play but not being included, defensively ironic about the gang's incapacity to agree on a game. Jesus was isolated not because he was precocious and learned, which is what Luke's Gospel piously claims (2:41–52), but because he was a *mamzer*.

All his life, Jesus was both intense in his personal vision and gregari-

---

7. This name was first used to refer to Jesus' followers in Antioch, around the year 45 C.E. (see Acts 11:26). Initially, it was a term of disparagement, meaning "partisans of Christ," much as we might call people "Clintonites" or "Reaganites," but it was eventually embraced with pride by Jesus' followers.

ous in company. These habits of temperament develop early: personal intensity comes of loneliness, and those who love company most know what it is to live without it. A critical, independent child with an ironic turn of mind, Jesus must have spent much of his time alone, wandering through the hills of Galilee, talking to the shepherds and vagrant rabbis who were regarded as shady characters in small communities like Nazareth. All the while, without training or conscious articulation, he was developing a sense of Israelite society that was radically inclusive and a vision of God that was not limited to the strictures of local institutions.

All the insults cast his way help explain why Jesus came to see God as his father, his *Abba* in Aramaic. If Joseph's fatherhood was in doubt, God's fatherhood was not. Jews of this time recognized themselves as God's children and addressed God as "our father, our primordial redeemer is your name" (Isaiah 63:16). To call God "father" was a daring metaphor in itself, because it signified that the creator of the entire world had entered into a special relationship with Israel, as a father to his children. And Jesus joined some rabbis in a further, bolder claim, asserting God's personal, fatherly care for his children as individuals.

Because of Jesus' love of this metaphor, calling God "Father" became systemic in Christianity. But its meaning is Jewish and especially strong within the unsettled Judaism of Galilee. When prayed to and worshipped routinely in Christian churches, God becomes everybody's father instead of *my* father, and the divine relationship becomes formalized and abstract instead of intimate, as it was with Jesus.

Aramaic stories in the Talmud vividly convey a reliance upon God as father. Although the Talmud was shaped during the fifth century C.E., it is largely written in Aramaic, and includes ancient traditions that sometimes open up new perspectives on Jesus. Jesus might have heard one Talmudic story about a rabbi who was himself known as Abba. Children came to him from a village plagued by drought, crying, *"Abba, Abba,* give us rain!" The rabbi lifted his voice to heaven, asking for rain on behalf of "those who do not know the difference between an *abba* who can give rain, and an *abba* who cannot!" (This playful wording works only in Aramaic, not in Hebrew.

In Hebrew, the term for "my father" is *avi,* not *abba,* so confusion with the name "Abba" only arises in the Aramaic language; Taanit 23b in the Babylonian Talmud.) Such stories show that "father" was indeed a Jewish way of referring to God, and when Jesus was a rabbi he instructed his students to pray regularly to God as *Abba* (see Matthew 6:9; Luke 11:2). Even Greek-speaking Christians addressed God as *Abba* because they remembered Jesus' original idiom (see Paul's letter to the Galatians 4:6).

Although Jesus referred to God as a masculine *Abba,* his childhood experience in Nazareth also led him to speak of God in images drawn from the domain of women. While the males of Nazareth, including his brothers, were gathered in the synagogue, Jesus was learning about God from his mother's daily routine. Once, he was looking at a little mustard plant that spread eagerly over other herbs in Mary's courtyard garden.

"What, my son?" asked Mary.

"Malkhuta delaha," Jesus replied. "The Kingdom of God."

If she felt puzzlement, it would have increased when she noticed Jesus staring at her while she kneaded yeast into dough.

"What is it my son?"

"Malkhuta delaha!"

These parables of God's Kingdom, as seed and as yeast, are linked in Luke's Gospel (Luke 13:18–21). Scholars and theologians have often cited them as proof of Jesus' later skill as a teacher. Skilled he indeed became; but before he was skilled, he was incisive. These were the kind of connections that he would have made as a child, watching Mary and working side by side with her. God was not only *Abba,* but his Kingdom could be seen, touched, and shared in the life of a woman in a Galilean courtyard.

Malkhuta delaha, the Kingdom of God, was the principal theme of Jesus' message throughout his adult life, and the pivotal hope of Galilean Judaism. Rule by a king was for Galilean Jews both the source of their oppression—under temporal emperors and kings—and their hope for the future—under God. The Roman emperor and his subordinates (legates, prefects, and vassal kings, one of whom, Herod Antipas, figured crucially in Jesus' life) exercised powerful and sometimes violent hegemony. Roman sovereignty kept Jews from fully practicing the Torah and therefore living as Israel in God's chosen land.

The world of Jesus made no distinction between politics and religion. The Romans not only obeyed the emperor, they worshipped him as God's son, *Divi filius*. Jews not only worshipped God, but believed that he ruled them and that one day his Kingdom would be the only power on earth and in heaven. That belief was wound into Israel's sense of itself as a nation and a people. Much of the Bible, from Exodus through the prophetic book of Malachi, claims that God helps his chosen people conquer their enemies when they keep his covenant, and lets them fall victim to oppression when they stray from righteousness.

Many Galileans believed that if they lived in accord with God's commandments and prohibitions, God would intervene in human affairs, drive the Romans from Israel, and institute a reign of justice. They had much in common with the Jewish group called the "Ultra-Orthodox" in Jerusalem today, and with some strains of Evangelical Christianity.

Part of the beauty of the concept of God's Kingdom was that it opened one's mind to see the divine hand in the natural world. A Galilean could stand under the stars, view the mountains, watch young animals gambol, and recollect the words of a well-known psalm that all the Lord's creations give thanks to him and attest his eternal Kingdom to all people (Psalm 145:10–13). Divine power was already present in nature, yet only just dawning in human affairs. Jesus came out of the Jewish tradition of seeing God's immanence everywhere, in forces as simple and powerful as a mustard seed and yeast. Later, as a rabbi, he took the leap of seeing the divine Kingdom in how one person relates to another. But even as a child, Jesus saw God's Kingdom not simply as a hoped-for future—he had a direct intuition of how his *Abba*, moment by moment, was reshaping the world and humanity.

———

Jesus eventually left his mother's side to apprentice as a journeyman with Joseph (Mark 6:3). He began his apprenticeship soon after he turned ten, when he was old enough to cope with the rigorous travel involved in journeywork: difficult walks over rugged terrain made dangerous by bears, wolves, and bandits.[8] The physical work of cutting wood, hauling stone, mixing mortar, working with mallet, ax, and trowel would have toughened Jesus' hands and broadened his shoulders.

Travel outside the village probably gave him a new sense of independence and self-worth, and, perhaps most important, introduced him to the oral tradition of Galilean villages outside Nazareth. Every village had its own cache of folk tales and a unique way of rendering Scripture in its *targum*. In later life, Jesus would demonstrate his acquaintance with the rich oral traditions of Galilee, which had taught him so many parables. He became a master in improvising with their themes and metaphors.

Jesus must have been about twelve when his father died,[9] probably from one of the deadly illnesses, such as malaria and tuberculosis, that plagued Galilee. His father's death had a profound, searing effect on him. In the eyes of the villagers in Nazareth, he was now not only a *mamzer*, but a *mamzer* without an Israelite who acknowledged his paternity; Joseph could no longer deflect the rumors that he was not really Jesus' father or give him work.

Joseph was buried the day he died, in accordance with ancient Jewish practice. An exposed corpse defiled the people and the land itself (Deuteronomy 21:23), and so had to be removed to sustain Israel's pu-

---

8. Only during the second century, after the major Jewish revolt of Bar Kokhba (132–135 C.E.), did the Romans develop—for purposes of defense—an elaborate system of roads in Galilee.

9. The Gospels themselves do not refer to Joseph except in relation to Jesus' boyhood; later Gospels from the second century such as the Protoevangelium of James and the Infancy Gospel of Thomas supplement them. On the basis of those sources, other reminiscences, and the lack of reference to Joseph later on in the Gospels, early teachers of the church such as Saint Jerome (who died in 420 C.E.) plausibly concluded that Joseph must have died during Jesus' youth. Still, we know he had time to teach his son a trade.

rity. The local synagogue would have gathered to mourn Joseph's death. On the saddest day of Jesus' young life, the synagogue would still have excluded him from their midst. Possibly because of the synagogue's disdain for him, one of the most striking characteristics of Jesus' later teaching was a deep skepticism about religious authority (Matthew 23:23, where my translation again conveys Semitic forms and syntax):

> *Miseries are yours, letterers and Pharashayahs, hypocrites! Because you tithe the mint and the dill and the cumin, and leave the heavier matters of the law: the judgment and the mercy and the faith.*

Moments of ostracism in Nazareth left their imprint on Jesus and on the entire culture of Christianity. The divide between Judaism and Christianity, between one Christian sect and another, and between "insiders" and "outsiders" century after century must to some extent be the result of this child's exclusion from public mourning for his own father.

The burial itself was the duty of the family, led now by Mary and James. They would have washed, anointed, and wrapped the body in flax. Sons carried their father to the cemetery, where they interred him in an unmarked grave: poor, illiterate Jewish Galilee had neither resources for nor interest in gravestones. In death, as in life, Joseph's monument was his family. All who touched the corpse became unclean (Numbers 19:11–13): they separated from the community for a week, bathing themselves on the third and the seventh days.

Mary and her sons would have recited the Aramaic Qaddish for mourners, a Qaddish such as is still recited today, praising God and celebrating his coming Kingdom in the midst of their grief:

> *His masterful name will be great and sanctified in the world he created in his pleasure; his Kingdom will rule.*

There were many forms of Qaddish, for mourning and for celebration, during this period of Judaism. But it is startling to realize that the Lord's

Prayer, which Christian teachers (and even scholars) have claimed is unique, derives from the Qaddish. When Jesus in later life taught people to pray (Matthew 6:9–13; Luke 11:2–4), he began in Aramaic, *Abba, yitqadash shemakh, tetey malkhuthakh:* "Father, your name will be sanctified, your Kingdom will come." Those words were burnt into his memory at the time of Joseph's death. The major themes of the Qaddish—God's sanctification and Kingdom—stayed with him.

I n his mature teachings, Jesus made God's Kingdom into the foundation of what he said and did. The vision of God in the Qaddish is a vital key to understanding how and why. There, in the midst of mourning, an Israelite affirmed that God remained sovereign and holy, a fundamental reality beyond Rome's oppression—beyond even death.

The death of his father brought an emotional truth home to Jesus: the Kingdom of God was his only support. As is often the case with great religious teachers, emotions led him to an insight, which could be put into words only later. God's Kingdom was not for him an abstract idea, but something for which he yearned at the core of his broken heart.

TWO

Pilgrimage
to Jerusalem

Mary now headed a large family: Jesus and his two older half-brothers (James and Joses), two younger full brothers (Judas and Simon), and several sisters (Mark 6:3). After consulting with the elders of Nazareth, she decided to undertake a pilgrimage to the Temple in Jerusalem during the fall harvest festival of Sukkoth, or Tabernacles, which celebrated family solidarity in Israel. It was crucial for a village to decide from year to year which families would take part in pilgrimages and which would not, because enough people had to remain to sustain the community. Synagogues made the communal decisions.

To sacrifice in the Temple was difficult for Nazarenes. The hardship of travel itself was not as great as if a family lived in Rome or Antioch, from which wealthy Jews made pilgrimages from time to time. Rather, it was because the Galileans lacked a currency-based economy that travel outside the region was hard. Within their little settlements, the Galileans had no regular use for money. They worked on a system of exchange: my wheat for your wine; my journeywork for your weaving. The synagogues regulated pilgrimage so as not to disrupt agricultural production, a difficult task since the great feasts of Passover (Pesach), Pentecost (Weeks), and Tabernacles (Sukkoth) occurred just when barley, wheat, olives, and grapes became ripe. The biblical ideal of pilgrimage to the Temple by all males at Pesach, Weeks, and Sukkoth (Deuteronomy 16:16–17) was not feasible, but Galileans showed an intense, sometimes violent insistence on their place in the worship of the Temple throughout the first century and undertook pilgrimages when they could.

The Temple to which Mary and her family were headed was by far the largest religious structure in the world at the time, known far and wide for its wealth and magnificence, the focal point for worship by Israelites, a physical manifestation to the rest of the world of the potency of the God of the Jews. The pilgrimage from Galilee to Jerusalem would have taken more than five days, even at a quick pace. I envision the family starting out from Nazareth before first light, crossing the familiar, rolling highlands of Galilee before descending into the wilderness of the Jordan River Valley. They passed the ancient settlements of Ramoth, Hammath, and Adam. Although predominantly Jewish, these towns largely lived off the currency of pilgrims, wanderers, and soldiers—including many non-Jews—and they did not share the more isolated Jewish culture of Galilee. Jesus' family would have given them a wide berth and camped their first night outside Galilee in the Jordan's wilds, rather than pay to stay in one of the towns. They were on their guard as they moved into the more desolate south. Sudden torrents of rain could wash through the wadis; leopards and jackals hunted in the thick brush. Thugs lurked, awaiting a chance to prey on the innocent. The family doused their fire after eating so as not to draw attention to themselves; they huddled in their cloaks, protected only by their vigilance and their walking staffs.

After eating breakfast, most likely consisting of bread and humus prepared from the ground chickpeas they had brought along (commonly used in the Middle East from the Late Stone Age on), they continued south. High cliffs rose on either side of the Valley. Through the breaks in the landscape they could see the barren moonscape of the dry Judean hills, so different from the textured green of Galilee. By late afternoon they were worn out but had almost reached the end of their hundred-mile journey. They came into a more developed region, where the river widened and slowed.

There were narrow, pebbly beaches and gentle pools. Perhaps they bathed in the late afternoon sun, refreshing themselves before wearily leaving the river valley for Bethany, a town one and a half miles east southeast of Jerusalem. They sought the house of two widowed, middle-aged sisters, Martha and Miriam, related to the family by Galilean descent.

The family felt out of place: the house faced a broad street and people were constantly passing. In Galilee, a stranger in the village was an event; Bethany saw dozens of new faces each day. The house had a spacious common room and a second story. Jesus did not know where the fields were: in Nazareth he looked out the window and knew where the day's work was to be done. But he knew there must be fields to support the luxury of rugs in the house, the patterns stitched into the sisters' clothing, and their jewelry of carnelian and turquoise. Jesus had never been this far south, and he couldn't understand why the Holy One would favor with riches those of his people who lived so close to the impurity of the oppressor. He and the family ate well that evening; perhaps even a goat had been slaughtered and cooked to welcome them. Good wine flowed, and they all slept safely in an upper room of this comfortable house.

The following morning, it would have been James who set out well in advance of the rest of the family to buy a goat for sacrifice. His walk to Jerusalem was accomplished before the sun rose. He transacted his business quickly at the place called Chanuth, "Market Stall," south of the Temple across the Kidron Valley on the Mount of Olives. Prices in Jerusalem were steeper than in Galilee, confirming James' innate Galilean suspicion of Judean merchants. He could rely on his own eyes and hands to make certain he was getting a sound animal by his own standards. But only the vendor could tell him whether the Judean priests who ran the Temple would accept a goat as a beast without blemish, depending on how its coat was marked.

James took the goat directly to the Temple. Priests at the north gate inspected and then accepted or rejected all the offerings for the day. The priest who met James was disappointed that the Galilean had no money for him. Nonetheless, he said the animal could be offered. James insisted that he would himself bring to the Sanctuary the grain and wine that the family had carried from Galilee. At least that would be completely their own, rather than what they bought in Jerusalem at inflated prices. The likelihood that a beast would be blemished during a long journey was what prevented the Galileans from bringing their own animals to the Temple. The priest assured him that the levite trained to slaughter the goat would let James lay hands on his offering prior to sacrifice. This treasured moment was mandated by Hillel, the greatest rabbi in living memory (see Besah 20a, b in the Talmud). Putting one's hands on one's own animal was an important moment for a pilgrim: it signaled the personal ownership of what was offered. But James knew he would be lucky to get through to any animal in the mob that was gathering, and that he would not know this goat from another.

Back in Bethany, after a breakfast of fresh fruit, Jesus and the rest of the family started out to meet James at the pool of Siloam, a prominent landmark south of the Temple. They walked without haste for just over an hour. Waiting for James was a pleasure; they were transfixed by the sight of the Temple looming above them. The stones of its enormous pedestal were gleaming white and beautifully fitted: the hill of Zion, as a result of Herod's building, had indeed become a mount, a brilliant rock which supplied the Temple above with more than thirty-five acres on which to unfold its splendor. From Siloam, far below, they could see a thick pillar of smoke that rose heavenward from the first sacrifices of the morning. The sun reflected off the gilt that covered the enormous rectangle of the Sanctuary, the courtyards around it, and the mammoth porticos that surrounded the entire edifice. Sunlight gleaming off the gold facades made the Temple blaze like a second sun.

The strain of the journey was behind them, but not its excitement. The family ascended the steps leading up from Siloam, broad, steep, and crowded with every kind of vendor and guide. The children gawked at offerings of fruit, nuts, and grain, neatly bundled and extravagantly priced as sacrificial offerings, as well as bouquets of flowers for personal adornment and pleasure. Jewish hawkers claimed they could convey non-Jewish travelers to any part of the Temple. But every Jew knew that was a lie. The Romans themselves had endorsed the regulation that non-Jews who entered the Temple's inner courtyards, which were reserved for only Israelites, were to be put to death. The Temple's priestly police and those who ran the bathing pools at the foot of the Temple mount had a close, working relationship with each other, and the presence of a male non-Jew would be as obvious as his foreskin. (Fathers, husbands, or brothers vouched for the religious identity of women.) The hawkers were there to exploit those who knew no better, the few non-Jews who had come this far without guides.

The older children stared in disbelief at the non-Jews. The women were unlike anything they had seen before, many without head covering—despite the festivity with strangers that required most Jewish women to be veiled—and some were even bare-shouldered. They might as well have been naked in their diaphanous, clinging tunics of cotton, decorated with purple bands and only partially covered by cloaks. Their decorated linen clothing marked them as Roman ladies (both Jews and non-Jews), making the journey to Jerusalem as tourists. The Jewish Temple guards, armed to preserve order, looked much like Roman troops, with their bare legs and stubby, glinting swords. Jesus was not the only Galilean—or the only Jew—to resent the easy access by Gentiles to most parts of the Temple, and the Gentile look of many Jewish guards. Although many of them were levites—from the caste of priests—they were appareled in short, toga-like tunics, as if they were soldiers of the empire, with whom some of them (especially the officers) had trained. They kept order on the steps and even better order inside the Temple.

Everyone entering the Temple needed to bathe by immersion. The entire southern slope up to the Temple entrance was developed with a system of canals, channels, and cisterns (visible today as a result of excavation), so that all Temple-goers might make themselves clean during this final ascent into the presence of the Holy One of Israel. There were installations for non-Jews, who, once immersed, were allowed to ascend with Jews to the magnificent esplanade of the Great Court and the porticos around it. The interior courts at the center of the Great Court were reserved for Israelites who had also purified themselves (one court for

THE TEMPLE MOUNT DURING THE SECOND TEMPLE PERIOD

The monumental extent of the Temple is plainly shown in this famous drawing by Leen Ritmeyer. The foundations of the platform built by Herod the Great are all that remain today; it has been estimated that its cornerstones weigh up to one hundred tons each. A wide stairway led up to the Double Gate, and interior stairs brought pilgrims to the south-

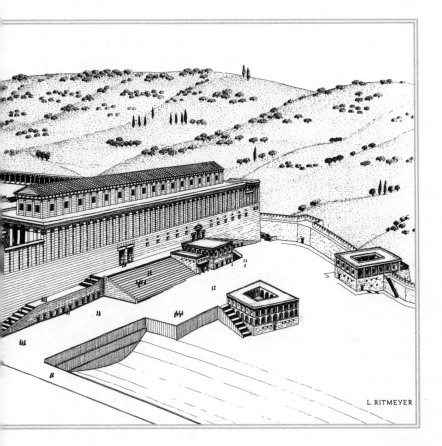

L.RITMEYER

ern end of the Great Court. Rome's Antonia Fortress loomed at the north end, while the sanctuary complex itself was laid out inside the Great Court, centered on the column of smoke that rose from the altar. (Illustration courtesy of Leen Ritmeyer)

males, another for females). Clustered around these inner preserves, chambers accommodated members of priestly families, prominent members of the Jewish council that governed Jerusalem under the aegis of Rome, and vying parties of Essenes and Pharisees.

The Pharisees were especially active in recruiting people for their immersion pools (*miqvaoth*), which pilgrims could use for a small sum. They were proud of their method of keeping a vat of forty *seahs* (some seventy gallons) next to the pool of forty *seahs,* so that a connecting pipe could be used at any moment to make the pool clean by contact with the water in the vat (see the entire tractate called Miqvaot in the Mishnah). There was enough water to assure that although it was still, it was like running, "living waters" (*mayim chayyim*), water that cleansed from God's point of view (Leviticus 14:5; Zechariah 13:1) in the Pharisaic interpretation of Jewish law.

Jesus and his family sought out a simple bathing pool, and asked a trustworthy friend of a friend to keep their outer clothing, sandals, staffs, and purses safe. The pool's personnel provided a thick, flax towel for drying. Pilgrims mounted toward the Temple itself barefoot, clothed only in their tunics.

As they made their way into the enormous gate on the Temple's south side, they could see nothing at first. The windowless staircase, climbing up inside the pedestal four stories to the Great Court, was as dark as a cave, despite the huge torches flaming along the outside of the staircase. Jesus and his siblings must have been as afraid of the height as they were of the smoky dark pressing in on them, the driving crowd, the press of strangers that became terrifying in its intensity. Perhaps they sang out bits of a favorite psalm (Psalm 24):

> *Who shall ascend on the mount of the Lord,*
> *and who shall arise in his holy place?*
> *Clean of hands, pure of heart, that*
> > *does not take up breath for lying and does not swear for deceit,*
> *shall take up blessing from the Lord, and*
> > *righteousness from the God of one's salvation.*

Singing built their courage. Jesus was especially susceptible to a later part of the psalm, which spoke of the same Kingdom with which he had already learned to console his loneliness:

Archways: lift up your heads!
Primordial gates: be lifted up!
And the King of glory shall come in!

It must have been a profound moment for him: here was the praise of God as the supreme sovereign of all, publicly proclaimed in the most magnificent building he had ever seen.

When they exited the stair, the sunlight on the golden edifice dazzled them. Every portico around the Great Court was overlaid with a shimmering intensity of gold and silver. Inside this area, in the interior court nearest the Sanctuary, there were only male Jews; women were consigned to a second court, closer to the sacrifice than non-Jews, but one step removed from the men. Finally, standing in the Court of Women with his family, Jesus saw within the court nearest the Sanctuary what he had been waiting for—the end of the pilgrimage, the holiest spot in earth, the timeless place.

Set near the courtyard's west wall was the white marble Sanctuary—whose inner recess was called the *qodesh qodashim* (holy of holies) in Hebrew, literally the sanctum sanctorum. This was God's Throne on earth, the focal point of divine energy, the link between heaven and earth, between the transient and the immortal, between the creator and creation. And it was empty—an enclosed room that no one but the high priest ever entered (and then once a year only, on the Day of Atonement).[1]

Before this Throne, in the open air of the first court, the altar fire

---

1. Once, this inner sanctum had housed the Ark of the Covenant, a box that contained the tablets of the commands to Moses and other holy objects, to seal the divine presence within Israel. But the Temple had been vandalized by an Egyptian expedition five years after Solomon's death (1 Kings 14:25–26), and the holy of holies probably remained empty after that.

raged, fed by huge logs. The altar itself was a rough structure of natural, uncut stones, some twenty-three feet high, surrounded by ramps covered with embers and ash and blood on which priests officiated. The animals bellowed and lowed on the way to slaughter. Dozens of priests slaughtered them, spattering their ornate garments with blood as they sliced throats, disemboweled carcasses, and divided meat into portions to be eaten by worshippers and priests or consigned to the flames. Flesh popped on the altar. Wine was poured into the fire, where it steamed. The explosive combustion of grain could be heard intermittently above the din of animals and the crowd's fervent prayers and ecstatic songs.

A short distance from James and Mary, Jesus stared towards the Sanctuary and the smoke mounting above it. The *mamzer* from Galilee had come to the place where God's presence was more palpable than anywhere else on earth. And he was part of it, in the house of his *Abba* (Luke 2:49). Gone was the exclusion he felt from Nazareth's synagogue, as he stood at the heart of the sacred, vouched for as an Israelite by his family. Here was Judaism in all its power. Here was what he had been searching for. His heart was overflowing. Conversation was pointless in the din, but Mary caught his eye for a moment.

"What, my son?"

"The Kingdom of God."

He disappeared into the crowd, and she would not see him for several years.

What exactly became of Jesus after he disappeared into the milling crowds at the Temple? The Gospels are nearly silent. There is just one lone reference in Luke (2:41–52): Jesus evades his family and remains in Jerusalem, compelled by the conviction that "it is necessary for me to be among those of my *Abba*" (Luke 2:49). Luke has Jesus eventually return to Nazareth after his family seeks him out in Jerusalem, but there is good reason to doubt that actually happened. Then Luke's narrative jumps forward to describe John the Baptist and Jesus' baptism by John in the Jordan River when he was "around thirty years old" (Luke 3:23); that long delay in his meeting John is also implausible. The whole time of Jesus' adolescence and young adulthood is a blank in Luke. Scholars have called these "the hidden years" with good reason.

Scholarship and piety both abhor a vacuum, and they have filled this one as best they can with Luke's picture: Jesus was "submitted" to his parents back in Nazareth, and steadily "progressed in wisdom and stature and grace" (Luke 2:51–52). During the second century, the Infancy Gospel of Thomas (13:1) made Joseph's occasional journeywork into a carpentry shop, and turned Jesus into Joseph's miraculously able apprentice. Once, the story goes, a piece of wood was too short for Joseph, so Jesus stretched it out to the right length! Jesus' adolescence was as mysterious to the early Christians as it is to us, and that mystery prompted legends.

The Gospels do not portray Jesus as maturing in Nazareth and becoming a peasant or journeyman eligible for marriage, which is what a village youth who simply stayed home would have done. Instead, Jesus moves straight from early adolescence into a close relationship with John, and is only referred to again in Galilee much later, as a mature adult. That suggests he never did return with his family to Nazareth, but remained near Jerusalem and sought out the company of John. His association with John supplies the key to what actually happened to Jesus during the transitional time of puberty.

The Gospels do not reflect these formative years, because they deliberately shove John into the background in their desire to portray Jesus as independent, the autonomous Son of God. What the Gospels conceal and what scholarship has ignored is the principal reason Jesus would have sought John out: he wanted to become his *talmid,* his student or disciple, in a way that was later formalized in institutional yeshivas during the fourth century C.E. He wanted to learn a *halakhah* from John, a "way" of living God's covenant with Israel. Jesus had a rebellious, venturesome spirit: he did not become a passionate religious genius by moldering in the conventional piety of a village that barely accepted him. He broke out. His pilgrimage to the Temple marked the beginning of an adolescent transition of explosive potential.

John is the key to Jesus' crucial teenage years. Jesus learned from John, disputed with him, and developed the ideas that would change his own life and the course of religious history. John led Jesus on the path that made an alienated *mamzer* and starving, wayward pilgrim into an apprentice in the subtleties of Judaic practice, and later into an acknowledged rabbi with a charismatic personality and a distinctive path to God that was all his own.

In order to explain how Jesus came to John, we must contradict the chronology of Luke, which has Jesus return to Nazareth when his family searches for him, and leave Jesus in Jerusalem after his experience at the Temple. Luke was right in one respect: Jesus' family would have searched for him, but Jesus had vanished into the crowd that filled the city for Sukkoth. He had no clear plan. All he knew was that he wanted to stay near the Temple. He longed for the wholeness of inclusion in Israel that he had experienced during his pilgrimage. Feeling and intuition moved him more than conscious intent. He couldn't face going back to Nazareth, to the look of judgment and distaste for a *mamzer* in the eyes of the village elders.

He darted down the Temple steps into the Upper City, skirting the palatial stone dwellings of the wealthiest priestly families (corresponding to the newest developments in today's Jewish Quarter) and turned into a warren of tight alleys in the Lower City, below Mount Zion. A bustling trade, unconnected with sacrifice in the Temple, catered to the masses that thronged the city at this time of year. Blood from butchered goats, sheep, and cattle ran through gutters into primitive sewers; offal was piled on cobbled streets. Market carts overflowed with onions, endive, leeks, muskmelons and watermelons, with bolts of wool, linen, and cotton. There were vats of wine and olive oil for sale, sometimes expensively scented and mixed with myrrh, oil-burning lamps of clay and metal, and garments: smock-like tunics, mantles and cloaks, even togas.

Jesus was overwhelmed with new sensations and odors. Food was cooking: the stews familiar in Galilee, but also rich combinations of skewered meats, grilled over charcoal, marinated and basted with herbs and oil. Asses, horses, and camels were tethered where alleys met wider lanes. He heard a wealth of languages, not only Aramaic and Greek, but also Phrygian, Egyptian, and Latin. He avoided the Temple area, knowing that his mother and brothers would look for him there. But wherever he wandered in the city, he could orient himself by the pillar of sacrificial smoke rising to heaven.

Jerusalem was like nothing in Jesus' experience, a major urban center of fifty thousand people. (As a boy, he had seen the garrison town of Sepphoris, but only from a distance; that impure, corrupt Roman outpost was avoided as much as possible by the rural Jews of Galilee.) He was preoccupied less with the city's splendor than with his own survival: How would he eat? Where would he sleep? The fall nights were cold, and there were no jobs in Jerusalem for vagrant pilgrims. He wandered the streets with no money, no possessions, his journeyman's skills superfluous in a city whose building trades were far in advance of rural Galilee's. He joined the legions of poor who sought alms around the Temple and begged among the merchants in the Lower City, many of whom had known similar poverty and showed more sympathy to beggars than the Temple police did. Pilgrims on the roads that led into Jerusalem from Jericho to the east and Joppa to the west could also be kind, mindful of Israel's duty to the poor. In Deuteronomy, God commands, "Open your hand to your brother, to your impoverished and your poor in your land" (15:11), and the Mishnah extends that imperative to poor travelers in particular (Peah 8:7). He probably considered seeking shelter from Miriam and Martha back in Bethany, but they would have insisted that he return to Nazareth. Breaking with the family brought dishonor, and those who left the community, by divorce or flight, brought shame on both themselves and those who harbored them. He was forced to take his chances on the street.

"Be compassionate!" he cried to passing pilgrims, asking for the same *chesed* (compassion or mercy) they sought from God at the Temple's sacrificial altar (Psalm 18:25). He held out his hands in the attitude of prayer, imploring.

"Get out, boy!" (*"Phaq, talya!"*) were the words often hurled at him when he strayed near the Temple, not so much from the pilgrims as from the cultic authorities. He yearned to ascend Mount Zion, to offer a meager sacrifice of grain or oil and once again feel the palpable majesty of God. But in order to enter the Temple, he had to be led by an adult male Israelite, a relative whose pedigree established those who accompanied him as Jewish. And relatives were just what the young vagrant had to avoid. To the Temple police, Jesus' scrounging and loitering was at best a nuisance and, in their minds, bordered on criminality.

Hunger dogged his days. Sleep was a troubled, semiconscious struggle against cold. His pilgrim's cloak, thrown over his shoulders, was his only blanket. Yet the Temple towered over all his suffering, a sign of Israel's joy before God.

As his face grew gaunt and his eyes glowed with his involuntary fast, he was filled with a deep and paradoxical confidence in the abundance God had promised to Israel. Years later, when his hungry disciples bought Jesus bread, he told them that *his* bread was to do the will of his *Abba* (John 4:31–34). That profoundly simple spirituality was the basis on which John's Gospel later identified Jesus himself as "the bread of life" (John 6:35, 41, 48, 51, 58). His hunger taught him to be acutely conscious of God's promise. When God's Kingdom was established there would be an end to hunger and strife; swords would be beaten into plowshares (Isaiah 2:2–4); the wolf would lie down with the lamb (Isaiah 11:6–9); and—as Jesus later said—the poor, maimed, blind, and lame would feast at God's table (Luke 14:21).

The promise of God's Kingdom burned so strongly within him that it seemed immanent. His grief over separation from the Temple made Jesus all the more acutely aware of how deeply God cared for man, even though he felt isolated and alone. He learned young what Julian of Norwich would discover only after a mature mystical experience in 1373: intense longing for God brings God's assurance to the one who longs that one is loved and cared for. Both Jesus and Julian were instructed by the simple yet profound spirituality of Psalm 42: the pure desire for God, like the pure desire for an absent loved one, is itself an assurance of the power of that love. In his mind, he was as close to the Kingdom as he was to the Temple.

The nearness of the Kingdom awakened more than love and compassion in Jesus. During his first, hard sojourn in Jerusalem, he also came to have a clear vision of an ideal world. In later life, he would become intensely impatient with anyone and anything that stood in the way of its realization. Truth, justice, and compassion were within our grasp, he taught, if only we would seize them.

As winter deepened, Jesus clung to a last, lonely hope. He had heard of a teacher called John the Baptist (Yochanan the Immerser), a rabbi known to most pilgrims from Galilee. With a roving band of followers, John offered purification in the Jordan River, along the route pilgrims from Galilee and Syria followed to the Temple. Jesus hoped that in John's company he might find a way to remain in Judea, in the vicinity of Jerusalem, and return to the Temple again. It was a desperate gamble to traipse into the wilderness after John, but that was his only alternative to an ignominious return to Nazareth.

He trekked over the rocky highlands east of Jerusalem, brown rolling hills dotted with green shrubs yet almost barren compared to the cultivated farmland around Nazareth. Broom trees, erect and spare, grew only to about eight feet, scraggly compared to the evergreens of Galilee. With the walking staff of a pilgrim that he had carried from Galilee, he trudged through heavy rain and occasional snow, blustery winds, a damp cold re-

HERODIAN JERUSALEM

First-century Jerusalem was a splendid confection of ancient buildings and Herod the Great's architectural ambitions. The Temple complex dominates on the east, with the Sanctuary towering within the interior Court of the Israelites. Herod's palace is promi-

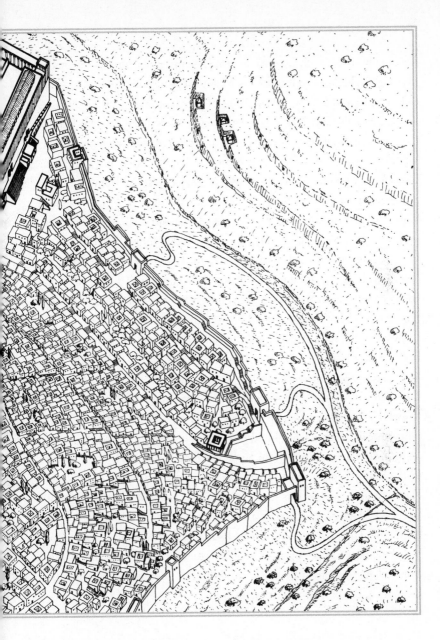

nently situated on the western side of the city. The Antonia Fortress guards the northwest corner of the enormous Great Court of the Temple, while the Lower City stretches out to the south of the Great Court. (Illustration courtesy of Leen Ritmeyer)

lieved only sporadically by the pale sun. The indigenous limestone made for rough walking, even for those accustomed to travel by foot. The paths were rugged at that time of year, some of them washed by the wadis that erupted with water from rain or melted snow on the highlands. He feared the bands of thugs that preyed on the unprotected. The adult Jesus told a parable of a man robbed and beaten by predators on his way from Jerusalem to Jericho (Luke 10:30–37); perhaps he spoke from bitter experience. He stopped only to beg in Jericho, the ancient site of Joshua's famous siege against the idol-worshipping Canaanites, before descending into the gravely wilderness of the densely wooded Jordan River Valley.

It became warmer as he descended to the valley floor, a thousand feet below sea level. Relieved to be out of the cold and wind, he was also on edge. Would John accept him even though he was a stranger, or spurn him as the religious community in Nazareth had?

Jesus wandered north along the Jordan, reversing the pilgrim route he had traveled just a few months before with his family. The valley was lush, green with tamarisks, vines, and swaying reeds, jungle-like even in the middle of winter. This wilderness, he knew, was as dangerous as the lions for which it was famous. He no longer had his brothers to protect him. He would not have wanted to spend a night on the Jordan's banks on his own. He was fragile from his lack of food and sleep, from huddling in doorways, begging on the streets. The ostracism he had known in Nazareth as a *mamzer* was nothing compared to the hostility and indifference he had experienced as a destitute vagabond after breaking with his family. The journey to find John had tapped into the last reserves of his strength. It was not until his final hour that we find him as completely alone; along the Jordan he must have felt even more vulnerable than he had among the crowds in Jerusalem.

THREE

The *Talmid* of John

Pilgrims traveling to and from Jerusalem knew of John and his whereabouts, so locating him would have been a simple matter. Yet it would have been with both relief and trepidation that Jesus approached the famous master.

He would probably have found the Immerser urging a group of pilgrims to dunk themselves in the Jordan. *"Tavu, teblu limshebaq dehovatkon!* (Repent, immerse for release of your sins!),"* he heard John call. He could quickly identify the rabbi, twenty-seven by the time Jesus met him, wild looking, with a straggly beard and long hair matted into dreads. He was dressed in a camel-hair tunic—a wooly garment caked with dirt—rough as a doormat against his skin. Around him were a handful of similarly dressed, younger disciples. A few new students were still wearing the fine linen tunits and cloaks (unlike Jesus' tunic of rough flax and his wool cloak) that showed they belonged to wealthy Judean families.

The pilgrims stepped gingerly into the water as John and the disciples, ranged along the pebbly shore, implored them to immerse fully in the river or a pool nearby, although the waters were frigid with snowmelt. Hills of limestone, marl, and chalk rose high behind them, from where the valley floor ended. Scoured clean by rain and wind on their upper reaches, they were swathed in scrubby bushes and dense vines as they plunged into the lower reaches of the gorge.

Jesus watched surreptitiously from thick scrub as the pilgrims came out of the water and wrapped themselves in their clothing. As the afternoon wound down, fires were kindled in camps; wool blankets and cloaks were spread on the ground, dotted with meager belongings. Equipped with little, these people nonetheless luxuriated in Israel's spiritual inheritance.

Perhaps it was the smell of food cooking and the warmth of the fires as the evening cooled that drew the cold, hungry adolescent from his hiding place toward the group. Jesus probably felt very much the outsider, intimidated as he approached John.

"*Shelama, rabbi,*" he would have said. He opened his hands by his sides in a gesture of vulnerability, went down on one knee, bowing his head, holding his breath, waiting to see if John would acknowledge him.

"Show your face," John finally said to this strange beggar-boy.

He saw a young man, dirty and disheveled.

"Who are you?" John asked.

"Jesus from Nazareth."

"Why are you not then in Nazareth?"

And Jesus found his voice by telling his story: how he had left his family because the Kingdom he intuitively discerned was palpable for him in the Temple, how he needed to remain near its center. In this telling, something loosened in him. He was at last able to express his emotional connection with Israel to a mature, recognized teacher. John was a famous rabbi, more notable than the Nazareth elders who could never see past his problematic birth and know what was in his heart. Even among his family, only Mary was familiar with his wonderful intuitions of the Kingdom; his brothers, especially James, resented his *mamzer* status and never associated him with the wisdom learned in the synagogue.

"Rabbi, I will remain with you," Jesus said, using the time-honored expression of an aspirant's desire to follow the teaching of a rabbi and learn directly from him (see John 1:37–39).

"Come after me," John replied.

They embraced and kissed. John motioned Jesus to join the circle around the fire and gave him food: roasted locusts, field honey, and bread from the pilgrims. Locusts and field honey were recognized in Leviticus (11:22) as a clean food one could eat in the wilderness, unlike game.[1] The locusts must have been oddly crunchy in Jesus' mouth, but by eating them he was initiated into John's rabbinic family.

Jesus' acceptance into the group around John was no doubt slow in coming. These disciples formed a tight clique, willing to endure hardship and deprivation, passionately seeking to master the way that brought access to God. Joining a rabbi was a luxury in a society where ordinary households needed every able-bodied member to work the land or pursue a craft, and the *talmidim* from well-off Judean families had a natural antipathy to Galileans. Obedience to John obliged them to accept the scruffy provincial, some four years younger than any of them and speaking Aramaic with a comical Galilean accent. Beneath all that, however, they eventually came to appreciate what John had discerned: a passion for the solidarity of Israel that would make Jesus into John's most famous student, a true *talmid*.

Our best historical guide to John himself is the Jewish historian Josephus, a religious seeker and consummate politician who dabbled in the different sects of first-century Judaism. Josephus portrays himself as having progressed to the most advanced level of his spiritual

---

1. In the conception of dietary purity taught in the Torah, "clean" animals were those that accorded with God's original model of creation. Living things that transgressed those categories were held to be monstrous, and unsuitable for consumption. So four-footed beasts with hooves that chewed the cud, real fish with scales and fins, and honest-to-God locusts could be eaten. But animals which missed these categories, like the rabbit (which looks like it chews cud but has toes, not hooves), catfish (which have no scales), and winged insects (that are birdlike, rather than terrestrial) were unclean, along with scavengers.

journey after becoming the *talmid* of a man named Bannus in the Judean wilderness near the Jordan (*Life* 11):

> *He stayed in the wilderness, using cloth from trees, supporting himself by food that grows of itself, washing with cold water day and night frequently for sanctification, and I became his zealot.*

The similarity to John is striking: Bannus' washing is for sanctification, and he takes disciples. Josephus' reference to "zeal" in describing his own relationship to Bannus reflects the political dimension inherent within discipleship in ancient Judaism. The loyalty one owed one's rabbi was complete and extended to every aspect of the rabbi's life. That loyalty and devotion is what Josephus gave Bannus, and what Jesus gave John.

In his *Jewish Antiquities* (18 § 116–117) Josephus described John the Baptist in much the same way he spoke of Bannus, and spelled out John's method of achieving purity:

> *For so indeed bathing seemed to him [John] pleasing to God, not in excuse for whatever sins people committed, but for sanctification of the body, with the soul indeed also already cleansed by righteousness.*

This program of immersion is what made John a "baptist" (*baptistes*) in the Greek language of Josephus and the Gospels. What Christians call "baptism" is their version of the Jewish practice of immersion: the Greek verb *baptizo* means to dip, dunk, or immerse. From Josephus we see how teachers such as Bannus and John, as well as their disciples, saw the purpose of their rituals. They claimed to achieve sanctification in a way others did not. Through John's teaching, Jesus entered the controversy in Judaism over how Israelites should purify themselves by bathing.

The Torah required Israelites to purify themselves by bathing following sexual activity, childbirth, contact with a corpse or other sources of impurity (for example, animal carcasses, foreign idols, and people with skin lesions). Bathing in this way—not for hygiene, but to restore and maintain one's place in the community—expressed Israelite identity by means of a common, basic practice. But how and in what should one immerse oneself? Priestly Zadokites (the "Sadducees" of the Greek Gospels) could afford luxurious bathing pools, sometimes in their own private dwellings. The Pharisees built stepped tanks (*miqvaoth*) with a reserve tank of water the same size that served entire communities and were financed cooperatively. The Essenes of Qumran had larger reservoirs for the exclusive use of their community. All these pools were carved and built in rock, as were their cisterns, channels, steps, and enclosures. Many Jews, however, had no access to a pool, and even when they did, the design often did not conform to that preferred by the Zadokites, the Pharisees, or the Essenes.

Immersers such as Bannus and John were successful because they tapped into popular discontent over attempts by factional elites to control how Israelites made themselves clean. They insisted that the Lord of Israel cleansed people in his own "living waters" (water flowing or collected naturally), so that the artificial pool of the sects were superfluous. John's message resonated with Jesus, who, as a Galilean, resented the elaborate bathing required by the Judean priesthood as a condition of entering the Temple. Were Galileans somehow impure? Did their own customs and practices make them anything other than Israelites? To Galileans and other Jews who did not cede to priests the exclusive power to decide who was and was not fit to offer sacrifice, John was a hero.

The pilgrims who came to John and Bannus knew that once they arrived at the Temple they would be confronted (as Jesus and his family had been) by a bewildering array of pools for purification. The Temple authorities required them to immerse before passing through the monumental double gate and ascending the stairs to the Great Court. Pilgrims who immersed with baptist rabbis such as John and Bannus enjoyed the confidence that came from purification in God's own waters before they even arrived in Jerusalem, whatever requirements others might impose on them. Pilgrims from rural Galilee, Syria, and the Judean highlands naturally resented having to use (and having to pay for) methods of purification not their own. The elaborate installations at the foot of Mount Zion seemed an inherent criticism of their own methods, and obliged them to bow to the theories of the ruling elites who ran them. Immersion in the Jordan was a silent protest against the urban cadres that controlled Judaism in Jerusalem, as well as a genuinely devoted practice.

As John and his disciples moved up and down the Jordan, they avoided the jackals, hyenas, lions, and leopards that hunted in the bush, and the Roman soldiers who were garrisoned in a dozen small forts built up from the ruins of Maccabean outposts to defend the approaches to Jerusalem. The garrisons helped to safeguard pilgrims from thugs, but the Romans themselves were a threat, authorized to take what they needed from pilgrims and force them into labor. Just as Jesus knew about thugs from personal experience, he had dealt with soldiers (Matthew 5:39–41):

> Yet I say to you, Not to resist the evil one, but whoever cuffs you on your right cheek, turn to him the other as well. And to the one who wishes to litigate with you, even to take your tunic, leave him the cloak as well! And whoever requisitions you to journey one mile, depart with him two!

This is not, as commonly believed, a timeless adage against resistance, but a strategy of coping with soldiers who took what they needed, by violence if necessary. In the face of an empire's evil, retaliate with the good, in the hope that by one's example justice might prevail and that one might avoid harm. Popular theology has persistently yanked Jesus' teaching from its original social context and made Jesus into a philosopher of complete nonresistance. But his powerful wisdom speaks from the conditions he faced. Mahatma Gandhi and Martin Luther King, Jr., rightly saw that Jesus did not teach acquiescence to evil, but an exemplary retaliation that shows evil for what it is.

John and his followers, Jesus among them, cried out a message of repentance while weary pilgrims dipped into living waters. They emerged refreshed, with a strong sense of their being Israel, the people covenanted to worship God. Baptized pilgrims sang snatches of the psalms of Israel, songs learned in family and communal celebrations (Psalm 51:7):

Purify me with hyssop, that I may be clean;
wash me, and I will be whiter than snow.

In a village ritual pool, men and women immersed naked, decently separated. In the Jordan, segregation was impractical; some pilgrims sought out a private spot within reach of John's voice, while others entered the waters in a light tunic, leaving the rest of their clothing on the bank. John was known to call attention to this clothing, and to press the pilgrims to be generous (Luke 3:11). After immersion, the pilgrims drank from their skins of wine and prepared for a makeshift feast, while John and the strictest of his disciples retired to their natural huts *(sukkoth)* of brush and persisted in their austere diet.

Not all John's disciples followed his rule completely or all the time. These were not monastics bound to a medieval abbot's rigid codes of conduct, but enthusiastic devotees of purity for whom John was a source of wisdom. What hungry Galilean adolescent, smelling bread baked over a fire from the newly harvested grain pilgrims brought with them, hearing his own distinctive dialect of Galilee sung and spoken around a festal fire of brush and tamarisk branches, lured by the sweet ambiance of early summer, would not leave his hut and join his own people for a celebratory meal? In this period, when as an adolescent boy he was growing quickly, Jesus was thin and scraggly, hungry much of the time. With his meager diet of wild food, he never reached his natural height as patristic writers knew. Dressed like John in a loincloth and camel-hair tunic (Matthew 3:4; Mark 1:6), he looked the part of a purifier in the wilderness—a thin, hungry, quasi-prophetic figure.

When the meal was over and children of the pilgrims were sent to sleep, the young Galilean disciple was dispatched to his hut. The adults turned to their private conversation, some of the married couples to foreplay. They felt free to indulge in sexual relations, since God's living water would make them pure the next day when they could again immerse with John, because John's baptism—like Jewish baptism generally—could be repeated as necessity arose. Jesus, comfortably sated by good food, slightly dizzy from several unaccustomed cups of wine, heard the comforting sounds of conversation and pleasure.

The morning sun brought not only its own comfort to John and his followers but also the imperatives of the day—to travel, forage, and purify. And, in Jesus' case, above all: to learn. When pilgrims flocked to John in large numbers, he relied on his disciples, in the midst of the throng in the water, to shout out his teaching of immersion with him. John told the pilgrims to repent and so release their sins (Mark 1:4; Luke 3:3). Then the pilgrims dunked.

For John, and in ancient Judaism generally, repentance meant a "return" (*shuv* in Hebrew, *tuv* in Aramaic) to God. By repenting, one acknowledged being headed in the wrong direction; by changing course, one was realigned with the divine. Repentance did not emphasize sin or depravity; the notion of original sin as a hopeless condition was a later motif in Christianity, developed by Augustine of Hippo during the fifth century C.E. John, far from preaching hopelessness, offered in repentance a pragmatic alternative to being estranged from God. In both Hebrew and Greek "to sin" (*chata, hamartano*) originally meant to miss the mark, as in archery. A rabbi's teaching showed how one could go right again, and only implied where one had gone wrong. After the Reformation, repentance was an individual act, but in ancient Christian as well as Jewish culture, it was social, involving how people in their communities and families ordered their lives.

John demanded repentance from all those who came to be immersed by him, so that Jesus stood on the same ground as everyone else. The hurt inflicted during his childhood, the sense that he was an outcast, in the wrong through no fault of his own, was healed through his repeated immersions. The Jordan's waters washed away his feeling of estrangement. He repented of the anger he had felt, of his resentment against his own people in Nazareth. He knew he was released from sin in John's baptism. And, in turn, he was prepared to release the grudges he felt against others. His reward was a place in a group dedicated to a respected religious practice.

Jesus joined the other disciples in John's practice only after he had watched, listened, absorbed, then mastered John's *mishnah*. A rabbi's mishnah was his "repetition," the words and actions that conveyed his teachings. His disciples soon learned the principle that "everyone who forgets one word of his mishnah, Scripture regards as indebted for his life!" (Avoth 3:8). Jesus never forgot.

Yet John did more for Jesus than teach his mishnah; he gave him the sense of belonging to a family. Luke's Gospel (without any support from the others) portrays Jesus' relationship to John the Baptist at his birth as that of a cousin (Luke 1:5–80). This portrayal is festooned with angelic manifestations, punctuated with little psalmic arias from the characters, and predicated on the assumption that travel over long distances was quick and easy for the pregnant women who feature in the narrative. The scholarly consensus that the whole story is legendary, like the nativity chapters as a whole in both Matthew and Luke, seems so well founded that it is now a matter of common sense. Yet for all that, Luke grasps that with John the Baptist and his disciples Jesus had a secure sense of family he would never know again.

John's insistence on the dynamic relationship between repentance and release from sin was the source of Jesus' emphasis on the same relationship throughout his own ministry. This release from sin, which is translated into English as "forgiveness," referred to the actual loosing or freeing (*aphiemi* in Greek, *shebaq* in Aramaic and Hebrew) of a person from the consequences of his own action by God. Jesus' conviction that release from sin makes every Israelite pure—and thus acceptable in God's eyes—is perhaps his most enduring legacy, and it was derived directly from his experience with John the Baptist.

The link between repentance and purity, the public emphasis of John's ministry, was readily understood by Israelites at large. The quest for purity was a common bond between Jesus and the hundreds of pilgrims he met while helping John with his immersions. But as Jesus advanced as John's *talmid,* he was also initiated into the esoteric side of his rabbi's teaching, the heart of his path to God. Behind John's public practice of immersion was an inner wisdom that explained why immersion was effective, where it came from, and how it was a part of God's plan to release Israel from both sin and oppression. In John's esoteric practice, Jesus began to refine his vision of the Kingdom of God and learn how to convey his vision to others.

John had forged a path into the mysteries of the divine mind through meditation. He was a part of the ancient rabbinic tradition that focused on the first chapter of Ezekiel. This text describes the Chariot, the moving Throne of God. The Chariot was the source of God's energy and intelligence, the origin of his power to create and destroy. By meditating on the Chariot, John and his disciples aspired to become one with God's Throne.

Ezekiel had prophesied in the wake of the destruction of the Temple by the Babylonians, when both the Davidic throne and God's Throne on earth, Mount Zion, had been destroyed. In response to the destruction, Ezekiel envisioned the *heavenly* Throne of God, where Yahweh still abided (Ezekiel 1:4–28), the many-wheeled Chariot of fire. In developing his conception of the Throne, Ezekiel used the biblical tradition that began with Moses, the first prophet to see the Throne during his ecstatic vision while receiving the Torah from heaven (Exodus 24:9–10). The Throne appears again in biblical tradition when Elijah, still alive, is transported into heaven by a divine, fiery chariot (2 Kings 2:11–12). Later, Isaiah sees an enormous Throne, hovering above Mount Zion, on which God sits, the flaming hem of his garments trailing into the Temple (Isaiah 6:1–5). Ezekiel brought these epiphanies together by conceiving of the divine Throne as a chariot. Because he saw the Throne as moving, Ezekiel was able to have his vision in exile in Babylon, rather than in the holy land.

The Chariot was to become the master symbol of Jewish mysticism. Ezekiel modeled his chariot after the war chariots of the Assyrians, which had roared over the plain of Esdraelon in successive waves during the eighth century B.C.E., sweeping through Samaria to grind up the Israelite armies of King Hoshea. The Babylonians later adopted Assyrian-style chariots in their devastatingly successful siege of Jerusalem in 587 B.C.E. By that time, the Jews knew more than they wanted to know about the Assyrian chariot, which put their own meager buggies—more perks for their officers than instruments of war—to shame. The Assyrian model was the tank of the first millennium B.C.E., an enormous vehicle, manned by up to four warriors, drawn by fierce steeds, and armored against attack.

The Assyrian chariot had rolled over the land of Abraham, Isaac, and Jacob, but now, in Ezekiel's mind, the greatest Chariot of them all rolled through the heavens. The steeds of the Assyrians had become monsters: "Every one had four faces, and every one of them had four wings, and their legs were straight legs and the sole of their feet was as the sole of a calf's foot, and they sparkled like burnished brass. They had the hands of a man under their wings on their four sides" (Ezekiel 1:6–8). On each beast, Ezekiel saw the four faces of a man, a lion, an ox, and an eagle (Ezekiel 1:10). (These faces were to become the symbols of the four Evangelists during the second century.) Magnificent wheels conveyed the four monsters, which propelled the Chariot at the speed of lightning in any direction, horizontal or vertical.

The Assyrian chariot, though deadly, was notoriously hard to steer, and Ezekiel improved its design. Each creature had four wheels beside it, reinforced not by spokes but by wheels within wheels. Depending on which of their wheels the creatures deployed, they were ready, without turning, to move in unison instantaneously in any direction, and even up or down (Ezekiel 1:15–21). The wheels implied that no place, no time, was beyond reach of the divine presence.

Ezekiel's vision of the Chariot was accompanied by the sound of roaring waters, imbued with the energy of the initial creation. A crystal rainbow shone above the surreal and frightening spectacle of the beasts. Above that was God's sapphire-like Throne (Ezekiel 1:22–28), the primeval reality, the vortex of creation itself that was timeless, still present, and moving with stormy force.

John taught Jesus and his other disciples to meditate on Ezekiel's vision of the Chariot. The Chariot text itself, of course, was not merely a written document, because the majority of rabbis in the ancient period, and many of John's followers, Jesus included, were illiterate. Ezekiel's words had to be memorized, his description of the Chariot mastered in all its detail, before meditation could even begin. The initiate's mind had to be on the text's meaning, not on the mechanics of recitation.

The disciples also had to master the text's intonation and cadence. The musical phrasing of the words (like mantras in Hindu and Buddhist traditions) was deemed essential to clear the way for divine realization. "Look at what you listen to!" Jesus told his own disciples later in his life (Mark 4:24), a technique he had learned from John. The words themselves were viewed as sacred, imbued with divine force. Without the correct intonation, they would lack the energy needed to transport the initiate to the locus of God's presence.

Jesus learned to *become* Ezekiel's text, embody its imagery, and master (as John had before him) the many other complex texts within Jewish tradition that embellished, augmented, and refined Ezekiel's vision. Like any aspiring rabbinic visionary, he needed a superb memory and concentrated devotion to pursue his quest.

Some of the mystical texts Jesus learned are still read today. Others have been lost over time. Still others, John's own vision of the Chariot among them, could only be known through personal familiarity with a rabbi. John was like a guru. His tone of voice, his attitude in mediation, his physical posture and gestures during hours of intense mindfulness and moments of ecstatic vision were as much the "text" that Jesus learned as the words from Ezekiel we can study on the page twenty centuries later.

As Jesus mastered the techniques of envisioning the Chariot, John began to teach him the secrets of God's Spirit, which flowed from the Chariot through all creation. This divine spirit was called *ruach* in Hebrew and Aramaic. John saw Spirit as palpable to Israel in the roaring waters of heaven that surrounded the Chariot, as well as in the "living waters" of the Jordan River. Water was moving and alive; it cleansed and purified the land and its people. John promised his disciples that just as he had immersed them in water, God would immerse them in holy Spirit (Mark 1:8; Matthew 3:11; Luke 3:16).

John's linking of Spirit and water, like his focus on the Chariot, was inspired by Ezekiel. Purifying water, Ezekiel had promised, together with God's Spirit, would bring with it a "heart of flesh" instead of a "heart of stone." Spirit would overcome the lack of compassion and disregard one Israelite showed another—basic to prophetic criticism of Israel—and ready the chosen people to live by the covenant with God (Ezekiel 36:25–27). Jesus learned from John that immersion in Spirit led not only to repentance and release from sin but also to compassion (Luke 3:10–11):

> *The crowds questioned him and said, So what shall we do? He answered and said to them, One who has two tunics, give over to the one who has not! And one who has food, do likewise!*

John taught Jesus that Spirit was not only water but "wind," another basic meaning of *ruach* that also appears in the Torah. *Ruach* as wind referred to the invisible, creative force of God that moved over the primal waters at the beginning of creation (Genesis 1:2), shaping all that is.

Both water and wind symbolize Spirit as the animating aspect of God, his infinite capacity to generate new forms of life. Jesus came to see that all creation was infused with the pulse of God: "He looks on the earth and it trembles; he touches the mountains and they smoke" (Psalm 104:32). Creation was not only primordial; it was happening anew each day, moment by moment. When God turned his face away or withheld his Spirit, his creations were instantly snuffed out and crumbled to dust, while that same Spirit constantly renewed life (Psalm 104:29–30). God was capable at any time of destroying the world and creating new heavens and a new earth (Isaiah 65:17). Yet as Jesus himself said, all living things, the simplest birds, find their nurture in God (Matthew 6:26; Luke 12:24).

John and his disciples built the expectation that God's Spirit was ready to be poured out on Israel anew as it had been at the time of Moses, when God liberated his people from slavery, gave them the law, and led them into the promised land. That expectation caused many people to see first John and then Jesus as a prophet who was inspired (literally "breathed into") by Spirit and spoke directly on God's behalf. The standard invocation of prophecy, "Thus says the Lord," is no mere figure of speech. It is a claim on the part of the prophets to pronounce the will of God.[2]

For ancient rabbis like John and Jesus, Spirit did not just animate life, put each particle in place and set it spinning. Encoded in that same animating force was God's omnipotent intelligence, his plan for the world.

---

2. John taught Jesus that people were capable of becoming aware of Spirit because each of us has a human soul (*nephesh* in Hebrew). In Genesis, God breathes into the nostrils of clay he shaped into the form of a man, and Adam becomes a living being, or soul (Genesis 2:7). Adam's soul is his most intimate connection to God's Spirit or breath. There is a direct connection between the esoteric insights of John and Jesus into the nature of God's Spirit, and the later Christian idea of "saving" one's soul. Our souls are saved when they fuse with God's Spirit; because Spirit is eternally becoming, one's soul, and, therefore, one's deepest self, attains immortality. German theologians since the end of the nineteenth century, following the lead of Johannes Weiss, have articulated this idea beautifully in the expression *Endzeit ist Urzeit*, The end of time is the beginning of time. Salvation is indeed apocalyptic, but it also signals a new creation: one's soul is made alive, as Adam's had been at the dawn of time.

Spirit was revealed in Israel's history, and Israel's prophets, when the Spirit was upon them, spoke with God's voice.

Whether that voice was really God's or a figment of the prophet's imagination, however, was always open to dispute. Moses, Jesus, and Muhammad were all at one time rejected by the people they sought to serve. Moses came down from Sinai to find his people kowtowing before a golden calf; Jesus, as we shall see, was derided, threatened with death, and driven from his native Galilee; the people of Mecca went to war against Muhammad. Long after the great prophets died, often violent divisions erupted between people and nations over whether those prophets spoke with God's voice. Jesus' life took the shape it did because he believed that holy Spirit was upon him and that he spoke for God. When he spoke, however, it was often not in the ways that traditionally have been supposed.

J esus' repetitive, committed practice, his sometimes inadequate diet, and his exposure to the elements contributed to the intensity of his vision of God's Chariot. Under John's tutelage, he altered his consciousness and entered the world of the Chariot and the Spirit. As he repeatedly immersed for purification, he came to have an increasingly vivid vision of the heavens splitting open and God's Spirit descending upon him as a dove. And a voice: "you are my son, the beloved; in you I take pleasure" (Matthew 3:13–17; Mark 1:9–11; Luke 3:21–22). Simple though the Gospel narratives may seem, they convey Jesus' revelation that Spirit could change the world. Spirit was the link between the Chariot and the Kingdom, the power by which God's will could be known and done. Spirit in this sense was what Jesus saw descend on him through the tear in heaven's veil.

The imagery of the sky opening and a dove descending may seem serene, almost cuddly, but we need to keep in mind the sense of cosmological disruption and potential for transformation that the Gospels convey. In ancient Jewish thought, the heavens are viewed as hard shells above the earth, so that the dove rends them in its descent. The term "firmament" designates the first shell in the King James Version of Genesis 1:6–8, where "heaven" is described, so people commonly think of it as being airy. But the "firmament" is literally firm and watertight in Hebrew. It is a *raqia,* a hammered-out metallic shell. It protects the earth, which was seen by the ancient Hebrews as a fragile, disk-shaped bubble surrounded on all sides by an infinite sea. Any break in the bubble's shell is fraught with danger, as when the windows of the heavens were opened at the time of Noah and the great flood poured down through the firmament and engulfed the earth (Genesis 7:11).

Ancient Judaism taught that at any time the bubble could be not only crushed but burst by the forces around it. These forces were not limited to primordial water in Hebrew cosmology. Just beyond the firmament, directly over the Temple in Jerusalem, the whole realm of God's unspeakably powerful court was arrayed. Seraphim—not the pink cherubs of Renaissance art, but enormous, burning, multiwinged snakes—thundered in praise of God (Isaiah 6:1–5). These were but a few of the ten thousand spirits and angels that served the heavenly King, the "hosts," "multitudes," or "armies" who stand at God's behest—a pantheon of fearsome, irresistible might (Deuteronomy 33:2). God's Spirit—with all its potential to create and destroy—could be revealed by any of these creatures as they descended into the human world.

The monotheism of Judaism and Christianity did not prevent either religion from developing heavenly cosmologies every bit as elaborate as the Olympian court of Zeus. For Jesus, God's Spirit was not just emanation and energy, and transcended the philosophical ideas of divine intelligence and voice. It was a force so potent that it could take any shape it liked. The sun and moon were dragged across the firmament by God's Spirit in the form of a host of angels, and at each thin spot in the firmament there was an angel, guarding the potential breach or portal into the pantheon. These thin spots were stars, the divine protection Jesus and other Jews of his time saw when they looked into the sky at night.

When Jesus perceived the heavens split open in the midst of his vision of the Chariot, he believed that, for good or ill, the panoply of spiritual power around God was being released into the world. And Jesus saw the Spirit of God not as a Seraph or angel of war but as a dove, hovering over him and descending, as it once had over the primordial waters of creation (Genesis 1:2). The divine Spirit, creating the heart of flesh predicted by Ezekiel, had come again into the world (Ezekiel 36:25–26):

> *I will pour upon you pure waters, and you shall be pure; from all your impurities and from all your idols I will purify you. I will give you a new heart, and a new spirit I will put in your midst, and I will remove the heart of stone from your flesh and give you a heart of flesh.*

Jesus related his experience of Spirit to his friends, and John and his disciples embraced it as the beginning of the fulfillment of God's promise. John called his *talmid* "the lamb of God," because in his innocence he embodied both release from sin and the arrival of Spirit (John 1:29–36). Perhaps that made Jesus cocky; he soon began to contradict his own master. In the wilderness of the Jordan, Jesus received from the close group of fellow visionaries the first sign of the special role he would play in Israel's destiny.

We can imagine how Jesus would have prepared himself repeatedly to receive God's Spirit as he stood naked on the banks of the Jordan or by a pool in one of its feeder streams. Hot sun baked his skin. He closed his eyes, held his breath, and plunged. The water covered and enclosed him. Sounds were muted and John's voice was faint, its urgency and edge softened, as he recited the *mishnah* that was now to Jesus as familiar and constant as his pulse. Then John's voice was loud again as Jesus emerged, waist deep in the chilly, living waters in the midst of the wilderness. A breeze, a natural Spirit, funneled between the mountains, tingled his skin, rustled the sedge, rippled the water.

As his mastery of John's secret teaching grew, his visions of the Chariot intensified, his sense of hovering Spirit grew stronger. He felt Spirit on the skin; he saw and heard it in the air. His experience was not his alone; some of John's disciples said they themselves had heard the voice that spoke to Jesus. Their communal vision welded them together.

When John called Jesus "the lamb of God," he conveyed his deep affection for the Galilean as a prime student of his discipline.[3] This painfully thin, short disciple, an adolescent with down on his cheeks, had experienced more than the purity of his teacher's immersion: the divine Spirit had given him its seal that this purification was complete, genuine, a connection between the realms of heaven and earth. John's trust in the spindly beggar had paid off. The gates of heaven were again open for the Spirit to descend upon Israel.

The close relationship between John and Jesus was not destined to last. As Jesus grew older and more confident, his success in gathering pilgrims for immersion, his ability to invoke Spirit, and the power of his vision of God's Throne put him into competition with John. One Gospel has John say in a stoic manner that Jesus "must grow, and I must diminish" (John 3:30). But that remark cannot conceal deeper tensions.

---

3. Nathanael—one of John's disciples—called Jesus God's "son" (John 1:49), and that is a key to the meaning of that term. Contrary to a popular fallacy, the language of divine sonship is by no means a Christian invention. The term "son" is used frequently in the Old Testament for the special relationship between God and others. Messengers before God's throne (*malakhim* in Hebrew, *anggeloi* in Greek) are called "sons of God" (Genesis 6:2); all Israel is referred to as a divine son (Hosea 11:1); and the Davidic king can be assured by divine voice, "You are my son, this day have I begotten you!" (Psalm 2:7). All these are expressions not of a biological relationship but of the direct revelation which God extends to favored people and angels; they are indeed "the beloved," as Jesus became as a result of his vision. When Jesus speaks of himself as divine son, he is not talking in the extravagant, metaphysical language of a later time, which claimed that he had no human father. Rather, he claims that he is of the spiritual lineage of Israel's seers, the visionaries who meditated on the Chariot and were blessed with the Spirit which pours out from the Throne of the heavenly father.

John's Gospel also speaks of a battle concerning "purification" (John 3:25) involving John and Jesus. Cleanness, the heart of John's program, was the cause of a break that became all but inevitable.

Jesus began to move out of John's stamping grounds near the Jordan into settled areas, and, as a result, he had the opportunity to immerse more people than John did. Just as Jesus had joined the pilgrims in their feasts by the Jordan, so he accepted hospitality in their villages, a persistent practice that all the Gospels reflect. Jesus was motivated not only by his hungry belly. He also had a deep conviction that the people he invited to cleanse themselves by immersion were *already* clean. That was why he could eat with them; within the Judaism of this time, eating with people was vivid testimony that one considered them to be pure.

Jesus actively sought out people in their hamlets and villages and towns around the Jordan, and he accepted their hospitality even before he had immersed them. He was their guest, but he was also an itinerant rabbi, known by his association with John to offer purification. As he joined in holy feast with them, Jesus spoke of the *Abba* of all who was the source of Israel's blessing. Major elements of the prayer Jesus later taught his own disciples, influenced by the Qaddish, were on his lips: "*Abba*, your name will be sanctified, your Kingdom will come."[4] Drinking and eating together, drawn together by Jesus' confidence in the divine Spirit within him, Israelites celebrated the all-embracing sovereignty of God in their midst.

---

4. The "Lord's Prayer" in the Gospels (Matthew 6:9–13; Luke 11:2–4) reflects the liturgical embellishments of the primitive church. Originally, it was a simpler, Aramaic epitome of Jesus' practice. This is my rendering of the original Aramaic, given in the notes:

> *My father, your name will be sanctified, your Kingdom will come:*
> *Give me today the bread that is coming,*
> *And release me my debts—not bring me to the test.*

As the story of his life unfolds, the genesis of every element of this meditative practice is revealed.

John's asceticism made him doubt that God's purity could be celebrated by wine and food. Jesus had made immersion unnecessary for release from sins, and had gradually replaced it with communal meals as the ritual symbol of the coming Kingdom of God. Jesus had been brought by John to see that every Israelite had the means of purity at his disposal, and he came to insist that every Israelite was in fact already pure, embraced by divine Spirit, as he had been. His tangible experience of God overwhelmed the feeling of rejection he had known as a *mamzer* in Nazareth, and he conveyed his newfound sense of inclusion to others. Jesus did not reject immersion, but neither did he require it. His theological differences with John were stark.

As his fame grew, he traveled independently of John, sometimes with a couple of John's disciples, still in the general area of the Jordan, encountering pilgrims and villagers. Sometimes he simply persisted in John's practice of immersion, promoting communal bathing and developing the visionary practice he had acquired from John and made his own. But he also shocked some of John's disciples when he entered settlements to celebrate the Kingdom in Israel with wine and food rather than immersion. This was more than a new twist on John's teaching: it was an alternative practice, and it intensified the competition between the rabbi and his *talmid*. Later Christian theology repressed this competition, as well as Jesus' early dependence upon John. As a result, the stark contrast between John's immersions and Jesus' celebrations at meals has been all but lost. An adolescent crisis with his father, precluded by Joseph's early death, was worked out in Jesus' deeply ambivalent relationship with John.

That fraught relationship was never resolved. John's movement was smashed by Herod Antipas, the son of Herod, who had ruled Galilee when Jesus was born. Antipas, obsessed with military and political threats to his rule, tracked down John after John had criticized Antipas' marriage to Herodias, his half brother's wife. Every bit as ambitious and libidinous as Antipas himself (Josephus *Antiquities* 18 § 110), Herodias had agreed to divorce her first husband to marry Antipas, the tetrarch, or governor, of Galilee and Perea. Perhaps she hoped the Romans might one day grant him the coveted title and prerogatives of a king.

Antipas' first wife (whom Josephus doesn't name), daughter of Aretas, king of Nabatea, decided to abandon Antipas rather than face the humiliation of divorce. She gathered loyal supporters around her in Machaerus, a splendid fortress in the hills of present-day Jordan, five miles east of the Dead Sea. With this fortress, Antipas projected his military power into Perea, his territory east of the Jordan. To humiliate Antipas, his wife set out from the fortress by camel in a caravan of sympathetic soldiers, armed and mounted, to cross the Nabatean border to the south and return to her father (who eventually waged war against Herod over the treatment of his daughter and a dispute over land; Josephus, *Antiquities* 18 § § 109–119). The message was clear: Herod was a poor husband and an inept ruler, with no scruples and no control over his own wife.

John stepped into this political maelstrom (Matthew 14:1–12; Mark 6:14–29; Luke 3:19–20; 9:7–9), condemning Herod's marriage because it violated a basic understanding of purity: marital intercourse with one's brother's wife was prohibited by the Torah, which spoke of such practices as the reason the land had vomited out the peoples before Israel (see Leviticus 18:16, 25). If his first wife's behavior had been a political and personal humiliation, John's attack on Herod's purity was a religious challenge with directly political implications: an illegitimate marriage implied that the ruler himself was illegitimate. No one needed reminding that the Herodians were Idumeans rather than Jews by origin, which meant they had been forcibly converted to Judaism—and circumcision—during the rule of the Maccabean dynasty in 129 B.C.E. Any Herodian was an easy target of the charge of impurity, and Antipas felt the sting of this challenge from John, a popular teacher.

With his first wife out of his reach, Herod Antipas moved swiftly to make an example of John, who had impugned the legitimacy of his reign. From his base in Machaerus, Herod sent a *contubernia* composed of his own men to seize John. A squad of eight horsemen equipped with short swords and lances, the *contubernia* moved quickly, acquiring information by terror, intimidation, and bribery. Surprise was crucial to their operation, since if John had known the danger he was in, he could easily have gone underground. Once the *contubernia* had identified John's whereabouts, they would have planned to attack in the morning, when John and his disciples were least ready to take flight or defend themselves.

Some of the *contubernia* spoke Aramaic and were Jews, but the language of most of these mercenaries was the Hellenistic *Koine*, the *lingua franca* of the Roman Empire, in their mouths a kind of pigeon-Greek. As they swept into John's camp at dawn with a cacophony of dialects and unsheathed short swords, the disciples realized immediately that they were helpless to protect their teacher. The name of Herod Antipas, tetrarch of Galilee and Perea, the same Herod whom John had attacked, was all they needed by way of explanation for John's capture.

John was forced by prods and blows to walk with arms bound to Antipas' palace in Machaerus—the site of his humiliation by his first wife—then was executed publicly outside the fortress. Wielding a long sword with practiced precision, a soldier hacked off his head. Had he been a Roman official rather than a petty governor subservient to Rome's military machine, Antipas would have had the power to crucify John, and he must have wished for that to reestablish his honor. Still, the beheading assuaged his Herodian dignity. Matthew (14:3–12) and Mark (6:17–29) portray Herodias and her daughter Salome as inciting Antipas to execute John with Salome's famous performance of her mother's choreography. Luke is probably more accurate in eliminating the song and dance (Luke 3:19–20). Fifteen years later, when Antipas suffered a military defeat at the hands of Aretas, many Jews saw the defeat as just punishment for his treatment of John (Josephus, *Antiquities* 18 § 116). In seeking to make John an example, Antipas had produced a martyr whose memory shadowed his reign.

The morning of John's capture, Jesus and the other disciples scattered; resistance against armed force was impossible, and they were relieved that only John had been taken. But even if Antipas had not specifically ordered the arrest of John's disciples, they had become targets of opportunity for any soldier's aggression or cruelty. The disciples knew the trails and hideouts of the Jordan better than the soldiers, and some simply hid, kindling no fire at night, avoiding the garrison posts along the pilgrimage route, sheltering in brush and in caves on the hillsides. Others, bolder, followed the *contubernia* at a distance to Machaerus and saw the beheading of their master. Antipas wanted them to see it; and he even permitted them to bury John (Matthew 14:12; Mark 6:29).

Jesus, now eighteen years old, felt John's loss even more acutely than the rest of the disciples. First Joseph, now John; worse, John had been killed while he and Jesus were locked in their controversy over purity. One story attempts to patch over this tension with an implausible tale of John sending emissaries to Jesus (Matthew 11:2–6; Luke 7:18–23), as if Herod Antipas would have granted his prisoner the leisure and liberty to discuss messianic claims. This was a moment of disorientation, fear, and confusion. No source, in the Gospels or elsewhere, puts Jesus with the disciples who were present at the scene of John's death. Jesus was one of those who had scattered. Just as he avoided Roman garrisons in the Jordan Valley, so he steered clear of Jerusalem now: Antipas was a client-ruler of Rome, and any *talmid* of John on the lam would instinctively give soldiers a wide berth. The death of John left him aching and lonely. But it also gave him a new sense of confidence and independence. He was a living link to a great master. That might have been what gave him the courage finally to go home. Nazareth was still a place of estrangement, but it posed nothing like the danger of being in or near Perea, and his family was there. He would return like the prodigal son he was; later he spoke of his return in a parable (Luke 15:11–32). But as he returned to his native village, any feast of welcome would be provided not by Joseph but by his *Abba*, whose Spirit had moved over him in the Jordan's living waters, in the wind that cooled him and rustled the reeds at night.

FOUR

$$\mathcal{A}$$

The Prodigal
Returns

J esus "retreated" into Galilee,[1] a relatively safe haven. Although it was
also under Herod's control, John had not been active there, and while
there were occasional garrison towns, it was only lightly patrolled by Herodian and Roman soldiers. Jesus simply avoided the pilgrim's route to Galilee
up the Jordan Valley, which was under closer Roman scrutiny. Instead, he
chose the more direct but rougher route through the highlands of Samaria.

He traveled into Samaria with two of John's former disciples (John
1:43–51), both from Galilee. Nathanael came from the hillside village of
Kana (John 21:2), four miles northeast of Nazareth, and Philip from the
more cosmopolitan fishing town of Bethsaida, northeast of the Sea of
Galilee. They traveled on footpaths through forests of oak, pine, juniper,
and cypress, alert for wild oxen and bandits. The valley floors were carpeted with meadows of wild mustard, dill, coriander, cumin, and mint,
and neat fields of wheat and barley climbed cultivable hillsides.

---

1. As Matthew 4:12 puts it. Many translations water down the meaning of *anakhoreo* in
Matthew's Greek, giving us "he withdrew." That is because they ignore the fraught political context that the execution of John by Herod Antipas produced for all John's disciples.

They begged bread and produce from small villages nestled in the highlands west of the Jordan River Valley. News of John's execution preceded them, and many villagers felt sympathy for these committed disciples of a famous master who had stood up to Antipas. There was a special feeling in Samaria for John's disciples, since John had asserted that Samaritans, too, could become pure and part of Israel after immersion.

John's view had been unusual. Typically, Galilean and Judean Jews viewed Samaritans as a people apart from Israel, even though many Samaritans were clearly of the progeny of Jacob, members of the twelve clans who had accepted God's covenant with Abraham and Moses. The Samaritans practiced circumcision and kept Shabbath. They also sacrificed to Yahweh, but they did so on Mount Gerizim, not at the Temple in Jerusalem. That made Samaritans impure idolaters in the eyes of other Jews.

The Samaritan people had deliberately broken with the mainstream of Judaism because they had been oppressed. David and Solomon are portrayed as heroes in the Old Testament, yet the first book of Kings makes it plain that they used the centralized power of the Judean monarchy to impose their will on all Israel. To build the Temple, they enslaved their fellow Israelites, especially those from the territory that became known as Samaria. Many Jews outside Judea hoped slavery would cease when Solomon died in 922 B.C.E. But his son Rehoboam only intensified the practice, taking more and more slaves to expand Jerusalem and to increase his army and retinue. In so doing, he followed the arrogant advisers who urged him to declare, "My finger is thicker than my father's loins" (1 Kings 12:10). The result was an overt and successful revolution (1 Kings 12) the same year Solomon died.

The rebels called their land north of Judea "Israel," established their own temple on Mount Gerizim, and eventually built their resplendent capital city, Samaria. The Samaritans became more prosperous and powerful than the Judeans, and might well have become the dominant force in shaping the religion of Israel. But the Assyrians besieged Samaria in

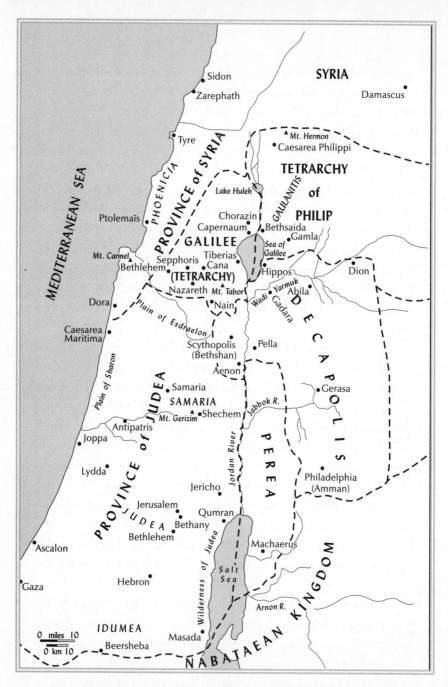

TERRITORIAL ISRAEL AND ITS SURROUNDINGS

722 B.C.E., exiled or scattered the political and religious leaders they did not kill, and settled non-Israelites in the Samaritans' land. The Israelites of Samaria fell victim to the cultural genocide of the Assyrians; they disappeared from history, persisting only in legends about the "ten lost tribes" of Israel. To the Jews (that is, the Judeans) the Samaritans were apostasy and defeat incarnate, a perfect example of what the people of God should not become: hopelessly mixed up with the Gentiles that the Assyrians and later conquerors settled in their land.

Having grown up in Nazareth, Jesus shared the Galilean prejudice against Samaritans, so it is ironic that Samaria was the site of one of his most profound realizations (John 4:4–42). Outside the small village of Sychar, he came to an abandoned well. Nathanael and Philip had gone on to the village to seek bread, but curiosity and thirst made Jesus stay by the well that local lore claimed the patriarch Jacob himself had dug (John 4:6, 8). The well was a hole in the ground, a couple of feet across. He stood in the hot sun, surrounded by thick brush, with no way to draw water in this disused place. A woman appeared, clearly past her youth, barefoot. She wore only her tunic, no pilgrim's cloak, which signaled she lived in the nearby village and was not a traveler. Her dark hair was pulled back in Samaritan fashion, and she carried a wooden dipper and flaxen cord. He was surprised and there was a moment when he hesitated. "Give me to drink (*Hav li mishteh*)," he finally said without preamble or greeting.

Bemused, she just stared at him. He had spoken first. In the steamy heat of early spring, thirsty and returning to Galilee, he needed water, and asked a Samaritan for help. This request was unusual not only because of the prejudice of Galileans toward Samaritans, but because rabbis were known to complain that Samaritan women in particular were perpetually impure, "deemed menstruants from their cradle," was how they put it in a crude, dismissive proverb (Niddah 4:1 in the Mishnah). Not only did Samaritans practice idolatry in their temple on Mount Gerizim; worse, they had been subjected to a policy of programmatic intermarriage by the Assyrian empire after the conquest of 722 B.C.E. The doubt about the parentage of a Galilean accused of being a *mamzer* paled in comparison to the suspicion with which Jews regarded Samaritans. Yet Jesus spoke to a woman more despised by the standards of Nazareth than he was himself.

She was amazed. "How is it that *you*, a Jew, ask of *me*, a Samaritan woman, to drink?" (John 4:9).

"Everyone who drinks from this water will thirst again," he replied. "Yet whoever drinks from the water I give will not ever thirst: but the water I will give will become in one a fountain of water welling up to eternal life" (John 4:13–14). She drew the water for him, bewildered by his pronouncement, but instinctively helping a stranger in need. He took the dipper from her, threw back his head, and let the cold water pour into his mouth, over his beard and neck. By taking water from her hands Jesus contracted uncleanness, but in his mind the water came from the same pure well of Spirit he had first tasted in John's immersion.

He spoke on about this "fountain of water" welling within to assure her, and to remind himself, that the purity John had promised was already inside both of them. His deep, disciplined sense of the Spirit within him unleashed a compassion for her that ignored the usual prohibitions of contact with Samaritans, especially Samaritan women.

In Jesus' mind, the esoteric meaning of immersion had become public, available to all Israelites. The "heart of flesh" Ezekiel and John had promised was now growing within Israel by the power of God's Spirit. Jesus expanded the scope of John's esoteric teaching of the holy Spirit and the divine Chariot. Instead of limiting the world of visions to the most advanced disciples, Jesus put that practice in the public domain. He saw that Spirit was flowing out to all Israel, even to Samaritans. Why should Spirit be felt only in John's immersions?

Philip and Nathanael returned (John 4:27). Jesus' easy conversation with the woman amazed them at least as much as the woman herself. As Jesus conversed with her and drank from her dipper, they remained stunned and silent. Thirsty as they were, they would not have touched the dipper or the water in it. They kept their distance, eyes on the ground, perplexed by this tableau of obvious impropriety.

Jesus himself was surprised at his extending the assurance of purity to a Samaritan. He must have guessed what had brought her to this remote place, outside the village, when the protected, equipped well of her own community would have been far safer to use. He told her in a mocking tone to call her husband. She replied that she had none. True, he said, you have lived with five husbands, and your current man is not your husband at all (John 4:16–18). He surmised that her notoriety, which probably included adultery, had driven her from Sychar, and that confirmed his Jewish prejudice against Samaritans. His deep conviction that God was in the process of purifying and pouring out his Spirit on all Israel, even Samaritans, did not completely wash away the cultural bias of his Galilean upbringing.

The woman went back to the village and spoke with pride and wonder about her exchange with Jesus (John 4:28–30). She called him a prophet (John 4:19). She would have felt empowered by Jesus' assertion of her purity; but, perhaps, she would also have been subdued, threatened by the ease with which he had discerned the shame that drove her from her people to seek water from a long-abandoned well.

The contact with the Samaritan woman must have deepened Jesus' rift with Nathanael and Philip as John's three former disciples continued toward Galilee. Even as Jesus mourned John's death, his conflict with his esteemed teacher could not be repressed. He crafted one of the paradoxes for which he was to become famous to express his complex relationship to his rabbi (Luke 7:28; Matthew 11:11):

> I say to you, no one among women-born is greater than Yochanan!
> But the least in the Kingdom of God is greater than he!

This declaration erupted from the tension between a conflicted emotional attachment to John and basic differences with John's religious orientation. His teacher was both greater than the greatest in his understanding of the preeminence of Spirit, and less than the least, because he had failed to see that God's sovereign Spirit was present even among Samaritans, and without immersion.

The emotional cost of embracing the Samaritans resounds in this assertive, stark statement about John, his spiritual father. Many popular writings about Jesus portray him as a perpetual compromiser, always eager to avoid being judgmental. He becomes the world's first liberal in his dedication to a God who is all love and no judgment. That picture gets Jesus exactly wrong. Struggling against the feeling that he had betrayed his background and upbringing, he was often testy and defensive, prone to overreact to any suggestion that he wasn't loyal to Israel. A harder side of Jesus' character shows up in what he said about John so soon after his master's death.

This conflict with John fed his resolve about embracing the Samaritan woman. In their encounter, which had required him to overcome deep-seated prejudice, he had transgressed his culture and his teacher. Likewise, he transgressed both by contradicting John's insistence that immersion was a prior condition of purification. But his transgression had brought him closer to his *Abba,* and there was no turning back. Spirit was pushing him to a new understanding of Israel. If God was there for an alleged *mamzer,* God was also there for a Samaritan. His pain and anxiety is part of the maturing of many religious personalities: the shedding of conventional identity in order to define a new self, framed by contact with the divine.

Jesus committed himself to this principle of self-annihilation as a lifelong process of renewal. He taught: Whoever loses one's life will save it (Mark 8:35). The world's mystical traditions center on the abandonment of the self, a dark night of the soul prior to union with God. Often that loss is a discrete event, punctuating one's life and signaling the first steps along a mystic's path. Jesus indeed took such first steps as he drank water drawn by the Samaritan's hands in the derelict clearing in the shadow of Mount Gezirim. But the moment of loss and renewal of self did not stop here; he turned it into a persistent principle. Again and again he embraced this shattering of self.

In a tentative, immature fashion Jesus pressed this program on Philip and Nathanael as the three of them crossed the Plain of Esdraelon from Samaria into Galilee. His homeland stood out from surrounding regions in the intensity with which it was farmed. Generations of reaping and sowing had made for ordered fertility, and the gentle hills were terraced, unlike the rougher terrain in Samaria, and supported vineyards and groves of olive and palm. They crossed into this Jewish land, and despite their closeness and the shared adventure of their recent flight, they went their separate ways. Jesus' refusal to preach John's immersion and his easy contact with Samaritans were radical departures from their master's teaching that alienated Philip and Nathanael.

Jesus was as alone in Galilee as he had been in Jerusalem when he was fourteen. He made his way back to Nazareth, a little village set on a rocky hillside, protected by a string of mountains north of the Valley of Jezreel. He came up the hill from the south, savoring the familiar configuration of the pastures, fields, and groves. The Galileans were harvesting barley. Men cut the crop with powerful thrusts of their iron-bladed shoulder scythes. Women and children gathered the whiskery stalks into sheaves and dragged them across the fields to their courtyards, where they set them out to dry on grass mats under the eaves of their homes.

We have no report of what happened when Jesus, unheralded and un-expected, walked into town on that late spring or early summer day in 21 C.E. But after he had become a master of parables, he embedded his homecoming experience in the parable of the prodigal son.

In this vivid, hyperbolic tale (Luke 15:11–32), a wayward child is re-duced to pig-tending for a Gentile after squandering his inheritance. When he at last returns home, his father treats him like a prince, order-ing a fattened calf slaughtered for a celebratory feast. An older brother, trudging back from the field, is angry and jealous when a servant explains what's happening. The father is sympathetic but firm: "It was necessary to celebrate and rejoice, because your brother was dead and lives, was lost and is found" (Luke 15:32).

There was no fatted calf for Jesus (and probably none was available in Nazareth), but Mary greeted Jesus as eagerly as the prodigal's doting father. James is clearly the older brother in the prodigal parable. He would have resented the joyous welcome given Jesus by Mary after the disgrace Jesus had brought on the family by abandoning them in Jerusalem. But for Jesus this return to Nazareth ended a long and dangerous nomadic period, and the emotional healing of his mother's embrace resonates in his parable of the prodigal come home.

Jesus' younger brothers were still living with Mary, while James and Joses had married and moved into their in-laws' compounds. Mary remained in the house where Jesus had been raised with her younger sons, Judas and Simon. The names of all Mary's natural sons—Jesus and Judas and Simon—convey a zeal for the heroic figures of Israel's liberation. We know nothing about Jesus' sisters, not even their names (see Mark 6:3), but some of them probably lived with Mary, too.

Nazareth's social fabric was woven from family ties. Despite the difficulty of her son's status—and precisely because she appreciated how marginal he had been—Mary did her best to bring him into the orbit of the community's life. Jesus' adult period in Nazareth brought him the only sustained, dependable comfort he ever knew. There was shelter and plentiful food, family meals of celebration, festive welcomes from friends—and even from people who had avoided Jesus before his association with John. John's fame only grew after his death, so that his Galilean disciple was greeted with a generosity to which he was unaccustomed. The prodigal in his parable was decked out with clothing and a lavish feast is made in his honor (Luke 15:22–23). These images reflect the welcome which greeted Jesus during the months after his return to Nazareth, as he entered his nineteenth year.

Galilean children lived with their parents until their marriages were arranged, and Jesus was now well into the marriageable age. Mary must have hoped that he would wed and settle in or near Nazareth. One reputed *mamzer* could marry another according to custom (see Qiddushin 4:1 in the Mishnah). Making a match for a *mamzer* was challenging, but a parent could look beyond the local community to surrounding villages for a suitable spouse.

Jesus helped in the fields, tended Mary's garden, and took up the trade he had been taught by Joseph, journeying through Jewish Galilee to repair and build. He might easily have married and made Nazareth or a nearby village his home. The pleasures of life in Galilee would have been especially satisfying after the austerities he had known during his time with John. In Nazareth he was a glamorous figure, part adept and part adventurer. He had studied with a folk hero and enjoyed firsthand knowledge of the Temple and of cosmopolitan Judea. He had survived the wilderness of the Jordan and had avoided Herod Antipas by traversing Samaria. Few in his little village could boast such a range of experience. What did his repute as a *mamzer* matter to this strong, mature young man, a survivor of hunger, cold, thugs, and Herod Antipas' attack on John? During festive parties with family, friends, or local hosts intrigued by his reputation, Jesus found his voice as a teacher and storyteller, entertaining guests with his direct, succinct style of speaking.

In this period of ease and honest pleasure, as he regaled fellow diners with stories of his adventures, he could see little point in fretting (Matthew 6:25–26 and Luke 12:22–24):

> *Do not worry about your life, what you should eat or what you should drink, nor about your body, what you should wear: is not life more than nourishment and the body than clothing? Look at the birds of heaven: they neither sow nor harvest, nor do they gather into storehouses, and your heavenly father nourishes them. Don't you matter more than they?*

Jesus taught that material concerns were secondary to the rich fulfillment that flowed from God: "seek first the Kingdom of God and his righteousness, and all these things will be added to you" (Matthew 6:33; Luke 12:31). Worry was unproductive; nourishment came from God alone. Here, in Galilee, the Kingdom was revealed in the weaving and stitching, planting and reaping, grape picking and pressing that assured a full life, not merely survival. Those activities find their way into Jesus' parables as images of God's Kingdom in a way that contrasts with the far less organic imagery of the Essenes at Qumran and the Rabbis in Talmud.

Galileans were enormously proud of the fertility of their land, which exceeded that of other regions in Palestine. The immediate, physical life worked out on the land provided food and wine for them. The rich bounty of the green Galilean hills mirrored their hope for the Kingdom that God yearned to provide for his people—if only Israel would honor his commandments, do his work, and cease to stray from the path of righteousness. Then justice, compassion, and truth would rule, and the oppressor would depart from Israel's sacred soil and go back across the Mediterranean to the land of the uncircumcised with its vomitoriums, orgies, and idols.[2]

Jesus took his place in Nazareth, and for perhaps the first time in his life we see him at ease. Not without reason German scholars have called this period in Jesus' life *die galiläische Frühling,* the Galilean springtime. But like all springtimes it was ephemeral, fleeting. Already, Jesus' activity was sowing seeds of dissent in Nazareth and beyond.

Jesus' work as a journeyman gave him the opportunity to develop his practice of holy feasts into an art form. Usually, journeyworkers were feted at the completion of a project. The meals were informal parties to eat the fruit and grain of the season, and stews of dried meat and vegetables ladled onto flat bread, and to drink local wine. They were not as elaborate as the feasts that marked circumcision and marriage, when

---

2. Jesus and other Israelites called the Mediterranean the *Yam* or sea. For them, this *Yam* was it—the one and only ocean, immeasurably vast. The people who came from its far shore might as well have been aliens coming from another planet. The ancient rabbis had a theory that in this vast sea there was once a reed (see Shabbath 56b in the Talmud). A floating piece of seaweed stuck to it. More and more seaweed collected until you had the plague that was Italy.

freshly slaughtered meat was prepared; still, the completion of journey-work meant festive eating and drinking.

A typical job for Jesus was to repair a household wall in a village near Nazareth. Mary would arise first, before sunrise, to prepare breakfast and send him on his way. The house was chilly and damp. It was expensive to light the tiny clay oil lamps; she worked by feel and the glow of dawn. She fetched salted fish (sprat from the Sea of Galilee) from the store-room just outside the door leading into the courtyard, placed a portion on an oak dish, and set it on a low pine table. She returned to the courtyard to draw water from the cistern and wine from the storeroom, then set water in a jug and wine in a smaller stone flask on the table next to the plate of fish and the stale remains of yesterday's bread.

By this time, the household had been awakened by the gentle rhythm of her work. Outside the courtyard, they relieved themselves in a crude latrine and rinsed their hands and faces with water from the cistern. They sat at the table on the floor atop rough woolen rugs.

Jesus left for work just after dawn, dressed in his basic flax tunic, a smocklike shirt in which he slept, and an overgarment of undyed lamb's wool that resembled a poncho, its color muted shades of grays and browns. He cinched a thick leather belt without a buckle around his waist and fastened its overlapping ends with leather thongs. In his belt he hitched his tools: a large wooden mallet made of seasoned oak and an iron chisel with a loop at the end, which doubled as a crowbar. He could expect to find a wooden shovel, if he needed one, at the job.

The walls of Galilean peasant houses were made from stacked stone (limestone and basalt), mortared with mud, then coated with a stucco made from a mixture of mud and clay. Because water corroded the stucco and worked its way into the crude mortar between the stones, the walls had to be repaired constantly. A journey worker had to fetch, mix, and water the dirt with which he worked. If the rocks inside the walls had slipped, he had to reset or replace them. Sometimes he would replace a rotten lintel by cutting and setting a new beam.

Jesus enjoyed his work enough to identify himself with it. In the

Gospel according to Thomas (saying 77) he speaks eloquently of his attachment to this rough, manual labor, referring to his materials as expressions of who he was: "Split the wood—I am there; lift the stone and you will find me there." Linked to Joseph by profession, touching the oak and iron his father had worked with, Jesus felt a connection with his fellow Galileans that was never deeper or easier. There was satisfaction in the hard physicality, the pleasure of working with one's hands and enjoying the tangible rewards of labor.

He wiped his tools and washed himself after finishing his work and then joined his hosts at an impromptu feast. The little banquet acknowledged indebtedness in the exchange economy of Galilee, a deposit toward a bigger gift that would be given to Jesus' family at harvest. A day's work was worth a midsized basket of almonds, apricots, pomegranates, or walnuts—a welcome addition to a standard diet of grain, vegetables, and beans. Now the extended family and friends from the village were gathered and the meal was eaten either in the courtyard or in one of the small huts, depending on numbers and the threat of rain. The head of the household asked, *Berakhah, rabbi?*" ("A blessing, rabbi?"), ceding to Jesus the invocation which would invite God's favor into the household during the celebration.

Jesus replied to the invitation of his host by taking a cup and raising it in front of him, then he said, "Sanctified are you, Lord, eternal King: creating the fruit of the earth." His eyes followed the cup, looking upward toward the heavenly Chariot as he recited the ancient, profoundly moving words. He did more than ask God to bestow fulfillment and prosperity on Israel, which was the usual mealtime blessing. Instead, he used the language of the holy feast that sanctified Israel before Shabbath and festivals. A blessing asked God to enter Israel's time; but Jesus was sanctifying Israel for entry into God's time. He was treating that house, these people, this little moment of social intimacy as God's place and time, as sacred as Shabbath or a feast of pilgrimage. A hush fell over the household. Then everyone drank.

"Sanctified are you, Lord, eternal King, bringing forth bread from the earth," he said, breaking the bread. The confidence and pleasure that emanated from Jesus, in his focus on the divine Kingdom and the divine Chariot, inspired his fellow Galileans. The bread of their land sealed the blessing that came from sanctifying the name of God. They sought Jesus out to preside over his empowering meals. He made their homes pure, a sacred space that God could inhabit.

Jesus had ceased practicing John's immersion altogether; he left that part of John's program behind in favor of his own practice of festive celebration. As he wined and dined his way around Galilee, he developed the simple prayer, much elaborated in the Gospels (Matthew 6:1–13; Luke 11:2–4) that would come to represent his spiritual vision:

Abba, your name will be sanctified,
Your Kingdom will come:
Give me today the bread that is coming,
And release me my debts.

God as father, divine Kingdom, and forgiveness had been woven into his experience on the Jordan. But now Jesus spoke also of "the bread that is coming." That simple phrase in Aramaic, *lakhma d'ateh,* was difficult to render in Greek and has provoked centuries of dispute, but its original sense is straightforward. "Bread that is coming" is the food that God provides for his people. It evokes the daily nourishment that comes from the fertile soil of Galilee, and also God's provision of miraculous bread (*manna*) at the time of Israel's exodus from Egypt (Exodus 16). Bread was both what you lived by and what you hoped for, the fact and the miracle of divine sustenance.

Meals rather than manual work progressively became the focus of Jesus' journeys. The Galileans understood, both emotionally and intellectually, what these meals meant. Their land was clean and acceptable to God. They were pure and forgiven. Their bread was an emblem of God's Kingdom.

As their enthusiasm for Jesus' banquets increased, he worked less and less and feasted more; hence the burden on his family steadily grew. Honor demanded they acknowledge Jesus' indebtedness to his hosts. They had to reciprocate by sending food or inviting the host family to eat with them. James and Joses, although married, still looked after Mary, and it was only natural for James to sound increasingly like the prodigal's older brother. To James, Jesus' activity must have looked like the reckless carousing of a prolonged adolescence. But, for Jesus, work had become inconsequential. His inner compulsion to celebrate the divine presence, to press all who would listen to enjoy God's power in the luscious fruit of Galilean soil, usurped his loyalty to family and convention.

Once he had established himself in and around Nazareth, Jesus ventured eastward along the valleys that made travel relatively easy in Lower Galilee. He sometimes reached the Sea of Galilee, fifteen miles away. There he came into contact with the economically advanced fishing towns of Capernaum and Magdala (*Migdal Nunnaya*, "Fish Tower" in Aramaic), ports with paved streets radiating from highly developed harbors with breakwaters, docks, and ingenious holding tanks for fish, fashioned from partitions of stacked stone. These towns conducted a brisk trade with Romans, non-Jewish Syrians, and Galileans, anyone who was fond of salted fish. Their wealth, while not comparable to that of Jerusalem, was unlike what Jesus was familiar with in the hillsides of Lower Galilee. Here was a Galilee committed to currency rather than exchange, to *mammon*—as Jesus derisively called money in his native Aramaic (Luke 16:13)—rather than the produce of God's own land.

He reacted fiercely. As a rural Galilean Jew he distrusted and even detested money. He regaled his dinner companions in Nazareth and other small villages by lampooning the attitude of the self-important materialists of the thriving ports. The most notorious case of his condemnation has long perplexed commentators (Luke 16:1–9):

*Yet he was saying to the students, There was some rich person who
had an administrator, and he was denounced to him as squandering
his belongings. He called him and said to him, What is this I hear
about you? Render the account of your administration, because you
are not able to administer still! The administrator said within himself, What shall I do? Because my lord will remove the administration from me! I am not capable of digging, and ashamed to beg. I
know what I shall do! So that when I am displaced from the administration, they might take me into their own houses. . . . He summoned each one of the indebted of his own lord and was saying to
the first, How much do you owe my lord? Yet he said, A hundred
baths of oil. But he said to him, Take your bills and sit: quickly write
fifty! Accordingly, he said to an other, But you owe how much? Yet he
said, A hundred kors of wheat. He says, Take your bills and write
eighty! And the lord praised the administrator for the injustice—because he had acted cleverly, for the ones of this epoch are cleverer
than the ones of light among their own generation. And I say to you,
make yourselves friends from the* mammon *of injustice, so that when
it fades they will take you into perpetual shelters.*

How can Jesus have advocated corrupt behavior? For Jesus the Galilean
rabbi, money really is *"mammon* of injustice," corrupt currency; it might
as well be used to buy friendship within Israel by any means necessary.
His depiction of the ambiance of dishonesty in what the Romans would
call a *latifundium* (an absentee landlord's estate) is as exaggerated as his
picture of the amounts due, which come to twenty times what an ordinary farm could produce in a year. Profit, in Jesus' provincial understanding, was a chimera unworthy of human effort; in his Galilean vision
of fertility and exchange, commerce was a blight.

In Nazareth, everyone was in debt. That is why Jesus and countless
other Jews referred to sin as "debt" in the Aramaic language of both
Judea and Galilee. The widespread use of the term "debt" (*chova*) to

mean a sin before God points to the extent to which indebtedness had become endemic. Peasants owed owners of the *latifundia* a rent in currency that they could not pay; year by year, they handed over much of the rich produce of their harvests just to be allowed to remain indentured on their land, owing more and more *mammon* they did not have. The burden of owing what could not be repaid became the principal metaphor of that alienation from God from which one prayed for release. When Jesus asked his *Abba* for forgiveness, he spoke from a cultural context alien to the developed economies many of us take for granted.

Jesus looked at Capernaum and Magdala through the suspicious eyes of an outsider, shocked at their prominent display of debt-acquired wealth. The bourgeoisie of these places, precisely because they were Jewish, offended him and many other Galilean peasants. They proudly built synagogues, but their efforts in Jesus' eyes were useless for the simple reason that "you can not serve God and *mammon*" (Luke 16:13; Matthew 6:24).

Jesus especially took aim at the banquets of the wealthy Jews, financed by debt, which stood in sharp contrast to the informal celebration of his holy feasts. These banquets were elaborate Graeco-Roman symposia, held in a special room in large houses designed to accommodate guests who lounged on scrolled oak couches (much imitated during the Victorian period), gleaming with walnut oil worked into the rich grain of the wood. The couches were covered with linen blankets and pillows of crimson, indigo, and a spectrum of greens and yellows embroidered with Syrian images of birds and trees. Orange dye for the cloth was made from henna, red from safflowers, yellow from saffron, purple from expensive murex snails from Phoenicia. Ornate end tables set beside a couch assured that its sole use was for the serious business of lounging. The richest merchants displayed their wealth with columned halls and floors tiled with mosaics laid in abstract motifs. Sometimes included among the motifs was the swastika, an ornate design that demonstrated both mastery of the mosaic medium and regard for the commandment not to make an idolatrous image. The total effect amounted to some kind of hybrid between a sheik's desert camp and a decadent palazzo in Rome. To Jesus, such dwellings were a travesty. What were they doing in Jewish Galilee?

The serving staff in these homes offended him, too. "Servants" or "slaves"—interchangeable terms in Aramaic, Hebrew, and Greek—were technically indentured for only seven years by biblical prescription. But that period was routinely extended, when the slave was willing to have his ear nailed through with an awl to the master's doorway to demonstrate his voluntary attachment for life (see Exodus 21:2–6). For the most part, these servants were Jewish: peasants who had lost their land because of debt or who were outcasts from their families. *Mamzers*, both male and female, were well represented in the serving class, which was itself like a caste in the ancient Middle East (as in the case today of Palestinian servants in Kuwait).

Non-Jews whom wealthy Jews took in service were mostly Aramaic-speaking Syrians, distinguishable by their love of bodily ornaments and their worship of household deities. Houses were often divided between the Jewish customs of the family and the practices of their servants; any accommodation (for example, allowing a statue of Tammuz, the Syrian shepherd god, to be kept in the quarters of the serving staff) spawned rumors of the family's apostasy and were abhorrent to rural Galileans like Jesus.

Bourgeois Jewish households catered to local dignitaries, the wealthier businessmen in the community who controlled the fishing fleets, fish-salting, and transport of their Galilean products by pack animals and ox-drawn carts. Every business transaction in ancient Palestine had to be sanctioned by both the Roman tax collector and the centurion responsible for order and security in his area. The tax agent (*telones* in Greek) was a private contractor who bid for the position of serving as Rome's agent, with a commission. The level of taxes he imposed on transactions could be sweetened by bribery and lavish entertainment. A centurion, similarly, was always alert for ways to supplement his income and enliven his austere routine. He needed an incentive to permit Jewish caravans to arm themselves and even more encouragement to agree to provide an armed guard himself. When a valuable caravan set out, either the local garrison provided mounted riders armed with short swords and javelins, or the garrison commander sanctioned the employment of mercenaries. Symposia were ideal occasions for currying favor with local authorities, however much they clashed with the ethos of Judaism and abrogated the commandments of Moses.

The principal customers of Galilean fish, rich foreign clients from around Galilee itself, Syria (including what is now Lebanon), and Decapolis, regaled themselves at these banquets. The foods included ox, a delicacy roasted slowly on a spit, producing a smell that tantalized guests as much as it reminded the host of its cost, the equivalent of a good Mercedes in a modern Western economy. There were sweets of honey, pistachio, and walnuts. Almonds were caramelized with honey and oil in a pan. Professional musicians of both sexes entertained with flute and lyre; they also doubled as acrobats and danced, deploying their skills to delight and divert. Their dance and song could be as lewd as required to move the party along, and their performances could be one on one. Flute players were renowned for their debauchery and many of the entertainers (both male and female in this Greco-Roman culture) were prostitutes.

The host's object in giving a banquet was to draw the best, most influential guests, whether Jewish or not, just as the intention of guests was to be treated with the greatest possible honor. Jesus' response to these banquets was trenchant and categorical: invite the indigent; prefer the lowest places (Luke 14:7–14). In short, stay in rural Galilee; abhor the depraved celebration of status in the symposia that infected Capernaum. The retreat to Nazareth had pushed him into an attack on the urban ethos that was undermining the purity he celebrated in his meals. The feisty young rabbi was feeling his oats. The decadence of Capernaum disgusted him. He went back into the small villages and hamlets of the countryside, to the people who welcomed him into their modest homes, kissed him, and awaited his blessing as they spread the bounty of the land before him on their rough oaken tables.

FIVE

The Spirit Chaser

As he ate and drank his way around Galilee, Jesus took every opportunity to lambaste the symposial game of maneuvering for status. His teaching became socially pointed, and he trumpeted judgment against wealth in the manner of Israel's ancient prophets. The rich will not feast; those who prize status will wind up ashamed (Luke 12:16–21):

> *Some rich person's area yielded well. And he deliberated with himself saying, What shall I do, because I do not have anywhere to gather together my produce? And he said: I will do this, I will level my storehouses and I will build bigger, and I will gather together there the wheat and my goods, and I will say to my soul, Soul, you have many goods laid up for many years, repose, eat, drink, celebrate! But God said to him: Fool, this night they demand your soul from you, what you prepared will be whose? So is the one who treasures for oneself and is not wealthy toward God.*

In this springtime of his public activity, at home in Galilee, among the people who embraced him for the first time, Jesus revealed the uncompromising side of his character. His vehemence was fed by the longstanding conviction in Israel (see Psalm 10:15–16) that God's Kingdom would sweep away all that resisted it:

Break the arm of the wicked, and evil;
search out his wickedness until it cannot be found!
The Lord is king for ever and ever;
the nations perish from his earth!

The vindication of the meek, fatherless, and oppressed required that the oppressor must perish (v. 17–18). The Psalms were sung by pilgrims traveling to the Temple—the texts still bear notations that mark melody and rhythm. During periodic outbreaks of violence in the Temple during the first century as Galileans tried to wrest control away from Zadokites and sacrifice according to their own system of agricultural exchange, these songs acquired a new and militant meaning. Jesus sang of the Kingdom with much the same meaning, but he sang against Herod Antipas and the entire culture he represented. Where God's justice was concerned, he did not advocate turning the other cheek. In this sense he was very much the Old Testament prophet.

Jesus' vehemence was often directed against specific opponents. Until close to the end of his sojourn with John, when he became independent and probed the edges of Judea and Samaria on his own, his experience had been circumscribed, involuted, with everything filtered through the medium of his master. But as Jesus traveled around Galilee he came into contact with powerful representatives of the different schools and factions of the Judaism of his day.

Now a rabbi in his own right, he came up against the Pharisees for the first time in Capernaum. He had seen Pharisaic teachers before, in the Temple, but at an age and time when he had not understood what they represented. Their movement, centered in Jerusalem, was driven by a passion to maintain the purity of Israel in an occupied land. They sought to separate themselves from the world of Greco-Roman defilement, somewhat as did the priests who served in the Temple. They kept themselves, their produce, and their food pure within households intended as a defense against the wider society, their comprehensive purity assuring their ability to offer sacrifices at any time. From its center in Jerusalem, the Pharisaic movement spread to the larger towns in Judea and Galilee, which faced the issue of what to do about Hellenistic culture. Jesus learned from them and participated in the kind of arguments typical of Pharisees, but his practice of fellowship at meals inevitably brought him into conflict with their teaching.

Just as John had taught that purity resulted from immersion in living water, the Pharisees had evolved a complex metaphysics around the purity of meals. Special attention was paid to how food was kept in the home: covered vessels of clay protected moist produce such as olives from the uncleanness of a lizard that might touch the rim of the vessel, or the impurity that radiated from a funeral cortege. Pharisees also judged whether purification by immersing one's hands and vessels prior to meals had been observed.

Jesus' holy feasts were celebrated widely in and around Nazareth, and these meals sometimes came to the attention of Pharisees, who rightly doubted whether Jesus observed their ritual practice of purity. Conflict with Jesus was inevitable (Luke 11:37–40):

> *While he was yet speaking a Pharashayah asked him so that he might dine with him. He entered and leaned back. But the Pharashayah saw and marveled that he did not first immerse before the dinner. But the Lord said to him, Now you Pharashayahs cleanse the outside of the cup and the platter, but inside of you it teems with plunder and evil. Fools: did not the one who made the outside also make the inside?*

Jesus is vociferous in this typical confrontation with an ordinarily pious Pharisee, because in insisting that purity in Galilee already existed, he opposed the Pharisaic assumption that purity had to be achieved. His object was not to make Israelites clean, but to use their innate cleanness to invoke the presence of God at their meals. Pharisaism was a movement

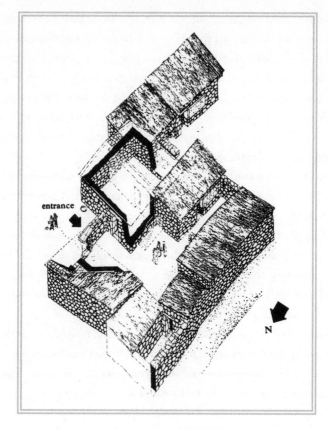

GALILEAN HOUSE

Reconstruction of a house in Galilee by the Studium Biblicum Franciscanum, on the basis of their excavation in Capernaum. Widely called "Peter's House" (and comparable to the sort of house in which Peter and Andrew would have lived), the courtyard structure is fairly typical of Jewish Galilee, although the plentiful basalt of Capernaum made for sounder and larger houses than were built in Nazareth. (Illustration courtesy of Studium Biblicum Franciscanum)

of towns and cities, such as Capernaum and Magdala, where the threat of impurity had to be countered daily. Jesus' practice was appropriate for areas accustomed to keeping their distance from urban corruption, and he disputed the logic of trying to clean outside with water what had already been tainted inside with *mammon*.

In a talmudic fashion, reflecting a teaching in the Mishnah, Jesus applied Pharisaic principles to respond to their objections. Rabbi Hillel (50 B.C.E.–10 C.E.) had argued that the inside of a vessel, whether pure or impure, determined the purity or impurity of the whole vessel (in the Mishnah, see Kelim 25:6). In his criticism of the Pharisees, Jesus adhered to Hillel's principle: cleanness proceeds from within to without and purifies the whole. But if that is the case with cups, he argued with an insight that disarmed his opponents, then all the more so with Israelites who are pure by their intention and the way they work the land.[1] It is what is *within* that makes a person pure. His well-known aphorism conveys just this insight (Mark 7:15, see also Matthew 15:11):

> *There is nothing outside a person, entering in, that can defile one,*
> *but what comes out from a person defiles the person.*

Washing did not make the produce of rural Galilee any purer than it already was, and no amount of rinsing could cleanse the symposial corruption of Capernaum. Against the Pharisees, Jesus asserted that purity was a matter of the totality of one's being. One was either clean or unclean; for Jesus, there was no vacillation. The Pharisees' policy of compromise with defilement, skillfully crafted to deal with the complexities of urban pluralism, found no resonance in his peasant's mind.

In the cleansing of the leper, one of the most dramatic and telling stories in the New Testament, Jesus pressed his program of purity into action (Matthew 8:2–4; Mark 1:40–45; Luke 5:12–16). But what Jesus was actually doing—and even what the story is about—has been lost to us, because the Jewish culture which was his context has eluded us.

---

1. In extending Hillel's teaching in this way, Jesus was invoking the principle of the prophet Haggai, who had once declared that just as uncleanness is contagious, so God's Spirit would one day make Israel clean by its holy contagion (Haggai 2:4–5, 10–19).

To begin with, the story is not about a leper at all. Jesus was dealing with a man with *tsaraat* (in Hebrew and Aramaic), which refers to an "outbreak" of the skin. It is clear that "outbreak" is not the disease we call leprosy; the book of Leviticus stipulates that walls and cloth—as well as people—may contract, and be freed of, *tsaraat* (see Leviticus 13–14). The term was rendered *lepra* in the Greek version of the Hebrew Bible: in Greek, *lepra* refers to a scaly or scabby condition of the skin, and the term was picked up in English for the specific, irreversible complaint clinically known as Hansen's disease, which we call "leprosy." That modern definition has nothing to do with the story's reference to a range of ailments that probably included eczema, psoriasis, and shingles.

In the Gospels, a person with outbreak approaches Jesus in an unnamed village in Lower Galilee and asserts that Jesus is able to "cleanse" him. "Outbreak" in humans (as distinct from cloth and houses) was signaled by broken flesh (Leviticus 13:14–15), or even a change in the pigmentation of the skin and its hair. Unbroken flesh and consistent pigmentation signaled a return to cleanness (vv. 12, 13). The fundamental concern was broken flesh: that brought proximity to blood, to which no human should have access. Sufferers from outbreak were banned from contact with the community during the period of their condition (vv. 45, 46).

Leviticus decrees that a priest must declare a person suffering from "outbreak" clean: that is, ready to make the twofold offering prescribed before rejoining the community. The first offering is a local sacrifice, which may take place wherever there is running water. The village priest twists the neck off a bird and lets the blood spurt into an earthen vessel, which is held over a stream. Into the dead bird's blood the priest dips a living bird, which has a scarlet cord wrapped around its neck with a pouch containing cedar bark shavings and a piece of hyssop. He then sprinkles the patient seven times with the blood drenching the living bird, and releases it (14:1–7). That first sacrifice symbolically releases the person from impurity. Afterward, the person immerses and shaves all his hair (cf. vv. 8–9), then goes to the Temple and offers two male lambs, a ewe, cereal, and oil. These actions bring the sufferer back into the sacrificial community of Israel (14:10–20). Release from the condition and reintegration within the communal body were the portals one passed through to rejoin one's people, one's family. The recent study of biomedicine has richly illuminated how health is not simply a physical condition but an interaction between a person and the surrounding community. The book of Leviticus permits us to see how the way to health was mapped by the priests who served the Temple.

But Jesus proved no more patient with the priestly program of purity than he was with the Pharisees' pronouncements. He skipped half the procedure set out in Leviticus. He told the outbreak-sufferer he did not need to see a local priest and could proceed directly to the Temple and offer a sacrifice. Jesus did not personally take over any sacrificial function, but he did pronounce on matters of purity. The Pharisees saw that Jesus abrogated their principles on how purity should be achieved and maintained (see Negaim 14:1–13 in the Mishnah). They were astounded that this provincial from Galilee had the chutzpah to pronounce on grave, complex questions and contradict traditional practice.

Jesus knew he was breaking barriers. He had been called out by the "leper" and challenged to act on his principle of purification (Mark 1:40). Jesus agreed, but then scolded the man and told him not to publicize what had happened (Mark 1:41–44). Jesus knew his actions would arouse the ire of the Pharisees and all other Jews with a traditional understanding of purity. The reputed *mamzer* who had experienced purity in himself with John and then knew its power in the Samaritan woman could not deny cleansing to any Israelite who desired it. But he might well have refused to deal with the scabby man had he not been confronted directly, or had he been on the turf of the Pharisees rather than in rural Galilee.

Just as Jesus applied in a radical way a principle articulated by Hillel regarding immersion, so his willingness to rule on the status of skin represents a remarkable revision of Pharisaic tradition. Pharisees debated in minute detail the cleanness and uncleanness of changes of skin color, bulges, raw flesh. A tractate of the Mishnah (Negaim 1:1–10:10) advises when to let the skin heal by itself and when to remove a spot by cutting it. Pharisees instructed priests (whom they constantly sought to influence) on how to declare on issues of purity; they advised on the removal of suspicious growths by minor surgery; and they counseled those blemished on how long to wait after surgery before visiting a priest to be pronounced clean. But the cleansing of Jesus presupposes that purity is not a status to be attained prior to sacrifice, but a power which one's offering releases. He had usurped the Pharisees' role.

Christian theology and scholarship have persistently overlooked Jesus' distinctive approach to the entire issue of purity. They have denied that Jesus was concerned with purity and rejected any consideration that his actions stemmed from his insights into what was clean or unclean. Their views are uninformed and misleading. At a later stage, obviously, primitive Christianity *did* eschew many facets of Jewish ritual practice, but only when it had become a predominantly non-Jewish, Hellenistic movement. Purity was Jesus' fundamental commitment, the lens through which he viewed the world.

The atmosphere of impurity that Roman culture engendered did more than simply repel the sensibilities of observant Galileans like Jesus. It heightened their sense that demons—supernatural agents of impurity—threatened them. Herod Antipas' regime was a particular source of distress: through a grandiose and deliberately Hellenistic building campaign, he had fomented an epidemic of impurity and released a host of unclean spirits into Galilee just before Jesus returned there in 21 C.E.

Antipas had been building from the start of his reign in 4 B.C.E. to buttress the ruling Roman culture of his Galilee. He was given ample scope for his architectural ambitions, in the same year as his accession, when a Galilean revolutionary named Judas (Yudah, son of Hezekiah) led an armed revolt in Sepphoris. The Romans swept in, led by cavalry, and quickly took back the city's strongholds, including the garrison won by the

Galileans. The Roman soldiers, trained in the use of javelin and long sword, carved up the revolutionaries, who had access to the same weapons in the garrison but had not been trained to use them. The residents of Sepphoris who were not slaughtered were stripped of land and sold as slaves by the Roman legate Varus (who was known for his military and administrative efficiency) after he had burned the city (Josephus, *Jewish War* 2 § 56, 68). He did all that through a subordinate, while he himself made his way to Jerusalem, where he crucified two thousand revolutionaries. (*War* 2 § 75). Architecture was the continuation of such ruthless measures by other means, a Roman response to revolt on a national scale.

Antipas rebuilt Sepphoris as his administrative center, with a three thousand–seat theater, a colonnaded street in the Roman manner, and a lavish palace for his own use. He turned it into a fortress—no doubt with brothels, baths, and crude circuses for the soldiers' entertainment—and gave it the imposing name of Autocratoris to honor the Romans with the Greek equivalent of their own Latin word, Imperatoria (Josephus, *Antiquities* 18 § 27).

Yet Sepphoris was little more than a practice run for what Antipas achieved at Tiberias, which he established in 19 C.E. while Jesus was with John on the Jordan. Tiberias, named in honor of Emperor Tiberius (who succeeded Augustus in 14 C.E.), was designed to replace Sepphoris as Antipas' capital. A stadium, forum, baths, and a royal palace were all constructed on fertile land overlooking the Sea of Galilee.

When an ancient cemetery was discovered on the land being cleared for the new city, Antipas arrogantly pressed ahead rather than change the city's design. He desecrated ground set aside to keep corpses separate from God and Israel and subjected residents to pollution. Many Jews were outraged. The cemetery excavation released unclean spirits, and contact with a tomb rendered a Jew unclean for a week and made immersion an absolute requirement for remaining among the people of Israel (Numbers 19:11–16). The defilement radiated outward across Galilee like a contagious disease. Unclean spirits were not perceived as a ghoulish flock of ghosts, but a seeping infectious miasma. It was no wonder, then, that Tiberias found no willing settlers among religious Jews. Antipas, however, was able to lure freed slaves and unobservant Jews to Tiberias with the promise of property—on the condition that they remained in the city. (Josepheus describes the Jews who came as a largely Galilean rabble; *Antiquities* 18 § § 36–38.) In Antipas' dominion, *mammon* had long since triumphed over God.

The corruption of Galilean Judaism by Antipas pushed Jesus into his confrontation with institutions of wealth from the time of his initial contact with Capernaum. The threat of unclean spirits in the midst of a land called by God to be pure turned him into an exorcist. He traveled through a Galilee traumatized by Antipas' actions in Tiberias, which had pushed observant Jews, already xenophobic, into a state that sometimes bordered on hysteria. An atmosphere of confrontation with ambient evil propelled Jesus into a new role, and pressed him to grapple with the issue of his own identity.

Jesus' purifications had celebrated the innate purity of Israelites. In his exorcisms, he removed "unclean spirits" so that Israelites' purity could shine through the plague of compromise with Rome. After Christianity became all but deaf to the issue of purity, exorcism gradually became the kind of practice it is today—a bizarre manipulation of unseen, spectral forces. Somewhat similarly, in Judaism the destruction of the Second Temple in 70 C.E. made purity an abstract concern, more a matter of obeying what Torah commands than of preparing to encounter the divine in sacrifice. As a result, Jewish exorcists are not common in the period of Rabbinic Judaism, from the second until the sixth century. But the literature of early Judaism, before the Second Temple's destruction, tells a different story. The Genesis Apocryphon from Qumran includes a full, inventive retelling of a story from Genesis in which Abraham rebukes an evil spirit for Pharaoh so that illness departs from him (Genesis Apocryphon 20:16–29). The story shows that exorcism, healing, and mastery over evil spirits were joined in early Judaism long before Jesus. Jesus focused them in a way that added to both his repute and to the mounting resistance he encountered in Galilee, particularly in Nazareth itself.

The Spirit Chaser

The people whom Jesus exorcised often suffered from affective disorders: depression, asocial behavior, violent fantasies, hallucinations, promiscuity. Jesus' exorcisms are remarkable in comparison to the records of exorcism in the ancient world because they involved unusually violent struggles. Other stories, whether from Greco-Roman or Egyptian literature, emphasize that the exorcist is in control; the demon obediently flees the body of the possessed and goes elsewhere. But in Jesus' case, exorcism amounts to vanquishing demonic energy, driving away the forces of impurity. These exorcisms were contentious, dramatic events.

Jesus' technique as an exorcist centered on the esoteric practice he had learned from John. He went into trance by meditating on the divine Throne. The living waters of the Jordan had long since been replaced in his consciousness by the primordial waters moved by God's Spirit. The vast ocean of spirit that surrounded the Chariot was a tidal force, pressing God's Kingdom forward and displacing the pestilence of Beelzebul's legions. As Jesus put it, "If I by God's Spirit throw out demons, then the Kingdom of God has arrived upon you!" (Matthew 12:28 and Luke 11:20). The Kingdom's coming, he insisted, brought not peace, but a sword (Matthew 10:34). His exorcisms, which produced an open break with his family and nearly got him killed, also defined in his own mind who he was in relation to God's Spirit.

In 24 C.E. Jesus was still living in Nazareth, still putting a strain on his family with the persistent feasting that obligated them to reciprocate his hosts in some way. Their growing annoyance with Jesus turned to antipathy one spring day when Jesus was teaching a crowd of Nazarenes, far too many people for Mary even to think of feeding, that had gathered in his family's courtyard (Mark 3:20–21[2]). Jesus sat in their midst,

2. Within Mark, this scene is placed in a later period, after Jesus was in Capernaum and had called his first disciples (Mark 3:1–19). But the prominence of his own family in the scene shows that the incident occurred earlier than that.

93

spinning parables on how the Galilean life of planting, sowing, and harvest reflected God's Kingdom. The hills were greening again around Nazareth, the ground was warming, new life was shooting up out of the earth. He spoke about the mystery of growth, how casting of seed, nutrition of soil, sun and rain all produced abundant food, a result no one could truly understand (Mark 4:26–29):

> And he was saying: The Kingdom of God is like this, as a person throws the germ upon the earth, and sleeps and is raised night and day, and the germ buds and sprouts. How, one personally does not know. Of itself the earth bears fruit, first blade, then head, then full grain in the head. But when the fruit delivers over, at once one dispatches the sickle, because the harvest has occurred.

The lack of any claim of special wisdom in these words emphasized that no one really knew how all this fulfillment occurred. The point was simply that it was possible. As he told his parables, the audience responded with their own observations of God's bounty. The scene had the feel of a revival meeting, with the crowd calling back to Jesus, erupting with encouragement and pleasure at his words, joining their own images to his. They especially loved the picture of the Kingdom as a luxurious feast more sumptuous than any they had ever known (Luke 14:15–24). They grew more and more excited, and then, in the climactic moment, a possessed man burst into the courtyard, shaking, jerking like a puppet on a string.

The enthusiastic crowd fell silent. Only a few of the onlookers found their voice and exclaimed in horror, "Beelzebul has him!" which expressed their fear of contagion from the prince of the demons.

Jesus stood and lifted his hands in silent prayer, fusing his mind with divine Spirit as the noises of celebration and confusion died around him. The silent tableau was swiftly ruptured when Jesus shouted "Come out from him, unclean spirit!" and physically shook the man. The violence of the scene convinced his family that Jesus himself had gone mad. According to Mark 3:20–21, James, with his siblings' help, restrained his brother and dragged him back into the family's house:

And he comes into the house, and there comes together a crowd again, so they are not even able to eat bread. Those with him heard, and went out to seize him, because they were saying that: He is deranged.

The Gospels downplay this part of Jesus' activity. The term "deranged" (*existemi* in Greek) strictly means "to be beside oneself," and corresponds to the usage of *michutz* in the Talmid to describe the distracted state of a sage engrossed in the Chariot (Chagigah 15a, in reference to Simon ben Zoma). Those around Jesus feared he was insane ("deranged") as a result of his obsession with meditative practice. His family must have been deeply worried by his willingness to have contact with people that Galilean Jews considered impure, declare them clean, and banish their unclean spirits on his own physical and disruptive authority. He was contradicting local custom and the respect in which Pharisees were held, as well as ordinary expectations of decorum.

The depth of his family's embarrassment increasingly pushed Jesus away from home after that spring. He had long been an economic burden on the family. He was called a glutton and a drunkard (Matthew 11:19; Luke 7:34), and his reputation of derangement tainted the family's honor.

Despite the shame his family must have felt, Jesus' growing renown enabled him to take his practice as an exorcist outside the family courtyard, away from Nazareth and into religious settings elsewhere. In Capernaum he received a warm welcome from at least some of the Jewish population. Twenty-one miles over hill country was far enough from Nazareth for Jesus' reputation as a *mamzer* to be unknown. Many of Capernaum's Jews were nostalgic for the rural Galilee they had left behind to find work in the religiously dubious atmosphere of the town. Jesus'

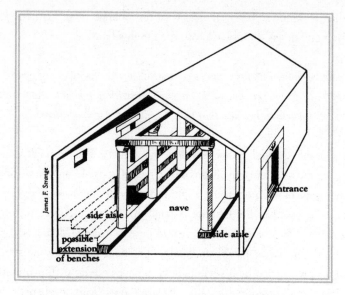

THE SYNAGOGUE IN CAPERNAUM

Beneath a fourth-century synagogue in Capernaum, the remains of its first-century predecessor have been excavated; on that basis, James F. Strange has proposed this reconstruction of the earlier building, which measured approximately 80 by 56 feet. (Illustration courtesy of James F. Strange)

teaching on purity was original, but also a vivid assertion of the value of their ancestral ways, and his exorcisms were a dramatic confrontation with offensive urban forces of uncleanness. Spirits as impure as the un-sealed cemetery in Tiberias were all around, but the rabbi from Nazareth seemed equal to their violence.

These were Jesus' kind of people, and they permitted him to enter into their synagogue, a small building fitted with benches, where the as-sembly could comfortably settle local disputes, hear and discuss Scrip-ture, delegate priestly duties, arrange for the collection and transfer of taxes to the Temple, and participate in rituals such as burial and *berith*. What happened in that synagogue would not soon be forgotten. Jesus entered into a shouting match with an unclean spirit (see Mark 1:21–28 and Luke 4:31–37). The stark confrontation between purity and impurity could not be plainer than it is here, because the encounter occurred during the meeting of the community on Shabbath, and the unclean spirit took the initiative in a verbal assault on Jesus.

The demon addressed Jesus as both "holy one of God" and "Nazirite," the latter an ironic reference to one who had made a vow to maintain purity and abstained from wine. The demon, by contrast, was an "unclean" or "impure" spirit, a designation unique to the Gospels and deriving from Jesus himself. The story does not even say what symptoms the possessed person manifested. All that matters is that the unclean spirit was removed after its violent argument with Jesus, screaming that Jesus' purpose was to *destroy* the demons, not merely remove them. The Galilean rabbi had achieved purity, but at a price. In that synagogue, the demon itself had identified Jesus as someone who opposed *all* impurity. He had put the entire ethos of Capernaum on notice: for all its urban prosperity and sophistication, its compromise with uncleanness would be swept away with the Kingdom's advent.

Jesus' family had become increasingly uneasy about his pronouncements on purity and his violent outbursts to drive out demons and restore cleanness in the land. The news of his exorcism in Capernaum came as no comfort to them. But what destroyed the last vestiges of good will initially directed at the prodigal and put an end to the Galilean springtime occurred, fittingly, in the synagogue in Nazareth itself, among the elders and the religious community that had spurned the *mamzer* Jesus as a child.

After his dramatic confrontation with the demon in Capernaum, Jesus' confidence grew to the point that he deliberately went up against the dignitaries of Nazareth. His *Abba* had assured his place within Israel, and no provincial congregation—not even in his home town—was going to deny that to him. Perhaps he thought he could win back the support of his family, if only the elders at long last would accept him into their company. But when he confronted them, the results were disastrous.

This confrontation has not been understood in terms of what happened, why it happened, or its significance for Jesus. Luke's Gospel presents it as if Jesus regularly attended synagogue in Nazareth, but it is obvious that it occurred on a singular occasion. The key to the elders' rage was not only Jesus' status as a *mamzer*, which the Nazarenes knew better than anyone, but what he said in the synagogue (Luke 4:16–30):

> *And he came into Nazara, where he had been nurtured, and he entered according to his custom on the day of the Shabbath into the synagogue. And he arose to read and there was delivered to him a book, of the prophet Yeshayah. He opened the book and found the place where it was written, The Lord's Spirit is upon me, forasmuch as he anointed me to message triumph to the poor. He delegated me to proclaim release to captives and recovery of sight to the blind, to dispatch the broken with release, to proclaim an acceptable year of the Lord! He rolled the book, gave it back to the assistant, and sat. And of all, the eyes in the congregation were staring at him. But he began to say to them that: Today this Scripture has been fulfilled in your ears! And all attested him and marveled at the words of grace that proceeded out from his mouth, and they were saying, Is he not Yosef's son?*

In response to that question, Jesus reacted with the bitterness of his memory of being marginalized as a *mamzer* when he was a child.

What he goes on to say may seem an irrational outburst on the surface, but it gave voice to the isolation of his childhood:

> *And he said to them, You will by all means say this comparison to me, Physician, heal yourself! As much as we heard happened in Kapharnachum, do also here, in your own country! But he said,*

Amen I say to you that no prophet is acceptable in his own country.
Yet in truth I say to you, there were many widows in Eliyah's days in
Yisrael, when the heaven was shut three years and six months, as a
great famine came on all the earth, and to none of them was Eliyah
sent, except to Zarafta of Sidonia, to a widow woman. And there
were many scabby people in Yisrael while Elisha was prophet, and
none of them was cleansed, except Naaman the Syrian. And all in
the synagogue were filled with rage when they heard this; they arose
and threw him out, outside of the city, and led him to an edge of the
mount on which the city was built, so as to hurl him down. But he
went through their midst and proceeded.

Luke smoothes out the narrative of the service to accord with a Hellenistic notion of what worship in a synagogue entails. This Gospel does
not, for example, mention the translation of the Hebrew Scriptures into
Aramaic, but assumes everything happened in Greek, and presents Jesus
as if he were literate. Because Luke presents the setting as routine, the
Nazarenes' response to Jesus seems completely irrational. That feeds another pet theme of Luke's: the senseless rejection of Jesus by the Jewish
people. By the same token, the reference at the close of the passage to
the acceptance of non-Jews such as Naaman by prophets tells us more
about the church of Luke than about the thinking of Jesus. Here the Hellenistic, non-Jewish idiom is obvious, just as much as it often is in John's
Gospel. Still, it is clear that who Jesus was and what he said brought
about an effort to stone him in Nazareth. What Luke misses is that Jesus
stood in the synagogue as an illiterate *mamzer* in his claim to be the
Lord's anointed.

The citation Jesus uses from Isaiah begins, "The Lord's Spirit is upon
me, forasmuch as he anointed me." Jesus told the congregation that
God's Spirit had been with him since his mastery of John's esoteric teaching, signaled by the descent of the dove as he immersed in the Jordan.
He claimed that he fulfilled Isaiah's prophecy of someone who would be
born into Israel, anointed by the Spirit, and, therefore, able to speak on

God's behalf. In Greek, as in Hebrew and Aramaic, the term "Messiah" basically means "anointed one." Its etymology is of more than academic interest, because the very verb used here (*khrio* in Greek, *mashach* in Hebrew and Aramaic) associated itself in the ear with the term "Messiah" (*meshiach*) or "Christ" (*khristos*). In Nazareth of all places, where from childhood he had been excluded from synagogue on suspicion of being a *mamzer*, Jesus entered the solemn congregation to insist that he was God's anointed, the bearer of his *Abba*'s spirit. Jesus is Messiah because that Spirit is upon him, and he made the text from Isaiah into a description of his own action.

The synagogue's violent response to Jesus was not only to his messianic claim; he also manipulated Isaiah's words. Jesus' "citation" is no citation at all, but a free paraphrase of the biblical book, different from any ancient version (Greek, Hebrew, or Aramaic). The dissonance is not a Lukan creation, because the pattern of the Gospel is to make the correspondence to the Greek version of the Bible (the Septuagint) in biblical citations as close as possible.

Fortunately, the wording of this speech in the Old Syriac Gospels (in a language closely related to Jesus' indigenous Aramaic) provides an even more radical paraphrase of Isaiah, closer to what Jesus actually said:

> The Spirit of the Lord is upon you, *on account of which*
> *he has anointed* you *to message triumph to the poor;*
> *And he has delegated* me *to proclaim to the captives release,*
> *and to the blind sight*
> *—and* I *will free the broken with release—*
> *and to proclaim the acceptable year of the Lord.*

Luke's Greek irons out a vital part of Jesus' originality for the benefit of Hellenistic readers accustomed to the Septuagint: the crucial change in pronouns (which I have represented with a change of font). By speaking these words, Jesus portrays himself as responding to a divine charge: "The Spirit of the Lord is upon *you*, on account of which he has anointed *you* to message triumph to the poor." Then he emphatically accepts that charge: "And he has sent me to preach to the captives release, and to the blind sight—and *I* will free the broken with release—and to preach the acceptable year of the Lord." Both the charge and the emphatic acceptance are produced by the signal changes in pronouns, attested only in Syriac, and other adjustments in the wording of Scripture to reflect the sense of purpose that his immersions with John had given him. (Both on the bank of the Jordan and here, Jesus was addressed directly, as the "you" whom divine spirit inspired.) Those changes are part and parcel of Jesus' conscious alteration of the language taken from the book of Isaiah.

The alteration is typical of his style of employing Scripture, especially the book of Isaiah (and especially in a targumic form). He manipulated and paraphrased the Scripture to explain his experience of God, and how God was active in what he said and did.

"Who is this illiterate *mamzer* who thinks he can manipulate Scripture?" the elders of Nazareth must have fumed. Jesus' prophetic claims were sufficient to appall the congregation; making them in a messianic context was an outrage! Because the term "Messiah" could be defined in different ways in ancient Judaism, he set in motion a controversy that has never ceased. Messiah could refer, for example, to one "anointed" to make war, or "anointed" to offer sacrifice, or "anointed" to prophesy, or "anointed" to rule as king. To which category of Messiah did he belong? The words from Luke discussed above, especially in their Syriac form, make it clear Jesus referred to himself as anointed to prophesy. But Messiah, the chosen of God from the house of David, had for centuries been at the center of the expected removal of foreign dominion. Through Joseph, Jesus claimed Davidic descent, even though the circumstances of his birth were disputed. How could Herod Antipas and the Romans respond other than violently to the news that a disciple of John the Baptist was using messianic terms to refer to himself?

To those in Nazareth, including Jesus' family, his explanation of who he was turned embarrassment into fear. Bad enough he pursued holy feasts just about everywhere, and with practically everyone. Bad enough he pronounced people free of "outbreak," as if his authority was commensurate with that of local priests and urban Pharisees. Bad enough that he exorcised, often with sudden, startling eruptions out of his trancelike meditations. Now he said in public that he could do such things on the basis of his access to God's Chariot, from which God himself spoke to him of his anointing. Although he might be using "Messiah" to speak of prophetic anointing, his family and friends feared that the people of Galilee, who prayed to be released from Roman rule, would see him as a new Davidic king come to rule. In the absence of resources to back up such a claim, he was a danger to himself, his family, and his village.

Luke's description of the attempted stoning of Jesus accords with the practice set out in the Mishnah (Sanhedrin 6:4). The victim was thrown from a cliff or wall, head first. If that did not kill him, first the witnesses against him and then all Israelites present were to heave large stones on him from above until he died. Jesus must have had sympathizers in Nazareth, because he escaped. But not even his family could (or would) shelter him any longer.

A stark passage from the Gospel according to John has Jesus' brothers saying to him, "Transfer from here and depart into Judea . . . because no one acts in secret and seeks to be personally famous: if you do these things, show yourself to the world" (John 7:3–4). The "world" is part of the Gospel's philosophical language, but this text points to the emotional turmoil of Jesus' second departure from Nazareth as a prophet unacceptable in his own village. From his brothers' point of view, his extravagant assertions about the divine Kingdom, the Throne of God, his anointing by the Spirit, as well as his profligate meals, controversial purifications, and violent exorcisms simply did not belong in Nazareth. His own family told Jesus that his messianic claim to bear God's Spirit could not be hidden in an obscure corner of Galilee. In words laden with irony, they in effect told him either to take his show to Jerusalem or to close it permanently.

SIX

❧

Chasid in the
Holy City

Jesus' near stoning in Nazareth must have happened late in the summer of 24 C.E. Where he went immediately after that is unknown. We pick up the thread of his life again when his brothers mocked him as they prepared to make a pilgrimage to Jerusalem for Sukkoth. If you claim you are anointed with God's Spirit, they said, demonstrate that in Jerusalem at the greatest feast of the year (John 7:2–5). Their words were laced with resentment. Eight years earlier, Jesus had deserted his family during their Sukkoth pilgrimage. After the attempted stoning in Nazareth, his brothers abandoned *him* at Sukkoth, telling him to fend for himself.

Mary must have felt ambivalent about Jesus. She had always supported him, believed in him, made a place for him in the family. But at this particular juncture she would have withdrawn from him. Jesus had taxed her patience, shamed her, and potentially endangered Nazareth. She must have breathed a sigh of relief when he set out for Jerusalem alone (John 7:10).

This break with his family would embitter Jesus for years to come. He made a lonely journey down the Jordan. He entered Jerusalem as a man who had broken away from his past but was without a clear plan for the future. He saw the city through mature eyes, filled with recollections of his hard months there before he had met John, grateful for the resilience and independence he had developed in the intervening years. He avoided the home of Miriam and Martha, where his brothers were lodged. Instead, he reestablished the connections he had made when he had occasionally accompanied pilgrims to the Temple with John's other disciples. Some of the disciples had come from Jerusalem, and Jesus would have met their families. When he showed up at their homes, his old friends were naturally curious to learn what had become of the "lamb of God" whom their master had both treasured and argued with; and they were intrigued by the word of mouth, filtering down from Galilee with the caravan trade, which conveyed Jesus' fame as an exorcist.

The young man who stood on their doorsteps was shorter than average height from his meager diet during his years with John. But he was broader in the chest than the scrawny adolescent they remembered. His beard had filled out and he had a new self-confidence about him. They kissed him on the lips and responded with delight to his rough manners and Galilean accent. These traits, which had put them off when they first met him, were now familiar and endearing.

For his part, Jesus greeted them warmly. He was going through one of his most vocal phases and probably approached his old comrades with exuberant good cheer. We know he could be charming; he displayed extraordinary skill at getting support for himself and his followers, and he had a remarkable ability to attract followers as well. A bipolar tendency is evident throughout his life, which caused him to swing between the kind of dramatic public display he put on in the synagogue in Nazareth and periods of silence and isolation.

The Judean families who gave him food and lodging were wealthy by Galilean standards. Jesus might have stayed in one of the Sukkoth huts built on Jerusalem's roofs at this time of year with branches of olive, myrtle, and palm. The huts had originated as makeshift shelters, set up in the fields during the grape harvest to keep workers near their task and allow them to sample the vintage and protect it from theft. By the first century, Jews in urban environments like Jerusalem ate and slept in these huts during Sukkoth, in remembrance of the "tabernacles" or tents Israel had used during the exodus from Egypt to the Promised Land. Jerusalem's Jews also used them to house pilgrims like Jesus who poured into the city for the feast.

Staying with these prosperous Judean families, Jesus was introduced to a new world where wealth was not a sign of alien domination, as in Capernaum, but the seal of Israel's prosperity. Wealth streamed into the Temple. The bounty of the land—its bellowing beasts, wine, incense, oil, and crops—were offered from the start of Sukkoth in an escalating pace that was maintained during the entire week of the feast. The altar flamed and smoked, pumping out seared meat and roasted grain. The Temple staff swelled with added reserves of priests who slaughtered, butchered, fetched, carried, shoveled, and heaved. The weather was bright and clear over the city. The gilded stones glowed with golden light, and the nights were cool, the stars close overhead as Jesus slept in his tabernacle. He might have been awakened by the reveling throngs that caroused all night through Jerusalem's streets, singing psalms (as well as bawdier songs), giggling, and drinking from skins of new wine. As the sky brightened in the east, the Temple fires were revived. Jesus would have heard the Great Gate (sixty-foot doors of Corinthian bronze that led into the sanctuary) creaking open on iron hinges—a sound which, it was said, echoed all the way to Jericho (see Tamid 3:8 in the Mishnah and Josephus, *Jewish War* 5 §§ 201–206). Worshippers hurried through the streets, their sandals pattering on stone, to fill the Great Court for the *tamid,* the daily offering, which occurred without fail each dusk and dawn.

The wealth, the heightened pace of sacrifice, the magnificence of the Temple, put many first-century Jews, Jesus among them, in mind of Zechariah's prophesy that "all the nations" of the world and their wealth would converge upon Jerusalem to keep the Sukkoth feast (Zechariah 14:14, 16). Zechariah was to become a centrally important text for Jesus, to some extent because of the Mardi Gras–like atmosphere he relished in Jerusalem during that Sukkoth in 24 C.E. He incorporated the apocalyptic motifs of Zechariah and his message into his own prophetic persona.

Zechariah announced that when the richness of the smoke streaming up from the altar was right, when the furnace of sacrifice finally got hot enough, when the critical mass of faith was attained, God himself would descend upon Israel as king "over all the earth" (Targum Zechariah 14:9). There would be earthquakes and cataclysms, and living water would well up from under the city and burst forth, flowing outward to purify the entire earth and reclaim it as part of the divine Kingdom (Zechariah 13:1; 14:1–8).

This might sound completely unrealistic to most of us, but the Zecharian prophecy was particularly poignant for first-century Jews. Roman hegemony was a fact in Israel by then, but only a recently established fact. (Pompey had claimed Jerusalem for Rome in 63 B.C.E.) Insurrection and criminality were part of the ambiance of Judea and Galilee during the first century, culminating in the great revolt that raged between 66 and 70 C.E. Rome eventually squelched this rebellion by burning the Temple. But even that could not destroy the Israelites' revolutionary zeal. It was only after the final crushing failure of the revolt of Simon bar Kosibah (132–135 C.E.) that the rabbis of the Mishnah backed away from the hope of a messianic revolution. Until that point, many Jews believed that finally getting the system of sacrifice right and living as God had commanded them in the promised land would trigger the realization of Zechariah's prophecy. Jesus, like other rabbis of his time, turned to Zechariah as a source of both vision and propaganda for activating God's Kingdom. He used Zechariah to galvanize the militant zeal of Israelites and impel them to live the Torah of Moses and cleave to the covenant with God.

After one night on a rooftop of Jerusalem, listening to the revelry below, Jesus wandered out into the city. It was the morning of Shabbath, and the city was quiet on this day of rest. The streets were cleared of vendors, shops were closed, and many people were sleeping in. Even the market stalls on the Mount of Olives were shut, all transactions having been completed before sundown the previous day for the sacrifices which were ongoing, even on this day of rest. Humanity's work was interrupted; the service of God never ceased.

The memory of John naturally drew Jesus to a large and public source of living water in Jerusalem. Near the Temple, adjacent to the Roman garrison called the Antonia, there was an enormous pool called Bethesda fed by several springs. It provided water for the Temple, especially during Sukkoth. Enormous quantities of water, and smaller amounts of wine, were carried by priests and levites from Siloam and Bethesda to the Temple in giant copper vessels. The water was poured onto the altar so it ran down the altar's plinth into the court of the Israelites, the Great Court, and down Mount Zion's steps. It was part of the Sukkoth sacrifice, a joyous remembrance of the past year's rain, offered in the hope that God would generously provide vivifying waters for next year's crop (see Sukkah 4:9 in the Mishnah, and, in the Talmud, Rosh Hashanah 16a; Sukkah 48 a–b).

Bethesda consisted of two large trapezoid-shaped pools, connected by a sluice that when opened caused water to run from the north pool into the south. The rush of water into the south pool made it bubble and swirl. (Indeed, Bethesda got its name from "place of poured waters" in Aramaic, or Bethzatha, "bubbling-over place" in Hebrew.) John's Gospel—the only source for what happened at the pool—portrays people with ailments waiting around the pool in the belief that when the water bubbled it released miraculous healing powers.[1] The quantity of water was so vast, it washed away their illness with their impurity, and retained the clean status of living water.

---

1. Recent excavations of the pool have revealed dozens of votive objects, gifts people had left to give thanks for their return to health. These finds both confirm John's portrayal and are remarkable in their own right. Remarkable, because no one expects to find votive objects—idols by the definition of the Torah—in a pool designed to serve the Temple. Most of the votive offerings come from the second century and later, after the Romans refounded Jerusalem as Aelia Capitolina following the debacle of 135 C.E. and excluded Jews from the new city; they were given in gratitude to non-Jewish deities. But the possibility remains that the idolatrous customs of non-Jews were tolerated in Jerusalem even during the first century.

Today you can stand beside Bethesda. There is no water, only a bleak aridity, broken stones scarified by time and bleached by the sun. The springs that fed the pool have dried up, the conduits that replenished its waters destroyed long ago. Even the archaeologists are gone. There is a desolate feeling to the place in the midst of the bustle of modern-day Jerusalem. But the pool's depth and scale are evident, attesting to the importance of the purpose it was designed to serve and evoking the power it had in the minds of people two thousand years ago.

Jesus stood by Bethesda. Levites opened the sluice gates and water bubbled and surged. Jesus watched as the sick and the lame were helped by family and companions into the roiling pool.

He noticed one man, ill, lame, unmoving, sitting on a stretcher-like contraption of rough cloth and two sticks (a *krabbaton* in Greek; John 5:2–9). Why didn't he try to immerse in Bethesda?

"Do you want to become healthy?" Jesus asked him.

"Master," the man complained. "I do not have anyone, so that when the water is shaken he can put me in the pool. When I come on my own, another goes down ahead of me" (John 5:7).

He embodied the plight of the sick: isolation, debilitating self-pity, misery. People with skin lesions, those possessed by unclean spirits, madness and despair in their eyes, had knelt in front of Jesus before imploring him to cure them. They had approached Jesus for cleansing, with the demand that he enact his *halakhah,* his own rabbinic teaching, which was a way to live in a manner God approved. But now, spurred by the taunts of his brothers, and perhaps intuiting it was time to take his next step into the power he knew surrounded the Throne, Jesus, without invitation or request, found the confidence to reach out with the power of healing.

"Rise, take your litter, and walk!" Jesus commanded, unbidden, to the paralytic. There was nothing routine about the rabbi's words; he had not acted as a healer before. A fullness arose within him. Eight years ago, as a beggar in Jerusalem, he had found that the focused longing for God's plenty awakened in him a deep sense of divine compassion. Now he invoked God's compassion on behalf of a fellow Israelite. He laid hands on the man's crippled legs, while his mind's eye soared to the Throne, bringing the cripple there with him. He told the man to walk, and that is exactly what he did (John 5:8–9). Jesus had spoken as *chasid,* a rabbi who was able to dispense the mercy of God, and his words had resounded in heaven, unleashing a compassion greater than the paralysis.

The cripple must have thrown himself at Jesus' feet, and the sick and the lame at Bethesda would have crowded around him (although the text of John moves on directly to recount the scandal Jesus caused by healing on Shabbath). They clamored for God's mercy, which this peasant from Galilee seemed to have at his fingertips.

Jesus had already been acknowledged in Galilee as a rabbi: a master of *halakhah* whose actions were equal to his words. His teaching had made him seem like other Galilean rabbis, who were known as *chasidim.* During the Maccabean revolt that followed the desecration of the Temple by the Seleucids in 167 B.C.E., the term was applied to Jews so faithful to the Torah that they preferred to die rather than to do violence on the Shabbath (see 1 Maccabees 2:29–48). Having known the *chesed,* the compassion of God, they refused to betray him, their compassionate Lord. The *chasid's* sense of integrity carried on long after the Maccabees. By the first century the word applied especially to rabbis who were shown to have obtained divine mercy not only for themselves but, more strikingly, for others. These rabbis cured sickness and relieved drought through prayer: that was the mark of divine compassion working through them. *Chasidim* were ancient Judaism's shamans, faith healers, witch doctors, and sorcerers. In one bold move, Jesus had joined their ranks. He had proved that he was anointed with holy Spirit: he was able to channel the energy of God.

To understand Jesus and other *chasidim,* we must move behind the scientific strictures of our own mentality and enter into the imagination of a world in which God's power transformed people physically, not just ethically and spiritually. *Chasidim* differed on how divine mercy was invoked and divine healing occurred. One famous *chasid* named Chanina ben Dosa, a contemporary of Jesus who lived near Nazareth, said healing stemmed from the fluency of his prayer.[2] Jesus' principal technique was not prayer in the usual sense of beseeching God. Rather, his confidence that he could ascend to the Chariot made him tell people, on the authority of Spirit, that God himself had released them from their sins, and from the consequences of those sins. "Your sins are released," became his characteristic, oft-repeated declaration to those who were healed by his touch; and his typical advice afterward, "sin no more," was its complement. His language reflects the Judaic conception of sin as constraint, a binding of one's natural capacity. For God to release sin—and "release" is what the terms in Greek, Hebrew, and Aramaic that are traditionally rendered as "forgive" actually mean—was therefore to break open an incapacitating shackle. This was how the crippled man was healed; his legs and his sins were unbound. The current, weakened conception of forgiveness as merely overlooking or forgetting the harm one has suffered is a far cry from the Judaic sense of liberation from the consequences of one's own deeds.

After the healing at Bethesda, Jesus told the healed man to sin no more (John 5:14). He was convinced divine release from sin produces health. In our time, it is fairly easy to construct a picture of psychosomatic illness that faith might heal, or of autosuggestion and other psychological explanations of healing. But no single explanation accounts for shamanic

---

2. Jesus has rightly been likened to Chanina. He lived only ten miles from Nazareth, in the village of Arab. He was so famous, a leader of the Pharisees in Jerusalem named Gamaliel once sent two of his *talmidim* all the way up to Galilee to have Chanina pray for his son, who was ill. Chanina told the envoys that the fever had departed. They asked him, "Are you a prophet?" He replied: "I am no prophet, nor a prophet's son, but this is how I am favored. If my prayer is fluent in my mouth, I know one is favored; if not, I know the illness is fatal." When they returned to Jerusalem, Gamaliel reported to them that the fever had left his son at exactly the time Chanina had spoken (in Berakoth 34b). Here indeed was a *chasid*, obtaining mercy on behalf of others.

power. Every recovery, just as every illness, has a unique value and meaning for those who experience it. For Jesus, the meaning of health was release from sin and the sense of full integrity as an Israelite. Healing followed naturally.

Several stories and brief references in the New Testament deal with people suffering from paralysis, or "palsy" in the language of the King James Version. In a culture in which sins were understood to be binding constraints, and demons could lay seige to a part of the human body, it was natural for illness to be manifested by one's becoming enfeebled, unable to move. The common experience of being weak, not quite in one's own body, was diagnosed as being alienated from God. Immobility signaled both disease and its underlying cause. There was no rigid separation in this ancient worldview between body and mind. Both were ruled by spirits, whether harmful or healing, which exerted their influence, producing times of sickness and health, sin and forgiveness, paralysis and ecstasy.

In his shamanic role at the pool of Bethesda, Jesus manipulated these spirits. The control he displayed over the supernatural world vindicated him. How could the elders of Nazareth or his brothers mock his claim that God's Spirit was upon him? He had met their challenge; but his trials were far from over. He was about to confront the ruling priests of Judea, covetous of power, venomous toward any outsider who challenged their authority.

The incident at Bethesda brought about a profound change in Jesus' self-awareness. He was now ready to begin conveying his *halakhah* publicly. He had gained not only visibility but real celebrity in the Jewish culture of his day. For the first time since he arrived in Jerusalem, crowds gathered around him. He quickly fell in with a group who felt a particular affinity with this provincial rabbi who seemed so often at odds with the ruling elite.

Among the many Jews in Jerusalem for Sukkoth was a young levite named Joseph, some four years older than Jesus, who had come to visit his aunt. The family was from Cyprus, the third largest island in the

Mediterranean and a wealthy, fertile land. Cypriot Jews were proud providers of wine for the Day of Atonement, which preceded Sukkoth (see Yoma 4:5 in the Palestinian Talmud). As a levite from the Diaspora, however, Joseph himself could not take part in the service of the Temple. He did not come from the land of Israel, and so was barred from undertaking any of the priestly functions in the Temple, even though he was an Aramaic speaker and a member of the priestly caste.

The honor of offering sacrifice was jealously guarded by the priests in Jerusalem, who refused to include levites from the Diaspora in their ranks. The priests had implemented a carefully systematized rota for service in the Temple, but only for men of levite pedigree who actually lived in Israel. The rota also shared in the immense wealth of tithes and the priestly portion of sacrifices, both treasured prerogatives. Some levites permanently assisted the principal priests, called Zadokites; they saw to the distribution among all priests of the portions of sacrifices to which they were entitled. The permanent Temple staff were the carnivores of ancient Judaism, near the top of the food chain. They were well built, bigger than their lay brethren from eating about as much meat from sacrifices each week as most Jews could expect to enjoy in a year. Including Diaspora levites like Joseph in the rota would have drastically cut the income of Jerusalem's priests. Joseph would have understood this. Money was not the issue: he came from a wealthy family. Let the priests keep their tithes! What rankled him was his exclusion from priestly duties.

More than once, standing in the Sanctuary or the Great Court of the Temple, he was consumed with the syndrome, common among the Diaspora levites, of turban envy. He would never be allowed to wear the imposing turban he admired on the high priest's head, or even the mini-turbans of the haughty levites who followed the high priest as he strode through the Great Court, handed him his shovel of incense as he intoned the blessings of sacrifice, and basked in their own importance. He would never even participate in the operation of the Temple as one of the lowliest from the house of Levi, who hauled muzzled and bellowing animals to their death, bespattering themselves with holy blood.

It was probably in the Temple, near the time of Sukkoth, that Joseph met Jesus. For Joseph, the spectacle of what Jesus was doing near the Temple was liberating: if a Galilean could enter Jerusalem with his bold declaration of purity and healing, perhaps a Cypriot levite might one day serve at the altar. Joseph befriended Jesus and invited him to stay at his aunt's house and enjoy their hospitality. And what hospitality! The home was furnished with tables and carpets, oil lamps burned at night, and the Cypriot wine was rich and satisfying. Jesus was so grateful for the kindness that he called Joseph "Barnabas," meaning "son of consolation" in Aramaic (Acts 4:36).[3] His experience with the families of John's *talmidim* had prepared him to accept and enjoy wealth as part of devoted worship. Now he tuned his ear to the strange, accented Aramaic of the Cypriots, and learned exotic and exciting new manners for eating and dressing.

The wonderful feasts with Barnabas, together with Jesus' vivid vision of Zechariah's promise of people everywhere streaming into Jerusalem, inspired Jesus' own prediction, which characteristically had to do with the pleasures of the table (Matthew 8:11; Luke 13:29):

Many shall come from east and west and recline in feasting with Abraham and Isaac and Jacob in the Kingdom of God.

Feasting on symposial couches was no longer simply a sign that unrighteous *mammon* had wormed its way into Israel; it symbolized the full glory to come.

---

3. Early contact between Jesus and the man he called Barnabas is attested in a source called *The Praise of Barnabas*, written by a monk named Alexander during the fourth century. Because Barnabas was simply a friend of the young Jesus, and not a disciple until after Jesus' execution, the New Testament only mentions him in connection with his later activity. But Alexander weaves together the evidence of the Gospels with the memory of Barnabas in the ancient church, and provides an interesting new resource for understanding the development of Jesus. In addition, modern archaeology has uncovered something of the luxury that was possible in dwellings in Jerusalem.

The household of Barnabas had swelled at the time of Sukkoth, and Jesus remained there with a few pilgrims afterward. The period around Sukkoth was one long, sacred celebration. Jesus' companions at meals were also his partners in sacrifice. They entered the Temple as a group, singing together and offering their fine Cypriot wine through the priestly personnel at the altar for Yahweh's pleasure. The priests and levites who shared in the wine would have been grateful for the quality of drink pro-

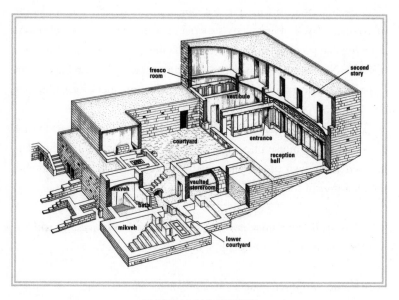

JERUSALEM HOUSE

This is the kind of residence that priestly families lived in, a two-story dwelling appropriately called "the Palatial Mansion" by excavators. The ground floor, centered around a spacious courtyard, contained the living quarters and a 33- by 21-foot reception hall preserved at one point to a height of more than 11 feet; in the basement were cisterns, a storeroom, and ritual baths. Lavish as this building was, it was relatively short-lived. A coin sealed beneath the entryway's mosaic floor dates to 34 B.C.E., giving the earliest date for the building's construction. Collapsed and charred cypress ceiling beams indicate that the Palatial Mansion shared the same fate as the rest of Jerusalem during the Roman destruction in 70 C.E. (Illustration courtesy of Leen Ritmeyer and Biblical Archaeology Review)

vided by the group, however leery they were of levite pilgrims from the Diaspora and uppity *chasidim* from Galilee.

In the evenings, Jesus and the Cypriots imbibed freely from the same wine as they talked the Torah, the Prophets, and politics, which were interwoven in their minds. Jesus was their guide in these discussions. His hosts and their guests would have deferred to him, looked up to him, hung on his every word. He was embraced more fully by them in intellectual terms than he had been even in the most welcoming villages of Galilee. The respect he was given was due not only to his chasidic reputation. They bowed to his expertise in the oral Scriptures of Galilee and the traditions of Judaism. From his childhood experience in Nazareth, Jesus had at his command the targumic, paraphrased rendering of the commonly used parts of the five books of Moses, the prophetic books, and the psalms. His folk wisdom (which also included his immense repertoire of parables) and his Galilean emphasis on the Kingdom of God were welded to the esoteric mastery he had learned with John. Much of his time with John had been devoted to the repetition and incantation of texts, which had further developed his already finely honed memory. His Scriptural expertise—along with his radical teaching of purity, dramatic healings, and showy exorcisms—made him an extremely attractive figure to the Cypriot circle. They took him to their hearts in a way Judeans never would.

As Diaspora Jews, these Cypriots keenly looked forward to the fulfillment of the promise Zechariah had made to all peoples, because it would assure their own position within Israel. If even Egyptians would join fully in the festival of Sukkoth (Zechariah 14:18–19), surely levites from Cyprus would also find their place.

The celebratory mood was strong within the Cypriot circle. These people had money, and, like Jesus, they loved to eat, drink, and delight God with lavish offerings at his altar. But there was also a dark apocalyptic side to their activity. The prophecy of Zechariah, as we have seen, was of judgment, as well as promise. Before the Gentiles came in supplication to offer the wealth of the world at the Temple altar, Zechariah prophesied, they would resist God's message and come into Jerusalem as conquering overlords, rifling houses and ravishing women (Zechariah 14:2). Their seemingly unbreakable onslaught on God and his people would be broken only by an overwhelming catastrophe. Both Gentiles and Jews had to pass through a crucible of fire (Zechariah 13:9), because all people had committed injustice. The final outburst of God's compassion, which brought about his eternal Kingdom and the vindication of his covenant, would be accompanied by Yahweh's exacting, unrelenting sense of justice. The pain of the Israelites and the ultimate defeat of the Gentiles were an integral part of the final, catastrophic end of history. Precisely because the appropriate punishment was to be meted out in a flash of violence, the full realization of the Kingdom could appear with lightning speed.

The Cypriot circle believed they housed a rabbi who could initiate the promise of Zechariah's prophecy, and they were prepared to see the resistance Jesus provoked as what Zechariah had prophesied. Jesus was still filled with the Spirit that had led him deliberately to alienate the elders of little Nazareth. In Jerusalem, in the aftermath of Sukkoth, he slipped easily into the adversarial pattern that became a leitmotif of his life.

The keen, sometimes feverish expectations of the feast had subsided, and the attention of many rabbis turned to their next favorite activity, argument. Jesus joined the fray. His healing of the lame man had occurred on Shabbath, when all Israel was to desist from work. Jesus' healing violated a fundamental precept of some Pharisees (John 5:9–18), but it was not such a terrible transgression. In fact, different schools of thought within first-century Judaism hotly debated the issue of whether or not healing was permissible on Shabbath. The debate was more pronounced in Judea than in Galilee, since the Temple was the center of the system of keeping purity. It followed that there was a heightened sense of urgency among Jerusalem's Pharisees to make sure God's commandments were kept in the Temple's vicinity.

Jesus was about to butt heads with the Pharisees, who reappear again and again in the Gospels as his opponents. To Jesus, as to many first-century Jews, the Pharisees were royal nuisances. They were not only sticklers for adhering to the letter of the Law (which they insisted they alone really knew, in its oral form), they were also busybodies, especially where priests and levites were concerned. They insisted on knowing the minute details of the pedigrees of the women the priests sought to marry and whether any priest had ejaculated the night before his appointed duties. The discharge of semen would render him unclean, unfit for Temple service; the Mishnah pictures the high priest being kept awake all night prior to the Day of Atonement to avoid a nocturnal emission (Yoma 1:7):

> *If he tried to doze off, young priests snap their middle fingers before*
> *him and say to him, My lord high priest, stand up and drive off sleep*
> *by walking on the cold stones.*

God forbid on this night of all nights the high priest should have a wet dream, which would disqualify him from his cultic duty.

That was the kind of regulation the Pharisees made sure was maintained. Sexual conduct and the maintenance of the caste system were central to their system of purity, and for that reason they deemed that what seem to us private matters belonged in the public domain. Equally important to the Pharisees were the laws of *kashrut* (dietary cleanness), which they fine-tuned, and keeping Shabbath. Of course, not all Pharisees believed that healing on Shabbath violated the law; they disagreed about virtually everything. But the Pharisees near the Temple were a testy bunch, innately conservative, not just a little paranoid, and unapologetically self-righteous. They quickly perceived that Jesus was playing fast and loose with their strictures, dabbling in matters that were not the business of an illiterate *chasid* from Galilee.

They must have challenged Jesus about his healing on Shabbath when he came to offer sacrifice in the Temple with Barnabas and his coterie soon after Sukkoth. Jesus could simply have apologized. After all, he hadn't realized he was stepping on toes. Healing on Shabbath was not a big issue in Galilee. Or he might have engaged the Pharisees in debate. Instead, he reverted to the difficult, reactive side of his personality, insisting that God was working within him. "My Father is working still, and I am working" (John 5:17). Just as sacrifice continued in the Temple on Shabbath, so, too, did God's compassion, which on this occasion had streamed from the Throne through his son. His statement must have smacked of arrogance to the Pharisees, but Jesus didn't stop there (Luke 10:21; Matthew 11:25):

> In this hour he exulted in the holy spirit and said, I own up to you, father, Lord of heaven and of earth, because you hid away these things from wise and understanding people, and uncovered them to infants!

He created a sensation as he mocked the Pharisees and their learning, proclaiming, in effect, that infants knew more about God than they did. Jesus' supporters from Barnabas' household would have howled with delight. Jews who had heard of his miraculous healing would have crowded around, too, gawking at him, paying obeisance, egging him on, begging for his healing touch.

Although the Gospels portray the Pharisees as the stock villains in the drama of Jesus' life, they were decent (if somewhat pompous) men, with a considered understanding of religion, grounded within the authority of the Torah and reasoned debate in the community. Why did Rabbi Jesus have to rub their faces in his personal, charismatic authority?

The confrontations about his healing in Jerusalem took him into new territory, bringing him into conflict not only with the Pharisees but also with the priestly teachers who also thought he had violated the observance of Shabbath. More important, they resisted Jesus' claims of an authority greater than their own.

The issue of authority haunted Jesus for the remaining weeks he spent in Jerusalem. It wasn't long before the priests directly challenged him, demanding to know where his authority came exactly from (Mark 11:27–33, see Matthew 21:23–27; Luke 20:1–8):

> *By what sort of authority are you doing these things, or who gave you this authority, so that you do them? But Yeshua said to them, I will interrogate you: a single issue. You reply to me, and I will say to you by what sort of authority I do these things. Was the immersion of Yochanan from heaven or from humanity? Reply to me!*

The priests were silenced. Denying that the Immerser effectively taught God's own purity would put them at odds with popular opinion, which favored John. But if they did affirm John's teaching, they would implicitly endorse Jesus' right to teach and heal, since Jesus was John's most prominent disciple. They refused to answer him. But their silence seethed with enmity; it was irritating to be embarrassed in their own Temple with onlookers present (and a particularly happy Barnabas).

Jesus could not resist besting the kind of men who had consigned him to the status of an outsider. In Nazareth, he claimed to be anointed with Spirit; in the Temple, he even called himself God's son, and in public. The smoldering tension between north and south in ancient Israel was playing itself out in this rabbi from Galilee. To the Judeans, the arrogance of many Galileans was intolerable; after all, it had taken the power of the Maccabees from Judea to establish Judaism in the land called "Galilee of the Gentiles" (Isaiah 9:1). With his poor clothes and rough, northern peasant accent Jesus fit the role of firebrand Galilean rebel, flouting the priestly authority, undermining the priests' claim that their authority was supreme.

He came from the proud oral culture of rural Galilee, from the visionary tradition of Elijah, from a people who cherished a Torah of insurgency and whose integrity resisted compromise with the oppressor and coveted the purity of their own land—and he let all who heard him in Jerusalem know it. He further spelled out his dependence on his *Abba* when it concerned his own deeds, and threatened his opponents with the power of deeds yet to come (John 5:19–20):

> *The son can not do anything from himself, except what he sees the father doing, because what he does, the son does this likewise. For the father loves the son and shows him all that he himself does, and greater deeds than these he will show him, so that you will marvel.*

What a weird combination he was! Both humble and proud, overflowing with compassion but adamant in his assertions of the terrible judgment of God. He seemed lost at times, the direction of his life unclear, but then he could turn around and flaunt his prophetic conviction. His certainty could be frightening.

Supported by Joseph Barnabas and his aunt, Jesus continued to live in Jerusalem for several weeks after Sukkoth, until the lesser but joyous feast of Chanukah, which celebrated the dedication of the Temple after it had been taken back from the Seleucid king Antiochus Epiphanes in 164 B.C.E. He had lucked into a sweet situation. Here were people who cherished him and were willing to lodge him in luxury and sit at his feet. He had come from the poor mud villages of Galilee and had jumped class. But as Chanukah approached, the Pharisees especially disputed whether Jesus' presence in the Temple should be tolerated. One of their rabbis, named Nicodemus, could find nothing specific with which to charge Jesus (John 7:50–51). After all, his healings were applications of his path of purity, which could not be condemned merely because it was different from the Pharisees' teaching. And the objection to his healing on Shabbath was easily answered: the Mishnah itself does not regard healing as work (Shabbath 14:4), since it derives from divine generosity, not human effort. Still, the reaction of Nicodemus' colleagues to his plea for moderation is telling: "Are you, too, from Galilee?" (John 7:52). The underlying antipathy to Jesus was aroused because a *Galilean* presumed to teach and practice purity by exemplary healings in the area of the Temple. He was a threat to Judean control—priestly, Pharisaic, and aristocratic.

Jesus and the Judean Pharisees had hardened their opposition to one another by Chanukah. Pharisaic opponents contemptuously challenged him, "Where is your father?" (John 8:19). Why should they accept instruction from a Galilean *mamzer*? They said to Nicodemus, "Search and see that a prophet does not arise from Galilee" (John 7:52). The power of the Pharisees resided in their influence over other Jews, their ability to convince them that the Pharisaic construction of purity was not only the best but was necessary. They did not have official control over what happened in the Temple: that belonged to the high priests. But they were represented in the ruling council, and—more important—their sway over large numbers of people in Jerusalem meant that they could call on a mob to enforce their positions, if the occasion demanded. Josephus reports that they incited a riot when the Maccabean king and priest, Alexander Jannaeus, tried to offer sacrifice on the Day of Atonement without first fasting and washing in the manner the Pharisees advocated. The mob picked up the lemons on hand for the imminent feast of Sukkoth and pelted Jannaeus, forcing him to retreat to his palace (see Josephus, *Antiquities* 13 § § 372–373). Josephus relates (with his customary exaggeration) that Jannaeus responded by killing some six thousand of the rebels; the Pharisees and others who opposed priestly control in the Temple learned the limits of their influence by painful experience.

It was much easier (and safer) for the Pharisees during the Roman period to enforce their position by inciting a small crowd to do violence against a local irritant, rather than against the hierarchy in the Temple, which was exactly what they did in the case of Jesus. They stalked him during the eight days of Chanukah, by which time the rainy season had set in. Time and energy were freed up from the labors of the field, for good or ill. Chanukah wasn't Sukkoth, Passover, or Pentecost, one of the great feasts of pilgrimage, but it was still a time of local celebration of the deliverance of the holy city from the Seleucids. It was known even then as the Feast of Lights (Josephus, Antiquities 12 § 325), because the menorah in the Temple was kindled afresh (1 Maccabees 4:50), and lamps were lit in Israelite homes (Baba Qamma 6:6; Sukkah 5:2–4 in the Mishnah). Light was among the first creations of God when the Spirit moved over the primeval waters (Genesis 1:3), so that light and Spirit are as closely linked in Judaic tradition as are Spirit and water. Given Jesus' claim that purity flowed out from him, we can see why he made the grandiose claim that he was "the light of the world" during Chanukah (John 8:12). He was inspired by the link between light in homes and light in the Temple, and he saw his own practice of purity and healing illuminating Israel, and Israel as God's light among the nations.

When Jesus called himself "the light of the world," he infuriated those to whom in the past he had been little more than a curiosity and an annoyance. For Jesus, the Spirit flooding out from the Chariot provided purity and healing by means of his own touch (John 9:1–7). He claimed a spiritual authority implicitly greater than the priesthood's. He did not actually blaspheme the Temple or the Torah; blasphemy required an explicit statement against what Judaism held sacred. But for his opponents, Jesus' assertion remained atrocious. How could he claim that he was the light of the world in the place that could alone claim that honor? A crowd in the Temple threatened him with stoning, not an organized group but an enraged mob, whipped up by Pharisees and priests (John 8:59; 10:31–32).

The Temple was a place of danger for Jesus, unless he could gather enough Galilean sympathizers to return in force. The time had come to retreat again to Galilee. But this retreat was not simple flight, as it had been after the execution of John by Herod Antipas. He departed now in order to gather disciples. His teaching had matured, and he was prepared to do what John had done and instruct disciples how to be what Talmudic tradition calls *yordey Merkabah,* riders of the Chariot. This was a strategic retreat, until the day he could return to Jerusalem and the Temple (Luke 13:34–35; Matthew 23:37–39):

Yerushalem, Yerushalem, who killed the prophets and stoned those delegated to her, how often I wanted to gather your children in the way a bird gathers her young under the wings, and you did not want? Look: your house leaves you! For I say to you, you shall not see me from now on, until you say, Blessed is the one who comes in the Lord's name!

Again, the compressed presentation of Matthew, Mark, and Luke leads to confusion: they attribute this bitter admonition to Jesus before he entered Jerusalem at the end of his life, when it is obviously a lament based on recent and painful experience there. It is the complaint and warning of a retreating, momentarily beaten *chasid,* not the triumphant challenge of the prophet who returned years later.

Newly confident in his practice, yet confronted with deadly opposition in Jerusalem, he escaped to the only town in Galilee where he could hope for a favorable reception: Capernaum. Barnabas, his aunt, and Jesus' other newfound supporters must have been sorry to see him go. But not the Pharisees, priests, and levites. They were more than content to see the back of this meddlesome troublemaker with his unpredictable outbursts, indecorous manner, *chasidic* powers, and sharp skills of debate, and were relieved that he had returned to the peasant backwater that had spawned him.

SEVEN

❧

Capernaum's Prophet

Three days of hard walking up the Jordan Valley had brought him south of the Sea of Galilee; he made his way to Capernaum on its western shore. It couldn't have been a pleasant journey. The golden light and balmy weather of fall had given way to cold. The skies were often gray, and he was chilled by the winter rains that swept over Palestine. He wouldn't have tarried on the way, and would have arrived in Capernaum with nothing to eat and no place to lodge (Matthew 8:20 and Luke 9:58):

Foxes have holes and the birds of heaven nests, but the one like the person[1] does not have a spot to lay his head.

Soon, however, he found a safe haven with Simon (later called "Rock" by Jesus; *Kepha* in Aramaic, *Petros* in Greek) and his brother Andrew, both professional fishermen, who knew Jesus from his occasional, and sometimes dramatic, visits to the synagogue in Capernaum.

---

1. "One like the person" refers here, as generally in Aramaic, to any human being. Later, in Jesus' esoteric teaching, the phrase would acquire a new meaning.

The Gospels portray Jesus as calling them, along with two other brothers named James and John, while he was walking along the shore of the Sea of Galilee (Matthew 4:18–22; Mark 1:16–20; see also Luke 5:1–11). Mark's version conveys the schematic quality of the story:

> He passed along the Sea of Galil, and saw Shimon and Andreas Shimon's brother rig-casting in the sea, because they were fishers. And Yeshua said to them, Come on after me, and I will make you become fishers of people. At once, they left their nets and followed him. He progressed a little and saw Yaaqov the son of Zebedayah and Yochanan his brother, and they were in the boat mending the nets and at once he called them. And leaving their father Zebedayah in the boat with the employees, they went away after him.

Jesus spoke of the necessity to repent in order to accept the Kingdom of God (Mark 1:15), and urged these fishermen to join him in fishing for people. The Gospels describe all four men as immediately dropping their professions and families to follow Rabbi Jesus. That is part of the New Testament's idealized, historically implausible portrait of discipleship. The realities of making a living pressed on these men, and the rabbi himself faced the issue of daily survival; their fishing did not turn all metaphorical in a single day. Nonetheless, what they did to enable Jesus to remain in Capernaum is a testament to the seriousness of Simon and Andrew, James and John: they opened their arms to Jesus, took him into their households, and supported him.

Jesus must have been pleased with his new accommodations. Andrew and Simon's house, where they had moved from Bethsaida to marry two sisters, had windows, two stories, and ornamental pebbles on the floors. It was not as luxurious as Barnabas' aunt's house in Jerusalem, but it was a far cry from the hovels of Nazareth. Jesus settled in with Simon and Andrew, their wives, children, and extended family, enjoying the relatively high standard of living from the lucrative fishing trade.

He knew nothing about fishing, but that didn't stop him from giving

CAPERNAUM

This rendering features the 2,500-foot promenade that lined the shore. Boats were tied up along the harbor's complex of curved piers and straight jetties. During the dry season in Galilee, the stone remains are visible still. The synogogue is represented here with a tiered roof on the upper left; one of these many houses would perhaps have been home to

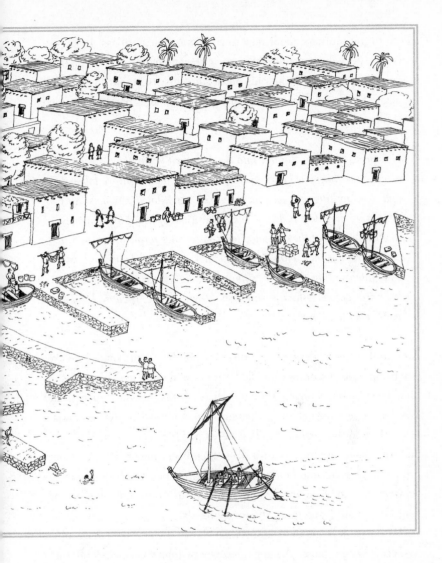

Peter and Andrew. A dwelling between the synagogue and the harbor has traditionally been called "Peter's House," but that precise identification strains credulity. (Illustration courtesy of Leen Ritmeyer)

advice to the brothers about how to go about their business. Luke presents an especially exasperated Simon, at the end of his rope after a fruitless night on the water when his houseguest insists he put his nets out yet again. Simon reluctantly plays along, getting more than he bargained for (Luke 5:4–8):

> He said to Shimon, Put out into the deep and lower your nets for a catch. Shimon replied and said, Master, the whole night we labored and took nothing, but on your utterance I will lower the nets. And doing this they hemmed in a great multitude of fish, but their nets tore through. And they signaled to the associates in the other boat to come take together with them, and they came and both the boats were filled so that they were sinking. Shimon Rock saw and fell on his knees before Yeshua, saying, Go away from me, because I am a man, a sinner, Lord!

Even in these early days, we see the dynamic that would mark Jesus' relationship with his prime disciple. Peter is obdurate, and Jesus pushes him. Peter relents, breaks through, shares Jesus' insight, repents, and asks forgiveness for his human failures and doubts. This dynamic was a key feature in the relationship that developed between them. Their productive tension matured into a deep friendship, and made Peter over time into the most important disciple, precisely because he can seem as slow-witted and uncomprehending as all of us often feel when we are confronted with Jesus' often strange demands.

We know less about Andrew than Simon Peter, and I have often wished we knew more. A stray reference in John's Gospel (John 1:44) fortunately tells us that both Andrew and Peter came from Bethsaida, and that explains their special relationship with Philip, who also came from that town. Andrew is a puzzling figure, because although apparently older than his brother Peter (who is mentioned after him in John 1:44), he quickly disappears into the shadows, named only sporadically as someone who supports and listens to Jesus.

Because Andrew is a cipher in the Gospels, he became a target of hagiographic treatment in Christian legend. In a document probably written during the second century called the *Acts of Andrew* (cited principally by Gregory of Tours during the sixth century), Andrew is a martyr to celibacy. He departed from Jerusalem after Jesus' death, traveled through Greece and Turkey, rescued Saint Matthias from cannibals, and engaged in a ministry of healing, exorcism, and raising people from the dead. He also convinced married people to abstain from sex, a characteristic practice of Syriac Christianity. Although it broke up families, celibacy was believed to be the best way to become angelic. (Syriac theology is an important source of the attempt to control sexuality throughout the Christian tradition.) Andrew's own life ended, the story goes, when he made one convert too many to celibacy, the wife of a proconsul, who promptly had him crucified by the seaside.

Other apocryphal tales are woven around the figures of James and John, the sons of Zebedee. James was known to have been beheaded by Herod Agrippa I in 44 C.E. (Acts 12:1–22; Josephus, *Antiquities* 19 §§ 343–352). But he miraculously comes back to life in a sixth- or seventh-century Spanish tradition, which has him sailing to Spain to preach in a ship guided by angels. John is paired with James, not only as his brother, but as a future martyr in the teaching of Jesus (Matthew 20:20–28; Mark 10:35–45). Church legend elongates his life by at least twenty-five years in order to make him the author of John's Gospel, the letters of John, and the Revelation. Not bad for an illiterate fisherman (Acts 4:13). Not only did he write several books, but he wrote them in different styles! According to later church martyrdom stories, John survived boiling in oil, drinking poison, and the deadly bite of a viper.[2]

Such accounts leave me cold. They offer virtually nothing of histori-

---

2. That is a minuscule sample of the rich legends about John. See the recent work of R. Alan Culpepper, *John, the Son of Zebedee. The Life of a Legend,* in the series Studies on Personalities of the New Testament (Columbia: University of South Carolina Press, 1994) 326–329.

cal value, although they are fascinating as a reflection of a certain kind of early Christian theology. When it comes to understanding Rabbi Jesus in his most important relationships, we often have to remain content with fragmentary evidence and inference. Trying to fill in the holes with legends only obscures what we can plausibly surmise.

The story of the healing of Simon's mother-in-law from a fever (Matthew 8:14–15; Mark 1:29–31; Luke 4:38–39) does derive from this period. Jesus had settled into the household, and would have been considered a member of the family. Mark describes the woman as "prone, fevered," when the disciples speak to Jesus about her. There was no such thing as a slight fever during the first century. Flu and infections could kill and often did, especially the young and the old. (Simon's mother, pushing forty, was on the threshold of being elderly in the ancient world.) Yet Jesus seemed unconcerned. His treatment of her is referred to as almost routine (Mark 1:31):

> He came forward, raised her—grasping the hand. And the fever left her, and she was providing for them.

"Providing for them" meant getting their lunch in the short term, and cooking, cleaning, and gardening for them on a regular basis.

We see in these early accounts of Jesus' healing in the Gospel according to Mark an emphasis on touch. He grasps the fevered woman's hand; in another episode he spits on his fingers, sticks them into a deaf mute's ears and mouth, then grabs his tongue and says in Aramaic, *"Ephatha* (Be opened up)" (Mark 7:31–37); and in yet another story he spits right into a blind man's eyes and lays hands on them in a healing that takes two treatments to be effective (Mark 8:22–26). This tactile focus of Jesus' chasidic power, the shamanic side of his practice, is greatly diminished in the other Gospels, which were written later. There, Jesus is logocentric: he just speaks and healing happens spontaneously (see, for example, Matthew 8:16). As Christianity took on an increasingly Hellenistic character, its portraits of Jesus became more cerebral, almost philosophical. He no longer spat or grabbed at hands and tongues; the carousing drunkard became a divine oracle. The earthiness of his rabbinic persona was lost.

Widespread healing in and around Capernaum (Matthew 4:23–25; Mark 1:32–39; Luke 4:40–44) punctuated Jesus' teaching. His confidence as a *chasid* corresponded both to his genuine fame as a healer and his conscious acceptance of Simon and Andrew, James and John as his first real *talmidim* (Matthew 4:18–22; Mark 1:16–20).

The crush of those who sought cures often became dangerous. Even the violent exorcisms of his period in Nazareth pale in comparison with the chaos that frequently swirled around him in Capernaum. The pressure on him there was sometimes unbearable. He sought relief from travel in wilderness areas (Mark 1:35; Luke 4:42), camping for days at a time, usually alone, but often with eager disciples and would-be devotees (Mark 1:36; Luke 4:42). Philip, who had returned to his native Bethsaida after John the Baptist's death and his separation from Jesus, accommodated his old friend from time to time and joined him in his travels. As they ran out of provisions, they sought the hospitality of small Jewish settlements and then returned to the wilderness.

When he was in Capernaum, even the protection of Simon and Andrew's house and courtyard was no match for crowds desperate for the healing purity of his touch. Mass hysteria gripped many in Galilee. For them, as in Jesus' vision during his immersions with John the Baptist, the heavens were splitting open. The Spirit was available to God's chosen people in this master rabbi who seemed to have almost limitless power as he strode the roads near the Sea of Galilee.

Once, when he had returned to his base in Capernaum after a brief retreat into the wilderness, he was teaching in a small house where a paralyzed man was brought to him. Those who carried him were prevented from getting to Jesus by the crowd that thronged around the house, for whom each healing was a new eruption of Spirit, a step toward the Kingdom of God. The bearers actually had to dig through the earthen roof and lower the man to Jesus on his litter. "Your sins are released for you," Jesus said, and the man walked (Matthew 9:1–8; Mark 2:1–12; Luke 5:17–26).

As Jesus' fame grew, we can see why he sought the quiet solitude of the wilderness. He needed to replenish himself and to teach those closest to him in a place where they could concentrate on the mysteries of the Chariot. These retreats offered a respite from the almost bacchanalian excesses that Capernaum offered, as well as from the busy urban routine of work and social life and the demands of Simon's and Andrew's families that cut into his meditative discipline. Desperate crowds that clamored for his healing were the final straw, and he would pick up a few belongings and leave Capernaum for days (Mark 1:35–37):

> *Extremely early (at night), he arose and went away into a wilderness place, and there he prayed. And Shimon and those with him pursued him, and found him and say to him that: Everybody is seeking you.*

These retreats were sporadic and short-lived, but they punctuated his movements in and around Capernaum with the solace of constant meditation on the Chariot. He deepened and redefined the visions he had experienced since his days with John. In the wilderness he began to use a vision from the book of Daniel, an angel beside the Throne of God called in Aramaic "one like a person," who brought him close to his *Abba* in the divine court of heaven. This "one like a person" was shortly to emerge as the anchor of Jesus' visions and of the visionary discipline he taught his followers.

The scrub land of wilderness around the Sea of Galilee was no desert, but it was reminiscent of the wilderness that Israel's patriarchs, as well as Moses and the prophets, had sought when they most needed direct communion with God. In this place of the burning bush and thundering commands, the earthquake and the still, small voice, Jesus—through his close identification with the "one like a person"—discovered what it was to become a rider of the Chariot, not only an observer of its splendor. The wilderness was the place where he and his disciples became one with the source of God's endless revelation.

Not all Pharisees were Jesus' enemies; many had at least a modicum of respect for him and were curious about his teaching. A Pharisee named Simon actually hosted a meal for him in Capernaum (Luke 7:36–50). Simon must have been wealthy, perhaps a merchant in the olive oil from Galilee which was treasured by Jews as far away as Syria for being *kosher* as well as of high quality.[3] The Pharisee's house would have been large and well appointed, without the decadent, Hellenic opulence of the homes Jesus had railed against when he had first visited Capernaum around 23 C.E.

By inviting Jesus into his home, the Pharisee opened it to Jesus' disciples, followers, and others who came to listen to the rabbi and sit with him out of simple curiosity. One of the curious was a woman described in Luke as "sinful." When she saw Jesus and heard him speak, she cast herself at his feet, repenting of her sins. She wept and "began with tears to wet his feet and with the hair of her head she wiped, and kissed his feet" (Luke 7:38). Her act must have silenced the chattering, rambunctious crowd. His feet would have been filthy from Capernaum's streets, which in places were little better than open sewers. The washing of his feet with her hair and tears is a beautiful, haunting image.

Legend has portrayed her as a prostitute, but there is no evidence she was. Still, the fact that the woman is simply called "sinful," without explanation, does intimate that she had been known somehow for sexual impropriety. She might have gone through a series of spouses the way the Samaritan woman did, perhaps out of her caste. But given her elaborate gesture with her own hair, it is more likely she pursued the forbidden pro-

---

3. Oil, because it was a fluid, was held particularly to convey uncleanness, so that having pure oil in one's household was vital to maintaining the laws of *kashrut*.

fession of a hairdresser, which many rabbis saw as just a step away from prostitution. The Pharisee was offended that Jesus accepted the touch of a notorious sinner, but Jesus pronounced that her sins had been forgiven, and articulated his principle (Luke 7:47):

> Her many sins have been released, because she loved much: but to whom little is released, loves little.

Those who are unaware of how much they have been forgiven love only a little. By contrast, those who consciously accept divine forgiveness, which releases them from their self-imposed shackles, are alive to the bounty which comes from God alone and are willing to extend that forgiving power to others, in generous, spontaneous acts like the hairdresser's. Her lavish embrace of Jesus was itself an extension of divine compassion, proof that she had been taken up and purified by God's love.

Love for Jesus was not an attitude of general tolerance, as it has been portrayed in romanticized versions of Christianity, but the power of divine creativity released in human relations. He said to the woman, "Your sins have been released" (Luke 7:48), because from that moment, she was to conduct her life in the purity which came from forgiveness. That is why Jesus sent her on her way as she rose to her feet, by saying "Your faith has saved you; proceed in peace" (Luke 7:50). His instruction was not to simply "go in peace," the weakened rendering of most English versions of the New Testament, which makes it sound as if she were simply to continue on her way. He said, "proceed in peace," proposing a new departure in her conduct. He made this moment the turning point which changed the direction of her life.

Jesus could not practice his holy feasts in Capernaum, as he had in Nazareth and other villages. His fame drew crowds too large for small convivial meals. He was pushed into the position of a public speaker. The crowds and even his disciples were often puzzled by his words. Why did he always speak to them in parables? What exactly was the Kingdom of God, the elusive concept at the root of his teaching? Often during this period we see Jesus frustrated. How could he reach these people, great in numbers but limited in comprehension? He compares himself to a farmer who scatters seed with no great expectation of the results. His hope is that the right conditions will see to a plentiful harvest of the little seed that is not lost in the process of sowing and planting (Mark 4:1–9; Matthew 13:1–9; Luke 8:4–8). Jesus admits to desperation in Capernaum and yet insists that people should be able to understand his message.

Instead of demanding their constant association with a rabbi such as himself or John and the practices he espoused (whether immersion or celebration at meals), Jesus announced that those who listened to him *already* enjoyed access to God's Kingdom. What Matthew calls the Sermon on the Mount (in contrast to the sermon on a plain in Luke) distills the approach that Jesus discovered. His words would carry through two millennia to provide the hope of transformation to the oppressed and exploited of countless societies. The Sermon's simplicity underlines its drama (Luke 6:20b–22):

> *The poor are favored, because* yours *is the Kingdom of God;*
> *Those who hunger now are favored, because you will be filled;*
> *Those who weep now are favored, because you will laugh;*
> *You are favored, when people hate you and when they exclude you*
>   *and censure you.*

Among those gathered on the shore or below the rock from which he spoke, Jesus could easily discern the poor, the hungry, those who were mourning the loss of loved ones who had supported them and had given them their status in the community, and those shunned by others because they were viewed as unclean. Jesus was speaking from personal experience; he had himself known poverty, hunger, the bereavement of a protective father, and ostracism. He knew when you are stripped down to bare bones, when you have been battered and threatened with stoning by fellow Israelites, when you are exploited and alone, you are in the best position to identify the sustaining force of God's compassion. The poor, hungry, and shunned were Jesus' people. Christianity at its best has remembered what Jesus taught and reached out with love and a complete sense of identification to the poor, persecuted, and oppressed, recognizing where the experience of God is most purely realized. Jesus' Sermon, like Moses' demand to Pharaoh to "let my people go," expresses a powerful and enduring truth of an Israelite prophet.

Jesus' Sermon identified a few of the different types of outcasts in first-century Judaism. Many were virtual untouchables, viewed by pious Jews (some of them Pharisees) as unclean. They were shunned because they oozed a contagious pollution that had to be avoided. Yet Jesus ate and drank with them. We often see him attacked for consorting with "publicans [agents who collected customs and taxes] and prostitutes" (Matthew 21:31) and claiming they enjoyed God's preference.[4]

Again and again Jesus is attacked for his acceptance of these people, and repeatedly his response is the same: he insisted they were fit for the Kingdom. For him purity, like uncleanness, was contagious. The trick was to activate the purity which came from inside a person (Mark 7:15). Once that purity was activated, it became an agent of the Kingdom. Through his purifications, Jesus was extending God's Kingdom meal by meal, person by person.

But it is wrong to see the purification process as occurring only within individuals. Jesus' primary concern was not with the single person, imagined in isolation. Recent scholarship has correctly seen that his insight of

---

4. Collecting revenues for Rome involved a person in a collaboration with the oppressor that alienated the Land from the inheritance of Israel, opened up the prospect of bribery, and necessitated transactions in untithed, impure produce. Prostitution was simply forbidden in the Torah, and became a primary symbol of impurity itself.

God's presence within the communities of Galilee was a distinctive element in Jesus' theology. John Dominic Crossan has referred to Jesus' teaching as that of the "unbrokered Kingdom of God." By that phrase he means that the usual brokers of power—the Romans, the Herodians, the priests—were bypassed in Jesus' insistence upon the community's accessibility to the divine Kingdom. What Jesus taught about forgiveness subverted the customary understanding that formal religious rituals alone wiped away sin, just as the mention of any sovereignty but Caesar's challenged the hegemony of both Rome and the Herodians.

But a Marxist reading of Jesus, as if he were engaged in a systematic redistribution of wealth, is tiresome and misguided: nothing Jesus did directly undermined any significant Roman or Judaic institution, and his teaching on possessions certainly does not amount to any sort of economic theory. There were and are political and economic consequences in applying his teaching, but that does not make it a political or economic philosophy in its context or motivation. The Kingdom was based on a community's acceptance of the poor, the hungry, the bereaved, and the shunned.

The meaning of Jesus' famous words, "the Kingdom of God is in your midst" (Luke 17:21), is all too easily twisted in their English translation. They are typically taken to mean that the Kingdom is the possession of each individual, but the fact is that the term for "your" here is plural (in Greek, as it would have been in Aramaic), and refers to a community, not a single person. The heroic individualism of a great deal of Protestant Christianity rests in large measure on a misbegotten English rendering. A community such as Capernaum could enjoy God's sovereignty if it embraced and associated with the poor. Especially for those who had recently come in from the Galilean countryside, this promise was especially poignant. Despite the currency of Herod Antipas, trade, foreign influences, and proximity to Romans and their agents, the Kingdom might be theirs. The *chasid* they increasingly called "the prophet: Yeshua from Nazareth of Galilee" (Matthew 21:11) announced that the Kingdom belonged to them, to Israel, to God's chosen people.

Jesus grew heavier over the years until he left the area in 27 C.E. Capernaum brought him times of plenty, and—as his message became more and more popular—little requirement for manual work. The emerging paunch only strengthened his voice, however, and his thick beard and thinning hair made for an impression of *gravitas*. Shorter than the norm, overweight, and tending to baldness, nothing about Jesus in physical terms (from what is attested about his appearance and from what we can gather from the likely results of his lifestyle) can explain his magnetism.

As Jesus honed his teaching, it began to set his disciples apart from other Jews. The Essenes of Qumran had taught that it was the duty of "the sons of light," those who followed the *halakhah* of their teacher, to hate the sons of darkness. Jesus insisted, by contrast, that his hearers love their enemies, and pray for those who oppressed them (Matthew 5:43–48, see also Luke 6:31–36), even if a soldier of the Romans or the Herodian regime should compel them with a cuff on the cheek to give up their supplies or to work in their service (Matthew 5:38–42). Jesus is known to have made only one direct allusion to the Essenes, and it is trenchant (Luke 16:8):

The sons of this epoch are cleverer than the sons of light among their own generation.

You could learn more from a crafty administrator who made friends with bribes (Luke 16:1–8) than from the prigs at Qumran! Everything in Jesus' Galilean identity rebelled against the dogma that all who were not Essenes were doomed. But as in the case of John the Baptist earlier, by resisting a sectarian understanding of Judaism, by insisting upon the unity of Israel, Jesus ironically found himself at odds with many in Israel. His own undoubted charisma did not overcome the divisions that plagued the religion of his time and ultimately introduced the most profound schism of them all.

He believed it wise to refrain from public displays of individual piety (Matthew 6:1–7):

> *Be wary not to do your righteousness before humanity, to be observed by them: indeed, otherwise, you have no reward from your father who is in the heavens. So when you make a donation, do not trumpet before yourself, just as the charlatans do in the synagogues and in the lanes, so they might be glorified by humanity: Amen I say to you, they get their reward. Yet when you make a donation, your left hand should not know what your right hand does, so your donation might be in secret, and your father who sees in secret will himself repay you. And whenever you pray, you will not be as the charlatans. Because they delight in standing to pray in the synagogues and in the corners of the roads, so they might appear to humanity. Amen I say to you, they get their reward. But when you pray, enter into your nook and—closing your door—pray to your father who is in secret, and your father who sees in secret will repay you. Yet when you pray, do not prattle like the Gentiles, for they suppose that in their verbosity they will be attended to.*

The practice of religion can too easily become a charade of trumpeting hollow prayers and pompously flaunting one's own piety. Jesus had not forgotten his treatment at the self-righteous hands of Nazareth's elders, nor did he ease up in his critique of Greco-Roman polytheists. The "prattle" of the Gentiles here refers to the vapid flattery of their gods, the enumeration of honorific titles like "all-wise," "all-knowing," "most revered," "most terrible," the standard invocations to magical deities who they assumed could swell their riches, restore their health, and improve their love life.

Rabbi Jesus resisted any tendency to prattle. His principle remained as he had articulated it in Nazareth—it is not what goes into a person, but what proceeds from a person's heart (the "secret" place Jesus referred to above) that purifies and brings one close to God. As we have seen, for

Jesus, Israelites were already pure and did not need to be cleansed by elaborate ritual observances or displays of public piety.

All too often, even perennially, Jesus has been portrayed as an antinomian, dedicated to tearing down the law that Judaism revered. That portrayal is simply off base. His attacks on public piety and his emphasis on one's "secret" relationship with God only enhanced the value of the Torah in his own mind. As he said (Matthew 5:17):

Do not presume that I came to demolish the law or the prophets. I did not come to demolish, but to fulfill.

The old Galilean loyalty to the Torah was in his bones, and for him it was a matter of what people actually did, how they practiced a *halakhah* that put God's commandments into action. After all, for Jesus the five books of Moses were a living word, the Torah upon the lips, rather than the objectified, written word. His disputes with literate experts in the law (the scribes of the New Testament) owe something to the difference of feeling between those who heard the words of Moses spoken and those for whom those words were consigned to writing. Written, a word loses the immediate proximity to action and the emotional resonance produced by the intonation, texture, vibration of the spoken voice.

It may seem counterintuitive to us, but for Jesus it was the spoken rather than the written word that was sacred. The word—spoken from person to person—was the whole thrust of prophecy. He was impatient with the notion that Torah's purpose was obscure. Torah was a program for living that should flow out of a person as naturally as Spirit flowed down to earth from the Throne. The abstract codification of word and law deadened and distanced religious feeling. What good was putting on phylacteries if they had been bought with interest charged other Jews? Where was the virtue in arguing over whether mint ought to be tithed, if the basic requirements of justice, compassion, and faith were forgotten (Matthew 23:5, 23)? Jesus' impatience could turn to scathing humor, as when he called scribes and Pharisees "Blind guides, filtering out the gnat and drinking down the camel!" (Matthew 23:24). Drinking camels! It was a deliberately ludicrous image, projecting a kind of mock outrage; he was engaged in a form of clowning that rabbis have relished throughout the ages.

I did not come to demolish but to fulfill . . ." Those words resound through twenty centuries. They seem to preclude making Jesus into the destroyer of Judaism which history has made him. Their meaning for him involved conscientiously living the Torah, not putting himself above the Law, as if he were its culmination, its ultimate object. By the time Matthew's Gospel was written, the Old Testament was being mined for texts that predicted the Messiah, which Jesus was claimed to "fulfill." That mining process undermined the regulative authority of the Torah (especially for non-Jewish Christians) by reducing it to oracles of messianic prediction. Influential though this procedure has been in Christian theology, that was not how Jesus understood the Torah.

Fulfillment, Jesus taught, was achieved when the Kingdom of God was made manifest in Israel's actions. Lending to those in need, for example, was required by the Torah (see Leviticus 25:35–38 and Matthew 5:42; Luke 6:34–35). Moses had taught that Israel was to remember its enslavement in Egypt, live with the memory of its liberation, and consequently not charge interest to debtors. That was just the principle Jesus had in mind for Capernaum. It was a specific imperative of his religion that he wanted applied to concrete circumstances. His teachings as a whole, in fact, can be traced back in one form or another to the Torah and the Prophets.

Dedication to the Torah joined Jesus with many rabbis and pious Jews of his time. Learning Torah and engaging with it—not just knowing the words of the Hebrew Bible but learning what they meant, and mastering the traditions within the ancient oral heritage also rooted in the revelation to Moses—set Jews apart from other peoples. Each point discussed or disputed involved the very identity of Israel, of how God's people should live. Rich debate, potent ferment, a rigorous exercise of mind that is not just philosophical but engages the heart as well, characterized this practice then as it does now. Torah was not simply a thing of the past but part of an unfolding story. By putting himself in that story, Jesus began a debate about the place of Torah in his movement that has never ceased.

Literate scribes and Pharisees were not the only ones who questioned Jesus closely. His disciples were all too aware that while the Pharisees and the disciples of John the Baptist engaged in fasting, they themselves did not. The Mishnah specifies regular fasts during the week (on Monday and Thursday; Taanit 2:9), and during highly public prayers for rain that included the application of ashes to one's head (Taanit 2:1). It was natural for the disciples to want to follow suit with an open acknowledgment of Israel's dependence upon its God. Jesus replied that his meals were like a wedding feast, a divine marriage with God's Kingdom (Mark 2:18–22; Matthew 9:14–17; Luke 5:33–39). He had known hunger and saw no need to impose it; rather, he preferred the playful joy of celebration as the ethos of the divine Kingdom.

Rabbi Jesus loved banter. By this point of his productive sojourn in Galilee, he had gathered around him the disciples who would figure critically in his life (and afterward). He gave his favorite disciples nicknames. James and John were noisy: he called them "thunder brothers," *bene rigsha* in Aramaic (Mark 3:17). Several of his followers were called Judas (after the patriarch Yudah); one he called "twin," *Toma* in Aramaic, because he kept himself always near to Jesus, and Jesus joked that he was like his shadow. Another Judas was dubbed "Kerioth man," *ish Kerioth* (the infamous Judas Iscariot), because he came from Kerioth (Mark 3:18–19). One disciple, called either Levi or Matthew, could never live down the popular knowledge that he once had collected customs, for even customs agents were included in Jesus' celebrations (Matthew 9:9–13; Mark 2:13–17; Luke 5:27–32). And there were two Simons. One he called "zealot," an appellation for an especially keen student; the other was the original Rocky (*Kepha* in Aramaic, *Petros* in Greek). That name must have stuck more than all the others because his physical stature was greater than that of Jesus and many of the other disciples. But it was also a teasing name: his was the lurching vessel Jesus stood on when he preached to crowds on shore. Calling him "Rock" was playfully uncomplimentary, a sly allusion to his being slow on the uptake, and maybe not quite as firm as he appeared.

The names of Jesus' disciples vary in the New Testament (see Matthew 10:1–4; Mark 3:13–19; Luke 6:12–16; Acts 1:13). There are two main reasons for that. First, there was a confusion between the large group who followed Jesus around Galilee to learn his *halakhah* as thoroughly as they could, and the select twelve whom at a later stage Jesus delegated to speak and act on his behalf. (Luke estimates the select group at around seventy people [Luke 10:1], but that is a symbolic number, corresponding to the traditional number in Judaism of all the non-Jewish nations of the world; Luke's Gospel manifests a particular interest in the promise of Jesus for the Gentiles.) A reasonable estimate is that twenty or thirty *talmidim,* some with wives and children, followed Jesus as best they could. Of course, not all of them could follow him all the time, and the identity of the group would change. That brings us to the second reason for the variation of the names: his disciples came and went, some defecting because they came to disagree with Jesus' *halakhah,* which simply was not as subtle as the Pharisees' for a community living cheek by jowl with the impurity of Rome.

Jesus acknowledged such defections in his parables. The parable of the sower, as we have seen, includes a theology of failure, the recognition that the word of the Kingdom would not always prove productive after sowing. He even trenchantly spoke of some who sowed bad seed in the midst of good (Matthew 13:24–30), and of fish caught, only to be discarded (Matthew 13:47–50). These are parables of harsh judgment, directed to those once associated with him, whom he felt had proved themselves useless, about as hostile as his growing opposition.

Opposition from other Jewish teachers, and defections within his own group, made Jesus more extreme in his judgment, but also more vo-ciferous in his insistence about the joy of the Kingdom he was celebrat-ing and the compassion that emanated from the divine Throne. Notoriously, he accepted women as disciples, implicitly proclaiming that their purity was as great as any male Israelite's, despite the uncleanness of their menstrual cycle. Rabbinic discussion in ancient Judaism *did* in-clude women, on the understanding that they could be fully associated with the community during the pure intervals of their cycles. Some stud-ies have falsely claimed women did not associate with rabbis, although Mishnah indicates the reverse (see Nedarim 10:1–11:12). What distin-guished Jesus was not that he spoke with women and valued them (a generic trait of Judaism); rather, women *traveled* with him, appearing dangerously like the camp followers of the Romans (wives, aspiring wives, and prostitutes). Their presence with him underscores his radical commitment to purity as the inherent trait of all Israel.

His practice of accepting female disciples opened him to the charge of sexual impropriety. Now he was called not only a glutton and drunk-ard, but also a friend of customs agents and sinners (Matthew 11:19; Luke 7:34), the last category referring especially to women of suspect sexual behavior. Simply remaining with a man in a private place (that is, without a third party present) made a woman suspect to some (see Sotah 1:2 in the Mishnah and, in the Jerusalem Talmud, Sotah 3:4). The anonymous woman in the house of Simon the Pharisee who touched Jesus by washing his feet with her hair, and whose touch Jesus accepted, was probably suspected of that sort of behavior. Being a *mamzer,* suffer-ing a broken betrothal, or even having a meager dowry could all give a woman the reputation of sinfulness.

Some, but certainly not all, of Jesus' women disciples were probably seen as sinful. Luke names three as a representative sample: Miriam from the village of Magdala in Galilee; Joanna, who had relatives in Herod's administration; and Susanna (8:1–3). Miriam, Luke states, had seven demons from which she was healed (Luke 8:2), and was evidently among the sinners. The enumeration of her demons suggests that Jesus exorcised her repeatedly.

Jesus' itinerant life precluded marriage and raising children. Loyalty to the Torah precluded adultery. But adultery was defined in Judaism as taking the wife of another, which, like seducing a maiden (who might become another's wife), is clearly forbidden (see Deuteronomy 22:22–29). But sexual contact with an unmarried woman who was not a virgin, particularly a sinner or a formerly demon-possessed person, did not fall under the definition of adultery or seduction. There is no evidence that Jesus did or did not enjoy sexual contact during his life, but seven-demoned Miriam remains the most likely candidate if he did so, because she is the only woman, apart from his mother, with whom he had persistent contact. Indeed, her status made her the kind of woman Jesus' mother might once have hoped her *mamzer* son would marry.

Celebration of the divine Kingdom was no abstract, puritanical affair, and I would caution against the sanguine assumption that Jesus was celibate. The celebration was, in Jesus' own analogy, a wedding feast. The inclusion of sexuality in the enjoyment of God's bounty is a classic feature of Judaism. Just as Jesus bantered with his disciples, so his disciples also bantered with him. Where is the rabbi, absent so late in the celebration? With seven-demoned Miriam. Again.

Femininity in Jesus' mind was more than a matter of gender. The image of God, impressed on every person, was female as well as male (Genesis 1:27), and the holy Spirit (*ruach*)—a feminine noun in both Hebrew and Aramaic, although not in Greek or Latin—was conceived as a woman. She joined in creation at the beginning with God (Genesis 1:2) and was first consort on the divine Throne, known also by the name of Wisdom. She actively created with God as the architect of the earth, and delighted humanity with knowledge (Proverbs 8:22–31):

Yahweh possessed me in the beginning of his way,
    Before his works of old.
From everlasting I was established,
    From the beginning, before the earth . . .
When he established the heavens, I was there,
    When he drew a circle on the face of the deep.
When he made firm the skies above,
    When the fountains of the deep grew strong,
When he placed the boundary of the sea,
    And waters did not transgress his command,
When he marked the foundations of the earth,
I was beside him as an architect, and I was daily his delight,
    Pleasuring him in every time,
Pleasuring the expanse of the earth,
    and my delight was with the ones like persons.

Wisdom was a crucial aspect of Jesus' vision of God, as poetic as Carl Jung's *anima* or world-soul, as organic as the veneration of Gaia among New Age practitioners, but also as powerful as the God who liberated Israel from Egypt.

When he spoke of a woman baking as an instance of divine Kingdom (Luke 13:21) or referred to himself as a mother bird gathering her young (Matthew 23:37), Jesus was not just inventing arresting images. The lush fecundity of Wisdom was as basic to God as sexuality was to the people who were created in God's image. On one occasion Rabbi Jesus even spoke in Wisdom's name (Luke 11:49):

> *For this reason also the wisdom of God said, I myself will delegate to them prophets and delegates.*

Wisdom was a source of revelation, part of the divine image of the Chariot. But Wisdom was also embodied in each female disciple, once she was freed from impurity—seven times over, if necessary, in the case of

Miriam from Magdala. If Jesus' relationship with her was not sexual, that in no way diminishes the intimacy of his exorcisms of her, the persistent, cherishing care that a lover devotes to the beloved.

Jesus' exorcisms embroiled him in his most contentious disputes. At the apogee of his success as a *chasid,* he healed a deaf man by casting out an unclean spirit. But those opposed to him charged that he acted by the power of Baal-Zebul, a Canaanite deity whom Jews regarded as chief of the demons (see Matthew 12:22–45; Mark 3:20–30; Luke 11:14–33). In an eloquent parable, Jesus insisted just the reverse, that his exorcisms represented the defeat of Baal-Zebul (Mark 3:23–29):

> *How can Satan throw out Satan? And if a kingdom is divided against itself, that kingdom cannot stand. And if a home is divided against itself, that home will not be able to stand. And if Satan has arisen against himself and is divided, he cannot stand, but is at an end. No one, however, can enter the home of the strong man and rob his vessels unless he first binds the strong man, and then he will rob his home. Amen I say to you, Everything will be released the ones like persons, sins and curses (as much as they curse), but who ever curses the holy spirit will never have forgiveness (but is liable for a perpetual sin).*

Just as opposition made Jesus more tenacious about his particular vision, so his own activity took on the character of a primordial conflict between good and evil.

When it came to freeing people from unclean spirits, one was either for Jesus or against him, one either gathered in the harvest of the divine Kingdom or scattered it (Matthew 12:30; Luke 11:23). His direct statement of how God was liberating Israel from its demons by means of the Spirit within him (Matthew 12:28; Luke 11:20) went hand in hand with Jesus' teaching that practicing compassion put the Kingdom in the midst of the community. The Baal-Zebul dispute defines, better than anything else, the disagreement between Jesus and both the Pharisees and his literate opponents. He stands for the purity of God in the midst of Israel; they stand for the purity of the practice of the Torah, whether written or oral. Convinced as he was that God's compassion was on his side, Jesus was even more vociferous than those who opposed him.

The close of his successful although chaotic period in and around Capernaum brought Jesus to a clear articulation of what made his practice of Judaism distinct from others. His differences from the Essenes, the Pharisees, and the literate elite are deeply ingrained in the Gospels, quite aside from their tendency to present Judaism as if it were uniform in its opposition to Jesus. Beneath a veneer of anti-Semitism, however, the diversity of Judaism, of which Jesus was an intimate part, shines through palpably.

The arguments around what Jesus was doing might have continued. All the disputants had followings, with disciples coming and going from movement to movement, and—more often than not—retreating eventually from religious controversy altogether into the life of their families and daily duties. After all, the link of pure Israelite families to the purity of the Temple and God's promise of the land was agreed by all sides to be basic to the covenant. Jesus and his opponents were arguing vehemently over what made for the integrity of Israel, but it was *as Israelites* that they disputed.

Their argument never matured. We shall never know whether it might have been brought to a resolution, whether some coalition of Pharisees and scribes and rural teachers such as Jesus might have found ground for agreement and common purpose. Herod Antipas intervened in Jesus' case and brought the debate to an abortive end (and the Roman intervention a generation later made any argument about the Temple moot). Jesus was warned by Pharisees, some of whom, although involved in a dispute with him, continued to sympathize with his dedication to the purity and liberation of Israel (Luke 13:31):

In that hour some Pharashayahs came forward saying to him: Go out and proceed from here, because Herod wants to kill you!

Jesus' exorcisms and healings, as well as his reputation as a *chasid* after the model of Elijah had come to Herod's attention, and he also knew of Jesus' connection to John the Baptist (Luke 9:7–9):

But Herod the governor heard everything that was happening, and was confounded, since it was said by some that Yochanan had been raised from the dead, and by some that Eliyah had appeared, yet others that some prophet of old had arisen. But Herod said, Yochanan I beheaded: but who is this concerning whom I hear such things? And he was seeking to see him.

There was every reason for Herod to "see" Jesus, indeed—to see to his removal. The memory of Elijah during the ninth century B.C.E. had always been linked to his resistance to King Ahab and Ahab's accommodation to foreign deities. Herod Antipas was just such a collaborator, who had already been challenged by John the Baptist and had reacted with deadly force.

Jesus knew that his reputation as a prophet brought the threat of death. Galilee was no longer the safe haven for him it had once been. Jerusalem, too, offered no security. That had been a place of resistance to the great prophets of Judah: Isaiah, Jeremiah, and Ezekiel. All those figures were portrayed as martyrs in Jewish tradition, put to death by those in Jerusalem who collaborated with foreign oppressors, rather than insisting on the integrity of Israel. So Rabbi Jesus needed to flee both Galilee and Judea, to escape territorial Israel altogether. At the same time, he faced the challenge of determining whether he was, as many of his followers increasingly claimed, a prophet of revolutionary resistance, in the manner of Elijah.

EIGHT

Beyond the Pale

Safety lay in avoiding Herod Antipas. Skirting danger for four years (between 27 and 31 C.E.), Jesus crisscrossed Galilee and parts of neighboring Syria. His hectic course has produced what many scholars refer to as "geographical confusion" in the Gospels, particularly in Mark. But the crisscross pattern is confusing only if you expect Jesus to be a sedate, itinerant sage who planned his journeys at leisure. That just was not the case. He was hunted, ready to move as soon as capture threatened. A few followers ran the same risks he did. They split up into tiny, inconspicuous groups of two or three to avoid patrols and seek sustenance, but they also needed to stay in close contact with Jesus to continue as his disciples.

The exigencies of rapid flight eclipsed the easy pace and loose planning of the three previous years in Capernaum. Now his core group included only men. The rabbi might ask many things, but it was unthinkable to demand that a female *talmid* expose herself to hard weather, robbery, and rape. Many beloved disciples were left behind, and the loss of women from his company made the group feel more like a squad of soldiers than a nomadic household.

Yet Antipas' malice, and the consequent hard changes in Jesus' life, were probably less painful for him than his doubts about his own identity. His healing powers invited comparison with the greatest of Israel's prophets: Elijah, who had brought the son of a widow back to life (1 Kings 17:17–24); and Elisha, who revived a boy who had been killed by a head injury (2 Kings 4:17–37). While Chanina ben Dosa had refused to be called a prophet or the son of a prophet (Berakhoth 34b in the Talmud), Jesus explicitly said that he spoke and acted with prophetic authority (Luke 11:49). Jesus knew, as Chanina knew, that prophets in the mold of Elijah or Elisha had entered into direct conflict with the kings of their time, demanding they accede to the rule of divine justice. But his commitment to the prophetic Spirit within him pressed Jesus to insist on just that demand. He and his followers were more than practitioners of purity and esoteric vision: they were a potential army, a band of rabble rousers who could ignite the tinderbox that was first-century Galilee. His prophetic stature marked Jesus as exactly the kind of revolutionary that threatened Antipas. But for the next four years, Jesus would agonize over the kind of revolution he should lead.

In Galilee, Jesus was being compared to Elijah (Matthew 16:14; Mark 6:15; 8:28; Luke 9:8, 19), and not only as a prophet of healing. Elijah confronted the rulers of their time with the threat of divine judgment, a threat he reinforced by means of signs (an *oth* or *neys* in Hebrew, usually *neys* in Aramaic; a *semeion* in Greek). His signs encouraged revolution in the name of God. Elijah's authority had been confirmed by prophetic feats that were often destructive: he brought about drought and deluge (1 Kings 17:1–7; 18:41–46), called down fire from heaven to consume a sacrifice (1 Kings 18:25–38), and killed the prophets of the god Baal (1 Kings 18:39–40).

By the first century, many Jews believed that God would again send Elijah, whose signs would herald the fire and healing of the divine Kingdom (Malachi 4:1–2):

For behold, the day comes, burning like a furnace and all the proud and all who do evil will be stubble, and the coming day will engulf them in flame, says the Lord of hosts, that it shall leave them neither root nor branch.

But to you who fear my name shall the sun of righteousness arise, with healing in its wings, and you shall go forth and gambol like calves from the stall.

This prophet's sign was not simply a healing, a restoration to the community of Israel such as *chasidim* could effect. Nor was the sign a "miracle" in the modern sense, a reversal of the laws of nature. In the epochs before scientific "laws," people were more apt to see the whole of natural experience interpenetrated with forces that were invisible but powerful. A sign was a moment in which that interpenetration became tangible; human experience became a transparent lens for the divine, and the sign promised irreversible change.

The first century saw several examples of men who took Elijah as their model. They promised their followers a sign, then a revolution. An unnamed prophet from Samaria scaled Mount Gerizim with armed followers to find the sacred vessels for sacrifice allegedly hidden there by Moses (Josephus, *Antiquities* 18 §§ 85–87).[1] A prophet named Theudas expected the waters of the Jordan to part for him, as they had for Joshua (*Antiquities* 20 §§ 97–98); yet another, a nameless Jew from Egypt who marched to the Mount of Olives, expected that the walls of Jerusalem would fall at his command (*Antiquities* 20 §§ 169–172).

On each of these occasions, when the would-be prophet announced the promised sign and then called for armed rebellion against Rome, the Empire reacted swiftly. Pontius Pilate, the Roman prefect of Judea and Samaria (26–37 C.E.) slaughtered the leading Samaritan rebels. The procurator

---

1. How, you might ask, did the Samaritans think Moses hid the vessels on Gerizim, when according to the Hebrew Pentateuch he had died on the east side of the Jordan, denied entrance into the land of milk and honey by God (Deuteronomy 34:1–8)? Well, the Samaritans thought that the Judeans had falsified the Torah. In their own tradition, Moses had led the Israelites into Samaria, scaled Mount Gerizim, and hid the vessels for the Temple that later generations would build there.

Fadus (44–46 c.e.) beheaded Theudas, and Felix (52–60 c.e.) killed four hundred of the men who had banded together with the Egyptian Jew. In each case, the aspiring prophet was killed before he could enact his promised sign.

Pilate, Fadus, and Felix understood all too well that no sign could be ignored, because no prophet was only what we would call a religious figure. Every publicly acclaimed prophet was—at least potentially—a military threat to Caesar, and was treated as such by his minions. After all, Octavian[2] had consolidated his imperial power only in 31 b.c.e. when he defeated Anthony and Cleopatra's fleet at Actium. The Roman Empire was a mere generation old when Jesus was born, and its policy of violently protecting its power was as necessary as it was ruthless. Antipas was no fool. Galileans compared Jesus to Elijah, and his prophetic fame branded him a potentially greater threat than Antipas' old enemy John the Immerser.

The first safe haven Jesus sought for himself and his followers was just outside Antipas' territory. Jesus set out in a boat across the Sea of Galilee with about fifteen *talmidim,* hoping for a quick, anonymous crossing to Bethsaida, the birthplace of Simon and Andrew. Philip, and some of Jesus' other disciples still lived there; a network of relatives could provide food and shelter for the rabbi and his followers.

This three-mile trip proved to be a prophetic journey into the world of signs, marking a dramatic surge in Jesus' charismatic authority among his disciples. His family was only a memory. His ambition to build a Galilean base from which he could teach and gather supporters around him had been quashed by Antipas. The threat of stoning in Nazareth had driven him from home, forcing him to confront who he was at the pool of Bethesda and take the next step in his unfolding quest for self-knowl-

---

2. Octavian was the adopted son of the assassinated Julius Caesar, later "Augustus," a title which invoked his supreme authority by divine and human mandate.

A GALILEAN BOAT

*One of the most surprising discoveries of recent archae-
ology has been a fishing boat found by the Sea of Galilee.
Dated to 40 B.C.E. (plus or minus 80 years) by radiocar-
bon techniques, the vessel measured 26.5 feet by 7.5 feet
by 4.5 feet; see Shelly Wachsmann, "The Galilee Boat,"*
Biblical Archaeology Review *14.5 (1988), pp. 18–33.
(Photograph courtesy of Zev Radovan)*

edge and divine revelation; now, Antipas forced Jesus' hand, compelling
him to grow and change.

Jesus dozed in the small boat. He had collapsed in uneasy weariness,
tortured by doubt over what direction he should take in flight from Herod

(Mark 4:35–41, see also Matthew 8:23–27; Luke 8:22–25). The disciples were anxious. They were hunted men, and Antipas had an extensive network of informers and spies, who were always ready to curry favor in exchange for the prospect of a lucrative arrangement with Antipas' court, the Romans, or even for a simple payoff. The disciples must have been torn, most having left their wives and children behind in Capernaum; this was to be no warm visit home. Had they made the right decision to follow Jesus? Was he asking too much?

The weather turned against them. The Sea of Galilee was and is notorious for its unpredictable storms. On their crossing, a squall blew up out of nowhere. The suddenly shifting wind made ominous patterns on the water. Trees heaved on the hillsides, bending and then snapping back. The sky turned dark and clouds rolled down over the mountain ridges. Before they knew it, whitecaps were slapping over the gunnels of their small, laden skiff, which they struggled to control with oars and sail.

Their boat was twenty feet long, a light, dexterous craft designed to drag a net fast enough to snare a school of sprat or carp. In a storm, a crew's speed and agility could save lives and avoid losing a catch. Andrew and Simon knew their boat and knew this water. Yet their fear as the storm blew up was larger than the storm itself, the panic of a small group facing capture, defeat, possibly death.

As they worked quickly and expertly, hauling in sail and pointing their boat into the wind, the disciples resented their rabbi being asleep. After all, he had gotten them into this mess in the first place. But Jesus was in no frame of mind to panic over fickle weather. His sleep was a meditation, a deep dreamlike trance. He was focused on the Chariot, oblivious of his surroundings. After years of the practice that he began with John, Jesus entered this state effortlessly, sometimes without conscious volition. The Chariot alone reassured and strengthened him.

The crew moved swiftly, reflexively, reefing the sails, adjusting the rudder. Their boat shuddered and pitched like a frightened animal. Wood, sail, and ropes groaned. But their rabbi could not be roused. He apparently didn't care that at any moment they could be swamped by the flattening power of the wind. A close translation from Mark's Gospel exhibits the rough, pidgin-Greek of the text, and the vivid, disturbed quality of the incident (Mark 4:37–41):

> And there happens a big storm of wind and the waves pile into the boat. Result: the boat was now swamped. And he himself was in the stern, sleeping on the cushion. And they raise him and say to him, Teacher, don't you care that we are perishing? And being roused he scolded the wind and said to the sea: Silent, shut up! And the wind ceased, and there happened a great calm. And he said to them, Why are you timid? Do you not yet have faith? And they feared a great fear and were saying to one another, Who then is this, that even the wind and the sea obey him?

In a single, sweeping gesture, Jesus had entered the realm of the miraculous. It now seemed that he controlled nature, taking a further step along the prophetic path, beyond purification, beyond exorcism, beyond chasidic healings. As frightened as the disciples had been of the storm, their fear in his commanding presence was even greater. "Who is this man?" they asked.

Safe for the moment, they could not know—any more than we can—exactly how their boat was righted. Had they moved out of the squall? Did the tempest shift or the wind suddenly drop? What they did know was that a prophetic sign had saved their lives. Elijah, it was said, had once—like Joshua—parted the waters of the Jordan (2 Kings 2:5–8), and now another prophet calmed the Sea of Galilee. The disciples who crossed the sea with Jesus would never see him the same way again.

From our perspective twenty centuries later, we ask the same question the disciples did. Who was this man? The part of us imbued with a scientific worldview recoils when we read that he stilled the storm. How can we take this story if not literally? How might we believe it without a leap of faith that flies in the face of reason?

Quantum leaps in human technology have come, paradoxically, at a moment when scientists themselves are much more willing than they were a hundred years ago to admit the probable existence of forces and substances in the universe that are beyond our perception or analysis. Given all the mystery around us, why not concede the possibility that Jesus was a miracle worker? When the Gospels speak of the supernatural world overruling the natural world, why not just believe?

These questions perplex and intrigue me, and I have found no neatly expressed formula to answer them. So I am not trying to finesse the point when I suggest that what happened that day on the Sea of Galilee had more to do with the inner workings of Jesus' visionary practice than with a miraculous event. The disciples must indeed have faced a storm one moment and not the next. But their belief that Jesus had delivered them came mostly from the discipline of the Throne that he had mediated to them, just as John had mediated it to him.

He had once taken the lame man at Bethesda with him to the Throne; now he took his *talmidim* with him to the Chariot. Their entry-way into that divine world was the angelic figure Jesus called "the one like the person." They were already familiar with this figure from their wilderness retreats with Jesus. In the visionary experience he shared with his disciples in the boat, it was "the one like the person" who vanquished both the deadly threat of Herod Antipas and the storm that threatened to swamp their skiff. As we enter the world of signs and miracles at this turning point in Jesus' life, it's important to understand exactly who this "one like the person" is and why he was so important to Jesus and his disciples, becoming, in fact, central to everything Jesus said and did.

Jesus used the phrase "the one like the person" to designate the angel described as "one like a person" in the seventh chapter of the book of

Daniel.[3] There Daniel has a vision in the night. The "one like a person" is an angel, standing beside God's Throne. He is called the "one like a person" (which can also be translated as "son of man") because he has a human face. His humanity stands in sharp contrast to the other angelic emanations around the Throne, which are bestial. The "one like a person" supplants a lion, a bear, a leopard, and a horned beast in God's presence (Daniel 7:1–13). Another angel interprets Daniel's vision for him (Daniel 7:17–18):

> These great beasts that are four are four kings: they shall arise from the earth. But the holy ones of the Highest shall receive the Kingdom, and shall possess the Kingdom for the age, and for the age of the ages.

The great kings of the Assyrians, Babylonians, Persians, and Seleucids have had their day; but when Israel's angel comes to rule, Israel's sovereignty will last forever.

Just as Ezekiel had built upon the earlier visions of Moses (Exodus 24) and Isaiah (Isaiah 6), so Daniel's vision extends and elaborates the depiction of the Chariot-Throne (Ezekiel 1). These successive visions evolve as a palimpsest (a text written over an earlier text), each seer inscribing new visionary insights, and inviting later seers to the inscription of further insights. Ezekiel's four beasts, propelling the Chariot at the velocity of lightning, become, in Daniel, the angelic representatives in the divine court of the greatest empires on earth, which seemed overwhelmingly powerful.

The visionary material in Daniel explores the cosmic battle between

---

3. The book of Daniel was written just before the success of the Maccabees in restoring the worship of Yahweh in the Temple in 164 B.C.E. But the "Daniel" it refers to was a figure in the Babylonian court centuries before. One of the characteristic traits of what is called apocalyptic literature is that it is composed in the name of a great person from the past, so that his or her alleged predictions of history seem accurate, at least as concerns the time until the actual composition of the book.

the "one like a person" and the angelic representatives of the great empires that had conquered Israel. It was written both as an apocalyptic prediction of the end of the world and as propaganda to promote the Jewish revolt launched in 167 B.C.E., which, to the surprise of everyone involved, actually succeeded. Daniel was written shortly after "the abomination of desolation" (Daniel 12:11), when the Seleucid king, Antiochus IV Epiphanes, ordered swine offered on the Temple altar (because roast pork was a favorite food of the god Zeus). Outraged Jews banded together to form an unstoppable guerrilla army, willing to go on suicide missions against a foe that greatly outnumbered them and whose equipment dwarfed their own. The revolt succeeded in 164 B.C.E., and the Maccabees came to power. The Temple was rededicated after the altar stones that the swine had defiled were hidden until a faithful prophet should arise to tell the king and high priest what to do with them (1 Maccabees 4:44–46).

In Daniel's cosmic battle, which mirrored the battles taking place on earth, the Seleucids are represented by the fourth and last beast, a ruthless creature, hideous beyond compare (Daniel 7:19–20a):

> And then I [Daniel] desired to ascertain about the fourth beast that
> was different from all the others, very dreadful, its teeth of iron and
> its nails of brass, devouring, smashing, and crushing what remained
> with its feet; And about its ten horns that were on its head and the
> other [horn] which arose and the three horns that fell before it.

These horns represent the various Seleucid kings and generals who vied for power within their corrupt empire. But Daniel's predictions have a particular target, the last horn which the text goes on to describe (Daniel 7:20b–21):

> And about the horn that had eyes and a mouth speaking great things,
> and an appearance bigger than its companions. And I saw that this
> horn made war with the holy ones and prevailed against them.

This last horn was Epiphanes (which means "Manifest God" in Greek) himself, the author of abomination who had offered swine at the altar.

In Daniel's vision, God himself intervenes and accepts the one like a person, Israel's angel, whom he elevates within the heavenly court. This changes everything (Daniel 7:22):

> The Ancient of Days came and gave judgment for the holy ones of the Most High and the time arrived, and the holy ones [qadishin in Aramaic] possessed the Kingdom.

The holy ones for Daniel were both the angels (especially Israel's angel) and the chosen people. When they are exalted, God's Kingdom would be realized on earth. This is the end of days when God's book would be opened, the dead would be raised, and Israel would rule the world (Daniel 12:1–4).

We can see why, as Jesus dozed in the boat on the way to Bethsaida, he would have been focused on Daniel and the "one like a person," the human figure who supplanted the wrathful pseudo-human deities of the past. The palimpsest of ancient visions was scrolling through his mind. His drowsy lips were muttering their words. Jesus reflected on "the one like the person" to face the wrath of Antipas, a beast with fearsome powers. He was drawn to the apocalyptic imagery of Daniel, as he had been drawn by the apocalyptic vision of Zechariah (especially chapter 14). Both texts are derived from relatively late portions of the Hebrew Bible, and both reflect the ferment and anticipation of Jesus' time. In his mind, the days of priestly corruption in Jerusalem and the beastly persecution of Herod Antipas were about to be dissolved in the end of days that was fast approaching.

In the books of Daniel, Enoch, and Tobit, sleep focuses vision. When asleep, the visionary adept perceives a different universe; his attention, undistracted by waking life, is intent on the angelic forces emanating from their divine source. Jesus, asleep in the boat, knew the peace of the

Chariot, his assurance that the *Abba* took pleasure in him, and that Rome's rule was only for a day. The angelic "one like the person," a human face before the divine Throne, assured Jesus that God remembered his chosen people (Luke 12:8; Matthew 10:32). His disciples saw that peace when Jesus turned from addressing the wind and waves. They entered his visionary world. And in that world, peace, *shelama,* was instantly reflected in the calmed lake around them.

Simon "Rock" and his brother Andrew initially found shelter for Jesus and his followers at the home of their parents; Philip's parents were also accommodating. Sharing hospitality meant spreading the economic strain among households, and it also made Jesus more difficult to locate for anyone in sympathy with Antipas. Bethsaida was at this stage a fishing town, smaller than Capernaum but prosperous, not yet the impressive city it would become after 30 C.E., when Herod Philip gave it the status of a polis and named it after the emperor's mother, Livia-Julia. But by the year 27 C.E., it had been well established as within Philip's purview—not Antipas'—and the old conflict between the brothers over Antipas' marriage to Philip's former wife offered Jesus a degree of protection. Philip's forces never opposed him directly, and Antipas had to be circumspect about taking action within Philip's territory.

Jesus stayed in Bethsaida several months with his little company of followers, out of harm's way. Bethsaida's Jewish community was less substantial than Capernaum's. It was surrounded by the wealthy Hellenistic culture that Philip (Jewish though he himself was) encouraged among his Gentile subjects: columned houses, coins with the image of the emperor, shrines to local and classical deities. Jews lived clustered in their courtyard complexes, valued for their contribution to the fishing industry but marginal in this largely Gentile world, without the impact on the intellectual and cultural life that educated Jews exerted in Jerusalem, Alexandria, and even Rome itself. In Bethsaida, Galilean Judaism lived quietly in the political jurisdiction of a tolerant but enthusiastic philo-Hellenist.

Jesus' teaching during this period addressed his own uncertainty, his disciples' fear, and the marginal status of Jews in Bethsaida. On the run from Antipas, he felt sympathy for the Jews of Bethsaida who lived in an ambiance of political and cultural estrangement. He stressed his growing conviction that the divine Chariot would see Israel through any threat: "my friends, do not fear those who kill the body, and after that have nothing more to do." Physical fear was nothing compared to the dread one should feel for the divine judge "who after killing has authority to throw you into *Gehenna*," the valley of judgment and oblivion beside the divine Throne. As the snare is to the bird, so is capture and death to a person, a pale reflection of the divine energy that makes a life, and then wipes it away with little more than a thought (Luke 12:4–7; Matthew 10:28–31, inspired by Amos 3:4–8). Take your fear, Jesus taught, and focus it together with your confidence before the Chariot, the swirling energy that both generates and removes life, the source of all that truly matters.

Fear and confidence, compassion and judgment all stemmed from that source, were all resolved in the Throne. His visions grew more vivid, etched by the violence he sensed around him and the remembered affections of easier times. The people who came to hear Jesus teach and to share in his sacred meals met a rabbi different from the one they had heard about from Capernaum. Jesus was changing. The carefree banquets, where people came and went in easy, chaotic harmony, were replaced by smaller feasts, which were quick and almost covert. Jesus did not want to draw too much attention to himself or enable Antipas' spies to predict where he could be conveniently and quietly taken. When Jesus spoke, it was to a smaller public than before, but the message was focused with a severe clarity.

Events were moving quickly, uncontrollably, both in the politics of Galilee and in his own spiritual quest. He was now in his mid-twenties, at the height of his strength. Deep in his visions, he had become expert in conveying their richness to his disciples. Those around him were having transforming experiences. He brought them again and again before the Throne of God, into the vortex of creation. Although they must have had many moments of ecstasy and transcendence, it was, in many ways, a terrifying, difficult path. "To find yourself you have to lose yourself," Rabbi Jesus taught them. He demanded nothing less than self-annihilation. In this he starts to move beyond our understanding, a holy man still made of flesh and blood but living in a visionary realm, not in the world of common experience.

In and around Bethsaida he found willing hosts prepared to run the risk of receiving him and his message. Not full disciples, these were nonetheless committed people, more attached to his teaching than the enthusiastic but whimsical crowds of Capernaum had been, ready to give, not only solicitous for healing. In these tight circles he spoke of the Kingdom of God and of the Chariot that was its source, and he explained the special blessing bestowed on those who were not afraid to commit to the power of the fiery Chariot (Luke 12:8–9; Matthew 10:32–33):

> But I say to you, everyone who will vouch for me before humanity,
> the one like the person will also vouch for before the angels of God;
> but whoever denies me before humanity, will be denied before the
> angels of God.

The Chariot's blessing had its dark double. When people refused to acknowledge where and how God was present in the midst of Israel, God would reject them in response. These damned would be pushed away from the divine Throne, judged by God, into a limbo of punishment between life and death, where apocalyptic seers such as Zechariah envisioned that divine justice would be exacted in a way unknown in the shadowy underworld of ancient Hebrew *sheol* or in Greek Hades. There they would pay for their own refusal of God's Kingdom; in a new universe in which the Chariot was the only source of life, they would be tortured by the absence of God's healing. That was "Gehenna" or hell, "where their worm does not expire and the fire is not extinguished" (the closing words of the Targum of Isaiah which Jesus quotes in Mark 9:47–48).

Biblical "Gehenna" was a physical place, the valley of judgment outside Jerusalem where God would destroy his enemies. In Jesus' apocalyptic vision, Gehenna became the black shadow of the Chariot, the consequence of rejecting the Throne, the destructive side of the Chariot's fire. His vision was not of Dante's metaphysical "hell," but his increasingly vivid images of judgment later fed the flames of medieval imagination. Just as the seers who handed on their visions in Daniel's name etched their descriptions with the violence of persecutions they knew all too well, so Jesus' apocalyptic imagination was fired by the threat posed by Herod Antipas.

"Faith" also entered the lexicon of Rabbi Jesus' characteristic themes in Bethsaida. From that time he used the word to refer not simply to trust in God but more specifically to confidence in his teaching as an authentic path to the divine Throne. He himself—or, rather, what he stood for—had become an issue in his own mind. In response to a question from Philip of Bethsaida, he said, "Believe me that I am in the *Abba* and the *Abba* in me, or else, believe for the sake of the works themselves" (John 14:11). His healings, his exorcisms, his meals, his teaching, all had become prophetic signs, incursions from the divine world into our own.

The seer's imaginative stretch from this world to the heavenly Throne was an act of faith, a trusting focus in the power of the Chariot to bring one to one's spiritual home, the true place of restoration. In the mystical tradition of Judaism of this time, a vision of the Chariot was also called an entry into Paradise, the primeval garden of Genesis from which the first woman and the first man had been banished. A rabbi of the second century C.E., Simon ben Zoma, was sometimes so caught up in trance that he failed to recognize those who greeted him (Chagigah 15a). Jesus entered such consuming trances, and saw faith as a means by which people could share his vision of the restored Garden, the original Eden, and be transformed by its eternal vitality. His healings were more than demonstrations of a *chasid's* alignment with God: they effectuated the restoration of Paradise that was part and parcel of God's primordial intent in making the world.

J esus' sojourn in Bethsaida came to end after one of his most famous (and misunderstood) healings. Jesus is called upon to cure a centurion's servant, who is gravely ill, "ready to die" according to Luke (Luke 7:1–10 and Matthew 8:5–13). The incident conveys Jesus' distinctive confidence that faith will restore humanity to the relationship man had with God in the garden of Eden.

The centurion, an officer in charge of eighty infantry, commanded a garrison in Capernaum or nearby. Although a Jew or proselyte (that is, a convert to Judaism) might conceivably have served in such a position, the centurion's exchange with Jesus hinges on his identity as a non-Jew, one of the many sympathizers with Judaism called "God-fearers" in antiquity who admired Israel's God and his ethics, although they could not accept circumcision. The centurion did not approach Jesus himself; a delegation of Jewish elders pleaded his case, on the grounds that he "loves our ancestry, and himself constructed the synagogue for us" in Capernaum (Luke 7:5).[4]

The centurion had sent delegates because Antipas was actively seeking Jesus; had any soldier personally encountered Jesus, he would have been obliged to arrest him. The centurion understood that Jesus limited his activity to the people of Israel, those demarcated by circumcision. He sought to contact Jesus through emissaries, relying on the spoken word instead of approaching him directly (Matthew 8:8–9; Luke 7:6–8).

Lord, I am not worthy so that you should enter under my roof. But only say by a word, and my servant will be cured. Because I also am

---

4. During this period, synagogues in Galilee were for the most part indistinguishable from private dwellings, and sometimes were incorporated within them. The generous benefaction of the centurion was within the means of an officer.

a person under authority, having soldiers under myself, and I say to this one, Proceed, and he proceeds, and to another, Come, and he comes, and to my slave, Do this, and he does.

The centurion said, in effect, that Jesus' control over unclean spirits mirrored his own authority over his troops; his confidence in Jesus prompted Jesus to summon divine compassion on his behalf, and his servant was healed. The centurion's faith was precisely the response to prophetic signs that Jesus had been demanding from his own disciples, which is why he said, "Not even in Israel have I found such faith" (Luke 7:9). If he can believe, why not you? He taunted them, as he had in the boat on the way to Bethsaida. "Why are you timid? Do you not yet have faith?" The pressure Jesus was willing to exert on his closest followers must sometimes have been unbearable. They buckled under the weight of his persistent challenge to them to see as he saw.

In sharp contrast to the way Christian scholarship typically portrays Jesus, the story also shows that he was wary of direct contact with Gentiles. Jesus' program was for his fellow Jews; only a delegation of Jewish elders from the centurion captures his sympathy. The episode provided every opportunity for Jesus to transgress the boundary between the circumcised and the uncircumcised—yet that is precisely what he does not do. Indeed, Jesus commended the centurion's awareness of the limitation of feasible contact between them.

The centurion never followed Jesus, literally or metaphorically; he remained in Capernaum, presumably saw his cherished servant restored to health, and said nothing. Yet how long he and his men would keep the secret of Jesus' location could not be predicted. It was time to move on.

In stark contrast to Jesus' acceptance of the delegation from the centurion, his reaction to an attempt at reconciliation by his own family was forbidding (Mark 3:31–35; Matthew 12:46–50; Luke 8:19–21). When they sent a delegation of family friends to him in Bethsaida, he would not interrupt his teaching to greet them: "Whoever does the will of God that is my brother and sister and mother." Obviously, his family's attitude had

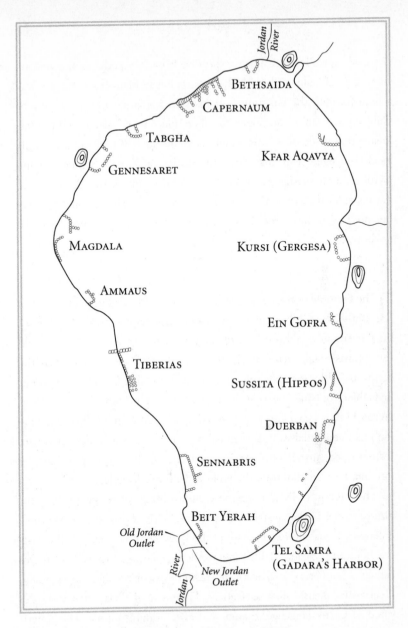

THE HARBORS OF GALILEE

As shown on the map, the harbors consisted of two basic elements (see, for example, Gennesaret, on the northwestern shore): a short pier jutting straight into the water, and a long curved stone breakwater, which protected moored boats from the violent storms that suddenly swept across the lake. To enter the harbor, boats slipped through the narrow passage between the pier and breakwater. (Illustration courtesy of Biblical Archaeology Review) changed radically since Jesus' expulsion from Nazareth. To the zealous Jews of rural Galilee, this Elijah-like prophet in flight from Antipas was a hero (despite the old rumors of his status as a *mamzer*), a symbol of Galilean resistance and hoped-for liberation. He at last enjoyed the following that made messianic announcements such as he had made in his local synagogue seem inspiring instead of ridiculous. But there was no joyful reunion among the Nazareans, and this time it was the prodigal, not his elder brother, who stood in the way of that. He was on the move, but not toward his home. Instead, he was about to cross into unknown territory.

The example of the centurion had opened a fresh, startling possibility. Rather than rely on the relatives of his disciples, whose support of his movement could result in retaliation from Herod Antipas, he could serve Jewish Galilee by means of the support of non-Jews such as the centurion. Why not stage his movement from *Gentile* territory adjacent to Galilee, outside the rule of "that fox" Herod Antipas, and even of Herod Philip? Having moved from Antipas' territory to Philip's, and having practiced Judaism in the midst of an enclave in a Hellenistic town, Jesus moved further into non-Jewish territory: that might give him the freedom he needed to ride the Chariot with his disciples.

His attempt to live among the Gentiles brings us to one of the most bizarre stories in the Gospels (see Mark 5:1–20; Luke 8:26–39; Matthew 8:28–34). Jesus and his remnant of disciples ventured south on the eastern side of the Sea of Galilee into explicitly Gentile territory. Called Decapolis ("Ten Cities" in Greek), this region was named after longstanding, Hellenistic towns—such as Gadara, Hippos, and Pella—that were devoted to Greek language, drama, and civic administration, their inheritance from the time of Alexander the Great. Their fertile lands and vigorous commerce in fish and trade with Persia and Syria buttressed their urban pride with genuine financial power, and the Romans permitted them latitude in the conduct of their affairs. As long as Roman garrisons were accommodated and taxes paid to Rome, the empire was willing to permit them a measure of autonomy. As a cultural region, Decapolis was the non-Jewish equivalent of Antipas' Galilee or of Philip's Trachonitis. When Jesus departed Bethsaida for Decapolis, he exiled himself and his disciples from their Galilean soil to seek, paradoxically, a haven among the unclean in order to concentrate on the Chariot. His visionary practice was all he had left, the one sustaining source of his personal strength and his communal movement.

He and the disciples, traveling again by boat, sailed down the east shore of the Sea of Galilee to one of the smaller towns of Decapolis (perhaps called Gergesa, although the Greek manuscripts of the New Testament offer several possibilities). Mark (again in an idiomatic translation from the Greek) describes what happens when they disembark in the land of the Gentiles and Jesus exorcises a madman who haunts graveyards and is possessed by a host of demons called "Legion" (Mark 5:1–13):

And they came to the opposite side of the sea, into the area of the Gerasites. He came out from the boat, and at once there met him from the tombs a person with an unclean spirit. He had the habitation among the tombs, and no one was any longer able—even with a chain—to bind him. (Because many times he had been bound with fetters and chains, and the chains were torn apart by him, and the fetters smashed, and no one was capable of subduing him. And all night and day he was among the tombs and in the hills, shouting and wounding himself with stones.) He saw Yeshua from a distance, and ran and worshipped him, and shouting with a big voice he says, I have nothing for you, Yeshua Son of highest God! I adjure you by God, do not torment me! For he had been saying to him, Unclean spirit, come out from the person! And he interrogated him, What is your name? And it says to him, Legion is my name, because we are many. And they summoned him a lot, so that he would not dispatch them outside of the area. Yet there was there by the hill a big herd of pigs grazing. They summoned him and said, Send us into the pigs, *so that we may enter into them. And he permitted them. The unclean spirits went out and entered into the pigs, and the herd rushed over the cliff into the sea, about two thousand, and they were choked in the sea.*

Decapolis was, by definition, impure, polluted by the refusal of its inhabitants to keep the laws of Moses. That impurity is underlined in the story: a maniac, possessed by an unclean spirit, approached Jesus. He inhabited a cemetery. Dead bodies in Judaism were, of course, considered a contagious source of uncleanness. The demon called itself "Legion," an allusion to Rome's control of the region and its relatively recent military occupation of Decapolis (under Pompey in 63 B.C.E.). The impurity of the scene is amplified when the demons asked to enter a herd of about two thousand swine.

Jesus was already known for his contact with Samaritans, women of doubtful repute, and tax collectors. But the story of the maniac pushes the issue of uncleanness well beyond any marginal impurity: here is a man who lives in a cemetery in a Gentile region occupied by the Romans, whose unclean spirit calls itself "Legion" ("troops"), and who likes to wound himself in the company of pigs!

The exorcism became a battle over territory, as the demon addressed Jesus directly, "I have nothing for you, Jesus Son of God Most High! I adjure you by God, do not torment me!" By using the word "adjure" (*horkizo* in Greek, whose variant *exorkizo* gives us the term "exorcism") the demon in the story attempted to control Jesus. By naming and adjuring, exorcists typically tried to manipulate the demons that infested their patients. Here, however, the demon wants to exorcise the exorciser, to ward off this incursion into the realm of the unclean. In the seesaw of exorcistic power, Jesus seems to accede to the demon's request, when he sends it into the swine. But then this heightened impurity—the uncleanness of death, the Romans, and the unkosher animals—destroys itself in his presence, as the pigs stampede off a cliff to drown in the Sea of Galilee. The sense of this story is plain: Jesus could abide in Gergesa, but the uncleanness there could not abide him.

The intelligence of swine makes them susceptible to fear. These were no lemming-like creatures, but animals startled by the screaming of the exorcist and his demonic counterpart. Jesus' disciples and interested locals also would have been shouting in support, derision, anxiety. No wonder, at the close of the story, the people of the village demanded that Jesus go away (Mark 5:17). He had destroyed their herd and the wealth it represented. However long this confrontation lasted in real time (impossible to determine, given the foreshortened perspective of the story), its result punished the local economy so thoroughly that Jesus lost any chance of receiving hospitality in Decapolis. There might or might not have been two thousand pigs, and the exorcistic combat might well have been more protracted than this single story indicates. Those are fairly minor details, compared to a much more basic observation: this story is told as if it were a triumph for Jesus, but it marks the failure of a desperate scheme. His foray into the land of the Gentiles had ended in disaster.

Jesus had no choice but to go back into Jewish Galilee. But he would always stay away from Sepphoris and Tiberias and avoid Tyre and Sidon on the Mediterranean coast, even when he might have been tempted to use the relative anonymity of a city to shield himself from Antipas. The story of the legion helps us see why Jesus avoided these centers of Roman civilization in Galilee and its outskirts: their uncleanness was simply incompatible with his practice of purity. His insistence on God's Kingdom over Herod's kingdom exiled him from Galilee, but his insistence on purity exiled him from the rich Hellenistic environment that otherwise might have supported him.

Jesus left Decapolis in the late winter of 29 C.E. He was at a crossroads, uncertain how God's Kingdom could be revealed. His visionary quest had taken him in a new, startling direction. He had become intimate with the "one like the person" (traditionally translated "the son of man") and his intimacy now bordered on identification. Indeed, Jesus could speak of himself as "the one like the person," meaning one human among others in the Aramaic of his time (Matthew 8:20; Luke 9:58). His use of the same phrase to refer to both himself and his angelic counterpart is characteristic of his playfulness.

Rabbi Jesus' spiritual discipline was the crucible of what would, within a century, become a new religion. The elements of this new religion—the Kingdom, the one like the person, Chariot, Spirit, exorcism, and purity—were all taken directly from Judaism. But Jesus' mind was like a nuclear reactor, fusing these elements and making new ones. It was at this point in his life that the new religion began to form in the netherworld between a desperate flight over a stormy sea and a mad exorcism that sent a herd of swine thundering into the abyss. Part of the heat in the reactor that generated Christianity was caused by the pressure from Antipas; part came from Jesus' insistence that his disciples have the same kind of faith in him that they had in his *Abba*. This was an outgrowth of his identification with the "one like the person." Jesus had begun to see himself as part of the heavenly court. That identification would lead, in time, to a fundamental mistake. Christianity would reduce the angelic "son of man" in all its resonance and complexity to Jesus as the one and only "son of God." In Jesus' exile from Galilee in the years between 27 and 29 C.E., we see how the Trinity began to take root in Christianity, gradually crowding out any other understanding of heaven until the angelic center of Jesus' own spirituality was lost.

Although the reactor at this point was only approaching critical mass, the principal characteristics of Christianity were already present: the apocalyptic fervor of the Branch Davidians; the mystical disciplines of Julian of Norwich and Hildegard of Bingen; the insistence upon full immersion in water and in Spirit among the Baptists; the charismatic healing of revivalists, whether under tents or on television; the political activism of Liberation theology; the ethics of Albert Schweitzer and the compassion of Mother Teresa; the compulsive socializing over meals, whether in the formal liturgy of the Mass or in covered-dish suppers in churches all over the world. Christianity in its pride and humility, with its emphases on sin and salvation, judgment and redemption, is rooted in the Jewish practices and beliefs that Rabbi Jesus welded together in his vision.

He would change the world. But for now he was still an outcast with nowhere to go. He feared Herod's Galilee. He couldn't abide Decapolis (nor it him), and he might be stoned in Jerusalem. The Kingdom of God could only come about in the land chosen by God for his chosen people. He had to communicate his vision to Israel. But how?

NINE

Three Huts

Afraid of Herod Antipas in Galilee itself, uncertain of safety within the domain of Herod Philip, repulsed by the Gentile population east of the Sea of Galilee, where could Rabbi Jesus go? How could he reach Galilee with his message?

His response to this dilemma was a stroke of genius: he dispatched twelve disciples as his delegates. The practice of sending a delegate (*shaliach*) as a personal representative was common in the Middle East, say, to seal a marriage or a business contract. The role of "apostle," from the Greek term *apostolos* (which translates *shaliach*) did not emerge from the desire to establish a high ecclesiastical office or to send missionaries into the heart of darkness to convert the heathen. It came out of the ordinary practice of sending a go-between to settle routine transactions. Rabbi Jesus proved himself a virtuoso of practical tactics, as well as of the Chariot vision: he applied this custom of personal, business, and military life to spread his own ideas and practices. He dispatched each *shaliach* to do what he did: proclaim God's Kingdom and heal.

Those sent by Jesus had crossed with him to Bethsaida. There was Simon Peter, his "Rock," the two noisy brothers James and John, Andrew,

Philip, Bartholomew (Bartholomayah), Matthew (Matthayah), Thomas, another James (son of Halphayah), Thaddeus (Thaddayah), Simon called "Zealot," and Yudah from the town of Karioth, known to history as Judas Iscariot (Mark 3:16–17; Matthew 10:2–4; Luke 6:14–16). Other disciples, such as Nathanael and Kleopas, had returned to their homes, Nathanael to Kana and Kleopas to Bethsaida. The role of a delegate involved more hardship than honor; it's not surprising that only twelve took on the task.

The delegates had to be skilled in Jesus' *halakhah* and masters of his esoteric teaching—in effect, *chasidim* in their own right. Jesus devoted most of the year of 29 C.E. to training them first in Decapolis and then in clandestine meetings in Galilee. He taught them the most intimate aspects of his wisdom. He had already initiated them into his visionary practice, but he now distilled and systematized his mystical insights and their practical applications for purification, healing, and exorcism into a personal tradition (*a kabbalah*), which enabled the twelve to act in his stead.

Kabbalah is routinely seen as a mystical tradition arising during the twelfth century C.E., but in fact, as we have seen, disciplined meditation on the Throne of God reaches far back into the prophetic period, and the term *kabbalah* is used in the Talmud (written in the fifth century) to refer to the private instruction rabbis gave their disciples. The term derives from the verb *qabal,* meaning "to grasp," and reflects the vigorous adherence to a master's visionary expertise. Where *mishnah* denoted a rabbi's public teaching, which a disciple learned in order to pass it on, *kabbalah* could refer to a technique of altering one's consciousness so as to enter "Paradise," the eternal garden of Eden adjacent to the Chariot-Throne. That altered consciousness was Judaism's equivalent of *nirvana,* fraught with both ecstasy and peril.

The terms of Jesus' commission to the Twelve reflect his visionary world and are so surreal they have long perplexed commentators (Matthew 10:1–16):

He summoned the twelve students and gave them authority of un-
clean spirits so as to throw them out, and to heal every illness and
every disease. . . . These twelve Yeshua delegated, charging them—
saying, Do not go away by a route of Gentiles, and do not enter into
a city of Samaritans! Rather, proceed to the lost sheep of Yisrael's
house! But proclaim as you proceed, saying that: The Kingdom of the
heavens has approached! Heal ailing people, raise dead people,
cleanse scabby people, put out demons: take freely, give freely. Do not
procure yourselves gold or silver or copper for your belts, neither a
bag for the way nor two tunics, neither sandals nor a staff: because
the worker is worthy of his nourishment! Yet into whatever city or vil-
lage you enter, locate someone worthy in it, and there remain until
you go out. When you are entering into the home, greet it, and if the
home is worthy, your peace will be upon it, but if it is not worthy,
your peace will return upon you. And whoever does not receive you,
nor hear your words, when you go out outside the home or that city,
shake the dust off your feet. Amen I say to you, it will be more bear-
able for the land of Sodom and Amorah in the day of judgment than
for that city. Look: I delegate you as sheep in the midst of wolves; so
be smart as snakes, and as untainted as doves.

In Luke, this charge develops the animal imagery even more strongly,
when Jesus speaks of his delegates having "authority to trample over
snakes and scorpions" (Luke 10:19) and explains the supernatural
reason for their invulnerability: "I observed Satan fall as lightning from
the heaven" (Luke 10:18). His apostles were to be the fire-walkers of
first-century Judaism. The peace they conveyed protected them from
harm; they walked in a healing trance of commitment to the Kingdom alone; they were invincible, imbued with the charismatic aura of
their master. They spread the triumphant message: the Kingdom was
at hand! Satan had fallen like lightning. They followed their rabbi into a
visionary world cleansed of Satan's influence, free from death, disease,
and pain. They threw out demons and raised the dead. The *Malkhuta*

spread before them, radiating outward from their bare feet and open arms.

Their perception of what was happening in heaven was played out in how they approached people in the little villages they entered. When a host was gracious enough to receive them into a house, the disciples were to pronounce their peace upon that house, and Luke's Jesus particularly insists that the disciples should eat what is set before them (Luke 10:8). That commandment presupposes that what the disciples eat in any house that might receive them is clean. Israelites produced what was clean from within themselves, ready to be shared with others. In his charge to his apostles he enacted the parable that "There is nothing outside a person, entering in, that can defile one, but what comes out from a person defiles the person" (Mark 7:15).

When we consider the commission to the Twelve in the light of Jesus' focus on purity, we can readily understand the reasoning behind a peculiarity which has confused all the commentators. In both Matthew and Luke,[1] Jesus tells his apostles not to carry a staff or wear sandals (cf. Matthew 10:10; Luke 9:3; 10:4). Mark's Jesus has the disciples without bread, bag, money, or a change of clothes, but he does permit them a staff and sandals (Mark 6:8, 9). That softening of Jesus' hard requirements in Mark's community makes sense: any significant journey would require a staff and sandals, even if you expected to beg for provisions. But Mark's deference to practical convenience only underlines the obvious question: why did Jesus tell people not to take what realistically speaking they would certainly need on any journey? They were to travel in pairs to avoid the danger of a solitary journey; other than that, they were vulnerable, right down to their bare feet.

If, however, we understand the commission to treat every village they

---

1. Matthew and Mark both were informed by a source of Jesus' sayings, amounting to some two hundred verses. Called "Q" in modern scholarship (as an abbreviation of the German term *Quelle*, "source"), in its earliest form this was the *mishnah* Jesus began to develop for his disciples, although his work was cut short by his death.

might enter as clean, pure territory, the perplexing hardship imposed by Jesus makes sense. At the same time, his exclusion of Samaritan territory at this time becomes particularly explicable. The disciples are to enter villages just as pilgrims were to enter the Temple within Pharisaic teaching: without the food, sandals, staffs, garments, bags, and money (see Berakhot 9:5 in the Mishnah) that supported their journey to Jerusalem. When a pair of delegates were offered hospitality in a village, that signaled two things. First, that their message of the Kingdom of God had been taken to heart. Second, by accepting local food and treating the ground they stood on as holy, they affirmed that the Galileans' practice of purity was fully acceptable to God. The apostles quickened the regional pride that had made Galilee a seedbed of revolt for generations. Through their acts, not just their words, they told Galileans that their culture, their produce, and their hands were fit for offering in the Temple. No one could stand between the Galileans and the Kingdom.

The Galilean zeal that greeted the apostles exhilarated Jesus and his followers. Jesus had charged them to report back to him every warm reception, as well as each painful failure. He himself risked a quick march through Antipas' territory in order to dispatch the delegates, coordinate their activity, and share the danger with them. He crossed the Sea of Galilee and landed at Gennesaret, a hamlet on the western shore (Mark 6:53–56; Matthew 14:34–36). When he disembarked, there was a crush of needy, sick people such as he had never seen before. A local rabbi named Jairus fell at his feet (Mark 5:21–24; Matthew 9:18–19; Luke 8:40–42):

Yeshua crossed in the boat again to the opposite side and a big crowd was gathered upon him, and he was along the sea. And one of the synagogue leaders comes, named Yair, sees him and falls at his feet, and summons him a lot, saying that: My little daughter is at her end, so come lay hands on her, so she might be saved and live. And he went away after him, and there followed him a big crowd and pressed around on him.

On the way to Jairus' house, however, the crush of people got so bad that Jesus panicked. He yelled out when an unclean woman, defiled by a constant flow of blood, seized the fringe of his cloak:[2] "Who touched my garments?" (Mark 5:30). His followers were no more sensible in their response (Mark 5:31): "Look at the crowd pressing around on you, and you say, Who touched me?" It was the woman herself, cured of her hemorrhage, who identified herself, apparently calming Jesus' apprehension (Mark 5:33).

But by the time Jesus actually got to Jairus' home, the little girl was thought to be dead: the distraught mourners ridiculed Jesus' own suggestion that she was still alive (Mark 5:35–43; Matthew 9:23–26; Luke 8:49–56). His reaction was fierce; he threw everyone out of the house but the parents, and took Simon Rock, James, and John with him to see the child. They heard the Aramaic words, *talitha kumi* ("girl, arise!"), saw the impact of simply being touched by Jesus, as the twelve-year-old got up and walked.

By their close observation of their rabbi, the apostles themselves became prophetic *chasidim* and seers, adept in the ways of their master to remove impurity, even the uncleanness of blood and death. They were to persist when others had given people up for dead, following the wisdom of the Talmud: when the end of life was as uncertain as life itself, even after preparation for burial and interment itself, life remained a possibility. An additional tractate of the Babylonian Talmud, devoted to mourning (Ebel Rabbati 8:1), recommends inspecting the dead for a period of three days. It supports the practice by telling of people who had been buried alive but then were found still breathing within their cavelike tombs; they came back from the dead and went on to enjoy their lives.

---

2. The fringe Jesus wore (see Matthew 9:20; 14:36; Mark 6:56; Luke 8:44) fulfilled the instruction in Numbers 15:37–41, that the people of Israel should sew blue tassels on their clothing to remind them of Moses' commandments.

Jesus made rapid, erratic progress across Galilee, confusing any attempts by Herod to discover his whereabouts. This last sustained period in Galilee, during the year 30, produced many false sightings of Jesus from Antipas' informers (including some Pharisees, see Mark 3:6; Matthew 12:14), as Jesus' delegates acted in his name.

His disciples were under intense pressure. Towns that had once accepted and even embraced Jesus now rejected him and his delegates. Although that reaction was only prudent under the circumstances, Jesus lashed out in condemnation of Bethsaida and Capernaum (Luke 10:13–15; compare Matthew 11:20–24):

> Miseries are yours, Korazin, miseries are yours, Beitzayadah! Because if the miracles which happened among you had happened in Tyre and Sidon, they would have repented long ago sitting in sackcloth and ash. Except it will be more bearable for Tyre and Sidon in the judgment than for you. And you, Kapharnachum, would you be exalted unto heaven? You will go down unto Hades!

Any trace of the "Galilean spring" was scorched away by the blazing hostility of Antipas and his sympathizers, as well as by the militancy of those who sided with Jesus and his apostles. Jesus fed the fire that he had started in Galilee with the virulence of his judgment against communities that he thought had repudiated God himself. Let those who couldn't see as he saw either repent or go straight to hell.

During this period, Jesus came the closest he ever did to embracing the full militancy of Galilean zeal. He even promised that his delegates would sit on twelve thrones, judging the clans of Israel (Luke 22:30; Matthew 19:28). Among the instructions in Jesus' commission, just after his naming of the twelve delegates, are detailed strictures for how to deal with towns that reject Jesus' message and refuse to accept his followers. The delegates are to call down the judgment of the Kingdom rather than its blessing, and wipe the unclean dust of such towns from their clothes and bodies (Mark 6:11; Matthew 10:14; Luke 9:5).

His treatment of non-Jews also became more severe. His exorcism of the legion of demons had been traumatic; earlier he had been eager for non-Jewish support, but after Gergesa his response to them was rude and phobic. An encounter northwest of Galilee, with a Gentile woman, highlights the ingrained prejudice and xenophobia that he shared with most rural Jews (Mark 7:24–30; Matthew 15:21–28).

While Jesus was staying in a house in that area, trying to keep a low profile, a woman described as Syro-Phoenician (that is, an Aramaic-speaking non-Jew who came from the ancient coastal region of Phoenicia) found him. She asked Jesus to exorcise her daughter from an unclean spirit (perhaps manifest by persistent bleeding after her period had ended). He refused, "It is not good to take the bread of the children and throw it to the dogs."

He had rebuffed her with the brutal comparison of female Gentiles to dogs. Expressing that sentiment in Gentile territory was asking for trouble. And the woman gave it to him, gently but to the point; the verbal victory went to her, at the expense of Jesus (Mark 7:28):

But she replied and says to him, Indeed, Lord: even the dogs under the table eat from the scraps of the children.

The contrast with the story of the centurion in Capernaum is relevant. The woman's location, her designation as a non-Jew with no evident interest in Judaism, as well as her sex and that of her child, all show that she was impure in ways the centurion was not. Yet her instinct to accept any help Jesus might give was stronger even than his reactive refusal of her; he relented and agreed to deal with her daughter's unclean spirit.

At this point, Jesus was honestly bewildered: the significance of this story is that he repented of his own xenophobia. After all these years, even after his steadfast commitment to his parable that it is not what goes into the person but what comes out of the person that defiles one, we can see his human uncertainty and the limitations that were part and parcel of his own culture. He was ambivalent about Samaritans: willing to accept them as Israelites but wary of their territory. And that ambivalence pales in comparison to his initial rejection of the Syro-Phoenician women. He remained torn between his belief that purity became contagious under the power of Spirit and his visceral antipathy toward non-Jews, a basic element in his Galilean upbringing.

After his contact with the Gentile woman in the vicinity of Tyre, Jesus returned again to rural Galilee. His growing fame as a folk hero made him welcome in one of the small towns which Antipas' troops mostly ignored, Kana. The visit to Kana marks the beginning of a sequence of signs that shaped Jesus' final sense of who he was and what he was doing.

In Kana, Jesus was reunited with his family. His mother and brothers had been invited there to a wedding. Kana was a little more than four miles northeast of Nazareth across hills that sheltered the village from the garrison at nearby Sepphoris, and they were friends or, perhaps, even distant relations of the betrothed. The years of homelessness after his Capernaum phase had taken their toll. He was ready for a reconciliation.

Weddings were big celebrations, often held in spring between the harvests of barley and wheat, when people were free from the most intense demands of their fields. The Mishnah designates Wednesdays as the preferred day for the marriage of a virgin, because "twice weekly are the courts in session in a town, on Monday and Thursday, so if the husband had a complaint as to virginity, he goes early to court" (Ketubot 1:1 in the Mishnah).[3] The countryside would have been blooming as Jesus and a few of his disciples made their way into Kana. This was his land and these were his people. They knew who he was. "Rabbi!" they would have hailed him, the men kissing him on the lips, making him feel welcome even though he was disheveled from his travels.

---

3. The weddings of widows can occur on Thursday according to this *halakhah*, but because this was such a large celebration we may surmise the bride was a virgin.

"*Shelama*," was his response. "The Kingdom of God is in your midst!"

In Kana, Jesus found a hamlet very much like Nazareth. There were houses of mud and stone around courtyards in close proximity to fields. Sheep, goats, and a very few cattle roamed freely or were penned in the larger enclosures of the most fortunate farmers. Perhaps a donkey pulled a mill wheel for grinding barley and wheat into flour at the center of town.

Women were in their best clothes, an outer mantel or cloak over a linen tunic, and some were wearing linen sashes or thick flax cords around their waists. The maidens pulled the hoods attached to their cloaks down over their hair, shielding their faces so they were modestly veiled. The young men were also in their best clothes, or at least cleaned up for the occasion.

Jesus and his small group entered the bride's family's courtyard where the contract of marriage (*ketuvah*) was to be formalized and festivities would follow. There he embraced his mother and his brothers. He was not the man they remembered from Capernaum. He was much thinner, almost gaunt, with a distracted air about him. The deference people paid him made them proud, but a little wary. Where was the son and brother they used to care for, play with, tease, and discipline?

The bride was kept sequestered in her own household. Her hair had been combed with olive oil scented with cassie flowers and aloes. She wore it in wound braids, covered by a net. On this exceptional occasion she also wore purple eye shadow, colored with an expensive Phoenician dye derived from simmering murex snails for nine days, along with henna, a more readily procured cosmetic, which was applied in abstract patterns with a thin feathered reed on her neck and hands. She was wrapped in two thick linen sashes: one accentuated the curve of her hips; the other was wound beneath her breasts.

The moment of marriage was scarcely what we would call a religious service. There was music from flutes, harps, and drums and dancing as the wedding party entered the courtyard. The bride and groom stood before the assembled guests as the *ketuvah* was read or recited by an elder.

Then there was singing of psalms and portions of the Song of Songs and lustier rounds. The new couple had their first dance as the feasting and drinking began.

The food would have been very much like what was served at Jesus' *berith*. Weddings and *berith*s were major festal events throughout Jewish Galilee. The wedding would have taken place in the late morning, and by the early afternoon everyone would have been well fed and tipsy. It was then that disaster struck. The party ran out of wine.

"They do not have wine," said Mary to Jesus.

"Woman, I have nothing for you!" Jesus replied. "My hour has not arrived!"

John's Gospel, where this scene is depicted (2:1–12), frequently makes Jesus implausibly prescient, as he is here. But we include the exchange to demonstrate what is nonetheless the way he would probably have talked to his mother (and most women most of the time).

His treatment of the crisis of hospitality at the wedding was similarly casual and abrupt, but also surreal. Jesus ordered that water used *for purification* be served up as wine, and the manager of the feast tastes and distributes what is explicitly called in John "water become wine" (2:9). It is perfectly understandable that in John's Gospel, written at the end of the first century in the cosmopolitan environment of Ephesus (a city in present-day Turkey), Jesus would have been portrayed as a new Dionysius, in order to compete with that perennially popular Hellenistic god. Much later in the text, the Gospel refers to what happened in Kana as a miracle: when wine ran out, Jesus "made" water into wine (see John 4:46). That is the slant of John's Gospel, not what actually happened. In its original Galilean context, what Jesus did had a totally different meaning.

Archeologists have discovered the kind of stone jars described at Kana (in John 2:6) in first-century Jewish settlements in Galilee. How Jesus used those peculiar emblems of Jewish identity was, in the symbolic language of early Judaism, even more radical than changing water into wine: by imbibing waters of purification during the festivity, and having others join him, he insisted that the purity of Israel was indeed to begin *from the inside,* and from Galilee. This concept of a new purity, enacted in Galilee but out of reach of Herod Antipas, was powerfully attractive to Galilean sensibilities. The sort of zealous pride that had made Galileans repeatedly dare to try to take over the Temple in Jerusalem was galvanized by this sign: not a miracle but an enacted parable of Galilean integrity.

The final victory of purity over uncleanness, of the divine over any human hegemony, of God's chosen people over all the nations of the world, was an essential hope of early Judaism. But the means of triumph were disputed. The Essenes of Qumran taught that a final, apocalyptic war would signal the end. The book of Zechariah predicted that Israel would envelop all the nations in an ultimate sacrifice on Mount Zion. The Pharisees and John the Baptist—for all their differences—simply put purity into practice with the trust that God would act in his own time. Jesus was now moving toward deciding when, where, and how the apocalyptic moment would commence.

S oon after the incident at Kana, Jesus left Galilee again. He created a sensation wherever he went. He was too visible, even under the cloak of the apostles who acted in his name, shared some of his powers, and attracted a little of the official attention that would otherwise have come all Jesus' way. Prudence demanded that he evade Antipas again by leaving his territory. Again, Jesus chose Syria, this time east of Bethsaida in a wilderness area called Gaulanitis, within the region now known as the Golan Heights. The delegates had done their work and reached literally thousands of people. Divine Kingdom, the Throne of God, purification and healing in the name of Jesus had become a Galilean movement. The strength of the land had found its voice in the *mamzer* from Nazareth.

The Gospels report that five thousand men followed Jesus into Syria, but it was probably more like a thousand. The total population of Galilee was about 150,000 at this point, less than half of whom were Jews living among 204 cities and villages (Josephus, *Life* 235); the thousand would have represented some 4 percent of able-bodied Jewish men, the most militant arm of Galilean Judaism. Jesus' movement had become politically significant, but militarily far short of overwhelming. Over a period of several months, these would-be zealots abandoned their families, left their peasant life behind, and streamed out of the hillside villages to covertly make their way north and east into the rolling countryside well outside Herod Antipas' jurisdiction. Jesus was waiting for them.

They camped in tents and shrub shelters, the kind of rustic base that Judas, son of Hezekiah, had used in leading his Galilean force to take Sepphoris in 4 B.C.E. (Josephus, *Jewish War* 2 § 56). Jesus stirred the Galileans' proud memories of resistance against Rome and of their determined onslaughts on the Temple. At night, fires dotted the landscape; the smell of wood smoke was thick in the air. An army in terms of numbers, yet unarmed and unsupplied.

Now outside Galilee and territorial Israel, Jesus no longer sent his followers into the surrounding towns and villages to seek hospitality and proclaim the divine Kingdom. When his disciples proposed that Jesus release the men to forage in the area, he refused (Mark 6:30–44; Matthew 14:13–21; Luke 9:10–17; John 6:1–15):

> *And the delegates gather together to Yeshua and reported to him everything, as much as they had done and as much as they had taught. And he says to them, Come on: you yourselves—privately— into a wilderness place and repose a little. For those coming and departing were many, and they did not have opportunity even to eat. And they went away by the boat to a wilderness place privately. And they saw them departing and many knew and they ran together there by dry land from all the cities and preceded them. He came out and saw a big crowd and felt for them, because they were as sheep not*

having a shepherd, and he began to teach them a lot. The hour being already late, his students came forward to him and were saying that: The place is wilderness, and already a late hour. Release them, so that going away into the fields and villages around they might buy themselves something to eat. But he replied to them, said: Give them to eat yourselves. And they say to him, Shall we go away, buy two hundred denarii of bread, and give them to eat? But he says to them, How much bread do you have? Depart, see! And they know, say, Five, and two fish. And he directed them all to recline for a meal—symposiums, symposiums—upon the green blades. And they leaned back by hundreds and fifties—garden plots, garden plots. He took the five breads and the two fish, and looked up into the heaven, blessed and broke up the breads, and was giving it to his students, so they would set it out for them, and the two fish he distributed to all. All both ate and were satisfied, and lifted full fragments—twelve baskets—and from the fish. Those who ate the bread were five thousand men.

This story resonated through the Gospel tradition, which amplified what was originally a vignette about living off the land into a miracle of a lavish banquet.[4] He expected his followers to live rough, in the manner of the great prophets of Israel. Elisha, the disciple of Elijah, had once provided for one hundred men from only twenty loaves of barley, and there was enough for leftovers (2 Kings 4:42–44). The original point of the

---

4. Written as they are to support the Christian practice of Eucharist in the Hellenistic world, the Gospels imbue this feeding with deeply symbolic significance. From only five loaves of bread and two fish that Jesus blessed and broke, the delegates fed the crowd, and collected remnants in twelve baskets. Twelve, the number of the clans of ancient Israel, marks the event as the promise of feeding all Israel. A different telling of the story (involving four thousand men; Matthew 15:32–39; Mark 8:1–10), had seven bushels filled, instead of twelve baskets, corresponding to the seven deacons chosen after the resurrection to give food to Greek-speaking followers of Jesus in Jerusalem from the common treasury of the movement (Acts 6:1–6). Just as twelve was the primordial number of Israel, seventy in ancient Judaism was the number of the non-Jewish nations. Even as embellished, these stories are rooted in the numerological traditions of Israel.

story was that Jesus and his men survived as the prophets of old had, sub-
sisting on the land around them and the generosity of those who had
sought them out. After all, Elijah himself had survived in the wilderness
on what the Lord of Israel provided (1 Kings 19:3–8), as had all Israel
during the time of Moses (Exodus 16). The wilderness was a place of
prophetic protest: for Elijah and Elisha, protest against Ahab and
Jezebel; for Jesus, protest against Antipas.

The regimen was hard, a return to the discipline of his days with John
the Baptist. The fuller statement Jesus now made about John reflects the
new conditions he faced, and his desire to motivate his followers
(Matthew 11:7–14; Luke 7:24–28; 16:16):

> *Yet while they were proceeding Yeshua said to the crowds about
> Yochanan, What did you go out into the wilderness to observe? Reed
> shaken by wind? But what did you go out to see? A man attired in
> soft clothes? See: those in kings' houses bear soft clothes! But why did
> you go out? To see a prophet? Yes, I say to you, and more than a
> prophet. This is he concerning whom it is written, See: I delegate my
> messenger [or: angel, since the word is the same] before your face,
> who will ready your way before you. Amen I say to you, there has not
> been raised among women-born one greater than Yochanan the Im-
> merser! But the least in the Kingdom of the heavens is greater than
> he! Yet from the days of Yochanan the Immerser until now, the King-
> dom of the heavens avails itself, and availers seize it! Because all the
> prophets and the law prophesied until Yochanan, and if you want to
> accept, he [Yochanan] is Eliyah who is going to come.*

It was time to risk all for the opportunity of bringing about God's
Kingdom, and it was necessary that Jesus and his followers endure
whatever hardships prophetic protest entailed. John the Immerser was
indeed Elijah, preparing the way, and Jesus implicitly compared
himself to Elisha, the disciple who had received double the portion of

Elijah's Spirit when he saw his master ascend by the divine Chariot (2 Kings 2:9–12).

Nearly two millennia of Christian preaching have made the term "messiah" or "christ" the title that best expresses Jesus' exalted power on earth. But in the early Judaism of his own time, "prophet" better conveyed the expectation of militant revolution. Jesus had long insisted on his messianic inspiration with Spirit, but the key to Jesus' encouragement of militancy lies in his assertion of prophetic authority.

The Galileans saw in Jesus an almost unspeakable hope: that their land would be free of Herod Antipas, free of the Romans, and that they would be powerful enough to enter the Temple with the pure offerings of their own hands. Revolt brewed in the wilderness of Trachonitis. Ordinary prudence would have required that such a hope not be spoken, but John's Gospel makes the matter plain: Jesus saw that his supporters were going to force him to become king (6:15), to take on an anointing not only of divine Spirit but of temporal rule. He had spoken of the necessity of seizing the Kingdom, and they wanted him to serve as the prophetic regent of God on earth.

Jesus had already claimed to be messiah from his time in Nazareth, although he had used the term to signal his empowerment by the holy Spirit. In Trachonitis, he had a potential army at his disposal, for whom there was nothing ethereal or otherworldly about the divine Kingdom of which he spoke. Would Jesus embrace their enthusiasm, and lead them as an army with the military authority of a descendant of David?

That issue perplexed Jesus, and he sought the solitude of the wilderness in order to wrestle with the possibility of direct revolution against Rome. Something within us may want him to sweep down from the highlands of Syria into Galilee, collecting supporters on the way, to fight glorious battles against Antipas, overthrow the despot against all the odds, even gather enough momentum to storm down from Galilee into Judea, force the Romans out of Palestine with signs and wonders and sit on David's throne as Israel's king. Our world would be a different place, and its religious landscape virtually unrecognizable, had Jesus attempted any program remotely similar to that.

Instead, Jesus did a very strange thing, which must have puzzled his supporters at the time, but which we can see in retrospect was completely in character. He dismissed the thousand militants, who had little choice but to return to Galilee. They went back to their homes without knowing whether Jesus would after all lead them in revolt. Traveling with only his closest *talmidim*, the Twelve, he continued north, toward Caesarea Philippi, built up by Herod Philip around the site of temples to the god Pan and the emperor, and named by Philip to honor Caesar. He asked the delegates a question (Mark 8:27–30; Matthew 16:13–20; Luke 9:18–21):

> *And Yeshua went out, and his students, into the villages of Philip's Caesarea, and on the way he interrogated his students, saying to them, Who does humanity say I am? But they said to him, saying that: Yochanan the Immerser, and others Eliyah, yet others that: one of the prophets. And he personally interrogated them, But who do you say I am? Rock replies and says to him, You are the Messiah. And he scolded them, so that they would talk to no one concerning him.*

At this point, Jesus vacillated. He had resisted any public acclamation as messiah, but he was unwavering in his conviction that God's Spirit had anointed him. His reluctance either to embrace or refuse the title of messiah produced a tension within himself and among his disciples. He turned to the world of vision, the perennial source of his confidence, to relieve his difficult ambivalence, and now he initiated a select group of his followers into a visionary experience of who exactly he was.

Jesus took three of his closest disciples—Peter, James, and John—and climbed above the villages, up the slopes of Mount Hermon (or Mount Lebanon, as Josephus called it in *Antiquities* 5 § 178), an ancient site of worship. More than twenty temples to various gods have been identified on its slopes, and the book of Enoch speaks of appearances of angels both on and near the mountain (Enoch 6:6; 13:9).

The mountain rose up from the valley of Lebanon to more than nine thousand feet at its snowcapped peak; its lower portion was blanketed in fruit and almond trees, vines, cypress, oak, and cedars. Halfway up, the lush forests gave way to shrubs and rock. The mountain was a resplendent and dangerous place, notorious for its lions and leopards (Song of Songs 4:8). Jesus encamped with the three apostles high on its slopes.

He had chosen his site carefully. Mountains in Scripture are places close to God, the sites where God had confirmed his covenant with Abraham, had given Moses the Law, and had found a place for his Temple. Jesus sat with his *talmidim,* perhaps around a crackling fire of brush, distraught in his uncertainty over whether his messianic anointing posed a military challenge to Rome.

The Transfiguration (Matthew 16:28–17:13; Mark 9:1–13; Luke 9:27–36) is one of the most majestic stories in the Gospels, both beautifully and simply written. Jesus is transformed before Peter, James, and John into a gleaming white figure, speaking with Moses and Elijah. Jesus' visions were not merely private; years of communal meditation made what he saw and experienced vivid to his own disciples, as well. On Mount Hermon, Jesus followed in the footsteps of Moses, who took three of his followers (Aaron, Nadab, and Abihu) up Mount Sinai, where they ate and drank to celebrate their vision of the God of Israel on his sapphire throne (see Exodus 24:1–11). But unlike what happened on Moses' mountain, Jesus' disciples, covered by a shining cloud of glory, hear a voice say, "This is my son, the beloved, in whom I take pleasure: hear him" (Matthew 17:5) and when the cloud passed they found Jesus without Moses and Elijah (Mark 9:8), standing alone as God's son. Divine "son" was the same designation Jesus had heard during his immersions with John the Baptist: now his own disciples saw and heard the truth of his own vision. The voice that came after the luminous cloud in the Transfiguration did not speak in the exclusive language of the later doctrine of the Trinity, which made Jesus into the only (and only possible) "Son of God." Rather, the point was that the same Spirit that had animated Moses and Elijah was present in Jesus, and that he could pass on that Spirit to his followers, each of whom could also become a "son."

In the midst of seeing the vision and hearing the divine voice, Peter offered to build three "huts," or *sukkoth,* for Jesus and Moses and Elijah, and Mark's Gospel presents that as an inept suggestion (Mark 9:5–6):

> *Rock responded and says to Yeshua, Rabbi, it is fine for us to be here, and we shall build three lodges: one for you and one for Mosheh and one for Eliyah. For he did not know how he should respond, because they were terrified.*

Frequently during the formation of the Gospels, when the significance of Judaic symbolism was forgotten, blame fell on the alleged ignorance of the apostles, rather than the cultural amnesia of the Church. In the present case, the *sukkoth* Peter referred to reflect both the great feast that was coming and the realization that great prophets—like Moses, Elijah, and Jesus—brought the Spirit of God to abide in Israel. There is a touching quality about Peter's impulse to provide shelter for the visionary experience of God's presence, and he no doubt built his huts on Mount Hermon. His act is an exact indication that he, with James and John, had indeed joined Jesus in the vision of the Chariot.

The Mishnah teaches that the Chariot should not be introduced to one person alone (Chagigah 2:1); the vision of the divine Throne was fraught with danger. Some initiates died, some went mad, and still others fell prey to polytheism by meditating on the Throne incautiously (Chagigah 2:1–7 in the Tosefta). It was part of his genius as a rabbi that Jesus led his disciples into a vision of the Chariot in a way that mobilized and safely transformed them. By sharing his vision with them, he shifted the center of his teaching away from what can be discerned of God's Kingdom on earth to what can be experienced of the angelic pantheon around God's Throne.

The Transfiguration represents the mature development of Rabbi Jesus' *kabbalah;* he was able not only to articulate his own vision but to initiate others into its richness. The nuclear reaction that had begun with his identification with "the one like the person" had reached critical mass and exploded into the consciousness of his disciples. They now saw him as a living presence in the pantheon of Israel's patriarchs and prophets around God's Throne. Their rabbi, favored by the power of the thundering voice of God (see John 12:29), stood at the flaming vortex of creation's source. It must have seemed to the apostles at that moment that all the hardships, struggles, and disappointments entailed in following this man were finally rewarded in the intimacy he gave them with the divine presence.[5]

Rabbi Jesus' esoteric teaching had grown in advance of his public teaching, a reversal of the pattern we would expect from the Mishnah and the Talmud. His early development of a *kabbalah* and its prominent place in his teaching was a result of Herod Antipas' pressure. The apparent oddity in the kind of rabbinic work Jesus pursued was one of the elements that caused early Christianity to separate from Judaism. Mystical currents certainly ran among other rabbis in the first century, and the kabbalistic tradition that began in Judaism long before Jesus has continued to the present day. But Jesus' unusual, even aberrant dedication to the practice of his *kabbalah* gave his movement a trajectory whose deviation from other forms of Judaism might have seemed subtle during his own time, but it proved to be radically important in leading to a new religion.

In Christian theology Jesus would eventually supersede the Temple as the locus of the divine. But that would not occur for another sixty years. Yet the Transfiguration was the beginning of a seismic shift in the center of gravity away from Mount Zion and toward a short, balding, charismatic rabbi with sharp wisdom and a wicked tongue. When the Temple was destroyed by Rome in 70 C.E., the Jesus movement and the

---

5. The presentation of the Gospels makes them less aware of what was going on than they should have been, but that seems to be part of the later development of the story. The portrayal of Peter as a stammering fool is, in particular, a reflection of controversies within the early Church, rather than a feature of the original story.

Pharisees were all that was left standing of the pluralistic ferment of the Judaism of the first century; even after that catastrophic event, Christianity moved only incrementally and gradually to the view that its Christ actually replaced the destroyed Temple. And it is in the Transfiguration that we see why Jesus came to take its place. He entered the heavenly court in the mind of his closest *talmidim* and took root there as a defining force in our consciousness of God and in our culture.

God had exalted his son in the Transfiguration, but he still hadn't told him what to do. Jesus wondered if he should take up the messianic challenge of his thousand zealous supporters and attempt to wrest control of Israel from Rome. He struggled with this question alone for days on the snowcapped mountain, having dispatched Peter, James, and John back to Galilee and his other disciples. From the top of Mount Hermon, he could see the Sea of Galilee and the Jordan Valley to the south, Galilee and the Mediterranean coast to the west— all the kingdoms of the world that mattered to him.

He later told his disciples that he had very nearly given in to the idea of a direct military assault on Herod Antipas. If he could have succeeded in the assault, he might have become the king of Israel, a tempting prospect. Knowing the power of the Chariot meant knowing the temptations of Satan: to rule people through their hunger for bread, their awe of signs and wonders, their fear of power (Matthew 4:1–11; Luke 4:1–13). As for the rabbis, so for Jesus—there was exhilaration and danger in the Throne. The Transfiguration on Mount Hermon had shown him and his disciples that he was God's son: who, then, could deny such a man the power to rule?

His vision of Satan suggests that Jesus had reached an advanced stage in his mystical practice. When tempted by the devil, Jesus, as a faithful son of God, insisted that his miracles and signs were a reflection of God's power, not his own. Satan's pressure on Jesus to dominate others was in Aramaic a *nisyona,* a test, a "temptation" or occasion of being pressed to the point of being disloyal. "The Lord's Prayer" was completed in the dark night of what has become known as the Temptation:

> My father,
>> your name will be sanctified, your Kingdom will come:
> Give me today the bread that is coming,
>> and release me my debts—not bring me to the test!

Temptation was constant in Jesus' life, and he conveyed to his delegates the necessity of resisting it not simply with one's own strength but with prayer. Jesus had spent so much time breaking the barriers of convention and prejudice that he needed to create his own personal form of prayer as a means of distinguishing the radically new opportunities of the Kingdom from personal opportunism.

The disciples, too, would be tempted to confuse God's Kingdom with their own power, especially as Jesus conveyed his heady visions to them and initiated them into the permutations of his *kabbalah* after the vision on Mount Hermon. As the select three, Peter, James, and John, joined the others of the Twelve, their vision of Jesus on Mount Hermon proved contagious (Mark 6:47–51; Matthew 14:24–33; John 6:16–21). Their rabbi appeared to them all in a boat once again as they crossed the Sea of Galilee from east to west. The whole group was now functioning on an astral plane, flipping back and forth between the practical demands of piloting their craft and the visionary conviction that their master would never abandon them. They knew very well they had left Jesus behind on the mount of the Transfiguration, but their impression of Jesus was so strong, their persistence in his discipline of vision so dedicated, that for them he was walking on water, calming the waves as he had on their crossing to Bethsaida. Elijah had been literally transported by God's Spirit to avoid Ahab (1 Kings 18:7–15); by appearing on the water to his disciples, Rabbi Jesus entered the world of prophetic signs once more. When he himself came to Capernaum again, the crowd asked in excited confusion, "Rabbi, when did you come here?" (John 6:25). Their rabbi was able to be in several places at once, a sorcerer, flying through air, breaking the bounds of time and space. He had stilled storms, raised the dead, appeared on the holy mount with Moses and Elijah. Why, they no doubt wondered, should he not break the rule of Rome? The power of Jesus' transformative vision of the world meant that the prospect of political and military revolution remained open. His return to the territory of Herod Antipas signaled his resolve to define the aim of his movement irrevocably.

TEN

❧

The Sword
of Rome

Jesus next met his disciples on the west side of the Sea of Galilee, near Capernaum (John 6:16–25), and went with them into the city. A crowd had gathered there, excited that he had returned from Syria. "Rabbi," they asked, "when did you come here?" (John 6:25). To them, as to his disciples, Jesus seemed unbounded by his physical body; he was like Elijah, defiant of time and space.

Jesus was still struggling to understand the meaning of his own prophetic vocation, but about one thing he was certain: God's Kingdom and God's Chariot were the only things that really mattered. When pressed to define when exactly the Kingdom would come, he insisted that its power was already working in Galilee (Luke 17:20–21):

> Yet interrogated by the Pharashayahs when the Kingdom of God comes, he answered them and said, The Kingdom of God does not come with observation, neither will they say, Look—here, or—there. Because the Kingdom of God is in your midst.

Nonetheless, awakening Galileans to the fact that the Kingdom was in their midst was not enough. How could he be part of the world's transformation, for which he so passionately longed?

His mission was to arouse his countrymen's yearning for the moment when the divine Kingdom would be revealed not only in Galilee but, more important, in the Temple. Scripture promised that Mount Zion was to be point alpha in the coming transformation of the world. Zion was the navel of the earth, the temporal gateway to the infinite, the *axis mundi* from which God had created the primordial *kosmos* and where he would commence his re-creation of the world.

The Targum of Zechariah (chapter 14) showed Jesus how to trigger that divine re-creation. Zechariah provided the formula and ritual program—the key that would unlock the magic door through which the transformation would flow. The Targum predicts that God's Kingdom will be manifested over the entire earth when the offerings of Sukkoth are presented both by Israelites and non-Jews at the Temple. It further predicts that these worshippers will prepare and offer their sacrifices themselves, in the Galilean manner, without the intervention of middlemen. Significantly, the last words of the book promise that "there shall never again be a *trader* in the *sanctuary* of the Lord of hosts at that *time*" (Targum Zechariah 14:21).[1] These words would prove fateful. Jesus' desire to realize the targumic prophecy brought on the dramatic confrontation that he would shortly provoke in the Temple.

The Targum emphasized the coming transformation, the final vindication of Israel that would give back the Land to the people of God. Zechariah's vision of the ultimate Sukkoth restored the Land to Israel and the Temple to the sacrifice God desired. The Romans would be banished and Zion's gates opened to all who would join with Israel there in worship (Targum Zechariah 14:9):

And the Kingdom of the Lord shall be revealed upon all *the inhabitants of* the earth; at that *time they shall serve before the Lord with*

---

1. In order to indicate where a targum innovates in comparison to the underlying Hebrew text, it has become conventional to change the printed font. In this case, the prophecy against trade in the Temple becomes stronger in the Aramaic version.

one accord, for his name *is established in the world; there is none apart from him.*

The Targum not only specifies that Zechariah's vision is of the Kingdom, it also spells out the immediate impact of that Kingdom upon *all* of humanity. Here it is prophesied that at the feast of Sukkoth the Temple will become the definitive tabernacle, the place where Israel would be regenerated. Sacrifice in the Temple would take on the character of a universal feast with God, open to all peoples who accepted the truth, which was to be revealed initially in Israel alone.

This feast was not to come easily, and its joy would be far from unalloyed. Rabbi Jesus believed the apocalypse was coming, and coming soon. His belief may be hard to fathom, although it is eerily close to the smoldering faith at the core of many so-called fringe groups in Christianity today. He was convinced that the world as he knew it would end. The advent of God's Kingdom was not just the wolf lying down with the lamb, a suckling child playing at the hole of the asp, a cuddly combination of love, faith, innocence, and compassion. It included cataclysm and catastrophe and cosmic upheaval. The gentle image of the seed in his mother's garden, the yeast she used to bake bread, remained with him as parables of the Kingdom. But his theology had evolved, and years of opposition, hardship, and kabbalistic meditation had focused his mind on some of the darkest aspects of Judaism's apocalyptic imagination. The fateful chapters of Ezekiel, Daniel, and Zechariah were not just intellectual exercises or speculative theology for him. He believed them. They were as real to him as is the ground under your feet. As surreal as the notion of the Zecharian apocalypse may seem to many of us, it was the kind of idea that could and did change history, although not in the ways Rabbi Jesus anticipated.

It was not only visionary fervor that propelled him toward Jerusalem. There was a realistic side to Jesus' strategy in turning away from a military campaign against Antipas. He was outnumbered and poorly equipped. He knew nothing about war or battles. He was a peasant turned rabbi, not a warrior. He had never raised a sword or thrown a javelin. His attempt to enact the Zecharian prophecy was a last desperate hope that everything might change without a military revolt. If only Yahweh's chosen people would keep his covenant! The ragamuffin band of Galileans would go to the Temple. Their rabbi had appeared with Moses and Elijah by the Throne. He was the Almighty's beloved son. He would lead them through the Great Court to lay their Galilean sacrifices on the altar. God would be moved to reenter Israel's history, and the Kingdom would come.

D riven by his vision, Jesus proceeded in his final campaign across Galilee. He had remained in the vicinity of Capernaum and its garrison only long enough to gather his most committed disciples, his core group beyond the Twelve, about thirty men and women. As he set out, he again used the Twelve as camouflage, confounding Antipas' attempts to capture him. He pressed southwest of the Sea of Galilee, but he did not travel quietly. He needed to draw attention to his plan to mount a Galilean pilgrimage that would trigger the prophecy of Zechariah. When he restored the life of the only son of a widow (Luke 7:11–17) near the spot where the prophet Elisha had also revived a boy (2 Kings 4:8–37, and see 1 Kings 17:17–24 for the story of Elijah and a widow's son), the news echoed through Galilee and must have been seen as a sign.

On this, his final pilgrimage, Jesus consciously played up the Davidic lineage he claimed through his father, Joseph. Those in Jesus' own movement never doubted he was Joseph's son (John 1:45); they rejected talk that he was a *mamzer,* and played up his David ancestry. His reputation as "David's son," a wise, healing master of demons in the lineage of Solomon, had long preceded him (Matthew 9:27). But now Jesus also referred to his illustrious genealogy in a different context (Mark 2:23–26, see also Matthew 12:1–4; Luke 6:1–4):

And it happened he was proceeding through on Shabbath through the sowings, and his students began to make a way, picking the heads. And

*the Pharashayahs were saying to him, See: why are they doing on Shab-
bath what is not correct?! And he says to them, Have you never read
what David did when he had need and hungered, himself and those
with him? He entered into the house of God when Avyatar was high
priest, and ate the bread of the Presentation[2]—that it is not correct to
eat except for the priests—and gave also to those who were with him.*

By associating himself with David, Jesus exacerbated the messianic fervor
of growing numbers of his followers and the enthusiasts that joined a
swelling caravan of pilgrimage. As David's son Jesus now led them to
Mount Zion, a new Galilean insurrection in the Temple seemed imminent.

In at least one respect, his revolution was already under way. As they
crossed Galilee, Jesus had urged resistance against paying the customary
tax for the Temple, which was exacted in addition to the tithes for the
priests and for sacrifice. When the 10 percent of tithe (Numbers
18:21–32) and what is traditionally called the "second tithe" (produce to
be consumed during sacrifice in Jerusalem; Deuteronomy 14:22–29),
were added to the taxes of Rome and the Temple, the result was a rate of
around 40 percent of one's income. No wonder Jesus lashed out against
the system (see Matthew 17:24–27):

*Yet as they came into Kapharnachum, those who took the double
drachma came forward to Rock and said, Your teacher does not pay
the double drachma? He says, Yes. And when he came into the home,
Yeshua anticipated him saying, How does it seem to you, Shimon?
Who do the kings of the earth take customs or tax from? From their
sons or from foreigners? Yet he was saying, From the foreigners.
Yeshua stated to him, Therefore the sons are indeed free! But so that*

---

2. These twelve loaves were kept in the sanctuary, before the Lord's presence in the holy
of holies, and were to be eaten only by priests (Leviticus 24:5–9). By referring to when
David permitted his men to eat this bread in 1 Samuel 21:1–6, Jesus both underlined his
Davidic lineage and emphasized that the target of his pilgrimage was the Temple.

we will not cause them to falter, proceed to a sea, throw a fishhook, and take the first fish that comes up. Open its mouth, and you will find a stater [that is, a coin sufficient to pay the tax for two]: take that, give to them for me and you!

Later Christian tradition made this *halakhah* of Jesus into a miracle story, but the original sense of Jesus' words points in a different direction. He is telling his preeminent disciple that all Israelites, as sons of a king, should be free of taxes for the Temple, and that those who collect such taxes can, in effect, go fish for them. While that is not quite a categorical rejection of the tax, neither is it anything like an obedient agreement to support the Temple with money. The "double drachma" was the name of the modest annual donation of a half-shekel (two drachmas) per Israelite male throughout the world (see Josephus, *Antiquities* 18 § § 312–313 and Exodus 30:11–16) and Jesus was refusing to pay it. The Temple for him was not to be supported with currency, but by the offerings of one's hands. He was speaking the language of Galilean revolution, centered on the act of sacrifice.

Enthusiastic followers swarmed around Jesus, including his brother James, who now supported him fully. James joined his brother once Jesus' program was defined in terms of sacrifice, rather than exorcism or military revolt. Jesus' focus on sacrifice in the Temple—which had perplexed the militant "five thousand"—was exactly what brought James to his side.[3]

In the early autumn of 31 C.E., about 150 people would have been with Jesus as he crossed the border into Samaria. Some of his followers

---

3. Two things about James stand out from the principal sources from which we learn about him (Josephus and the historian Hegesippus from the second century): he never participated in armed revolt and never wavered in his loyalty to the Temple. He remained devoted to the practice of sacrifice and became famous for his piety in Jerusalem, where he was ultimately killed in 62 C.E. by a high priest who was jealous of the reverence in which he was held. For an assessment of these traditions, see *James the Just and Christian Origins:* Supplements to Novum Testamentum 98 (edited by B. D. Chilton and C. A. Evans; Leiden: Brill, 1999).

had been among the thousand in the wilderness; they still clung to the hope that his intention included direct action against Rome and its minions. For them he was Elijah, the preeminent prophet of resistance, despite his attempts to temper their zeal. Jesus was playing with fire and he knew it: these zealots could easily turn violent as he led them to proclaim the Kingdom of God in the holy city.

He conducted his throng through Samaria, pronouncing people with skin lesions pure on his way (Luke 17:11–19). They, too, were invited to join in the climactic sacrifice of all Israel which finally dissolved Jesus' ambivalence about Samaritans. Some Samaritans did join him, increasing his ramshackle ranks. Whole families would have been marching with him, a bedraggled caravan, singing psalms, asking for food in villages, sleeping around fires at night. Jesus had no regrets about not sweeping out of the highlands with his little army and attempting (no doubt with dismal results) to overthrow Antipas and take Galilee. He saw himself as on the verge of triumph, pressing on to offer the sacrifice at Sukkoth that would transform the world.

He moved quickly through Samaria with his ecstatic company of militant Galileans, crossing into Judea near Mizpah. The company camped that evening on the outskirts of Jerusalem. Perhaps in the dusk they could see the thick plume of smoke still rising up over Mount Zion from the last sacrifices of the day and hear the distant clamor of the carnival-like festivity of Sukkoth. They were poised to enter the city the following morning and trigger the prophecy of Zechariah, initiating the greatest sacrifice the world had ever seen.

In order to understand the perilous situation Jesus would confront the next day, we must leave him for the moment on the outskirts of the city, full of expectation, sharing a simple supper with his band of assorted followers. We look instead over the flat rooftops of Jerusalem, where the good Jews of the city are dining in their Sukkoth huts and, helped along by sweet new wine, reveling in tales of their ancestors' wanderings in

Sinai, in local gossip, and in the wealth of the harvest flowing into the city.

Toward the eastern edge of the city, the Antonia Fortress stood adjacent to the north wall of the Temple. The Antonia was Rome's center of command in Jerusalem. It housed a cohort of troops, around 480 men. Josephus offers a remarkable description of the place: "It was built upon a rock seventy-five feet high steep on all sides. . . . The rock was covered from its base upwards with smooth stones, both for ornament and so that anyone attempting to ascend or go down would slip off. . . . The interior resembled a palace in its spaciousness and arrangement because it was divided into apartments of every description and for every purpose, including porticos, baths and broad courtyards for the accommodations of the troops. . . . The whole design was that of a tower-form with other towers at each of the four corners; of which three turrets were seventy-five feet high, while that at the southeast angle rose to 105 feet, and so commanded a view of the whole area of the Temple. . . . For if the sacred place overlooked the city as a citadel, the Antonia overlooked the sacred place. . . ." (*Jewish War* 5 §§ 238–245).

Within the Antonia's elegant accommodations sits a forty-year-old man in a chair with scrolled arms. Addressed as "dominus" (lord) by the soldiers that serve him, he is dressed like a Roman soldier. But his tunic is immaculate, of the highest quality linen, cinched around the waist with an ornamented belt. His hair is cropped short, carefully styled and coifed with scented oil. His cheeks are smooth; a barber had shaved his face that morning with a straight razor and rubbed olive oil mixed with aloes into his skin. His appearance and demeanor are a far cry from Jesus and his bearded Galileans, smelling of campfires, sweat, spilled food and wine. But there is nothing soft or pampered about the Roman. He has killed with the short sword and dagger, the standard weapons of soldiers and officers alike, which are sheathed but near to hand, ready to be strapped on and holstered at each hip.

The man in the chair, of course, is Pontius Pilate, and he might have had a preoccupied air about him, for his career had taken a bad turn in

31 C.E., just as Jerusalem was gearing up for Sukkoth. Pilate had recently received word that his mentor in Rome, named Sejanus, had fallen out of favor with Emperor Tiberius. This apparently invincible regent, prefect of the nine-thousand-soldier Praetorian Guard, had become the target of ambivalent messages from the emperor himself. Writing to the Senate from his Villa of Jupiter on the island of Capri, Tiberius trenchantly criticized Sejanus' use of the legal system to make life miserable for anyone who opposed him in Rome, while flattering Sejanus personally. Speculation grew in Rome that Sejanus' days were numbered.

Sejanus' suddenly precarious position boded ill for Pilate. He was a protégé of Sejanus who, like him, had come up through the equestrian ranks. Both men were members of the subaristocratic class of warrior-bureaucrats, a virtual caste in Rome, similar to the *kshatriya* or warrior class in India. They came from wealthy households that had bought educated Greek slaves to tutor their children in arithmetic, Latin and Greek grammar, and the rich literature of the Hellenistic world. Knowledge of Greek made such men particularly attractive for foreign postings, and during their military training they had mastered strategy and accounting. They knew exactly how to mount a siege, provision troops on the march, and (perhaps most important) assure that all the taxes due Rome were collected. But they had not enjoyed the full elegance of learning and manners reserved for the nobility.

Pilate was not surprised that Tiberius had withdrawn his support for an underling who had flaunted his power. The emperor was notoriously querulous and changeable in his moods (and, rumor had it, promiscuous to a scarcely imaginable degree). Pilate could easily see how Tiberius had grown insecure about Sejanus' power, influence, and taste for conspiracy (see Josephus, *Antiquities* 18 § 182). It was common knowledge that Sejanus had used the Roman courts to carry out witch hunts against his enemies, bullying judges, with bribes and threats to their own lives, to convict and execute innocent men on spurious charges of treason. It was also well known that Sejanus particularly liked to slander Jews.

For a long time now, Sejanus had been pressing his luck, thinking, perhaps, that he was untouchable because of the crack soldiers he had quartered in Rome since 26 C.E., turning the city into a virtual police state. That same year Pilate had been posted as prefect to Judea and he still would have felt some loyalty to his senior colleague.

Judea was not a posting that Pilate would have preferred but, of course, he accepted it. Refusal would have meant the end of his career, or worse. Judea was no plum. The uppity Jews with their jealous deity, barbaric custom of circumcision, and inexplicable dietary laws were unpredictable and difficult to govern. And his own power was limited. His title as prefect gave him a lower administrative rank than a full governor; he was subservient to the Roman legate in Syria.

This administrative arrangement was in place before Pilate took office. From 4 B.C.E. until 6 C.E., Herod the Great's vain and dithering son Archelaus had governed Judea and Samaria for Rome. It had surprised no one but Archelaus himself when revolts broke out during his reign. Jews rioted in the Temple, attacked Roman soldiers, and, worst of all, from Rome's point of view, refused to pay their taxes. The revolts proved that Archelaus was an inept ruler, and Rome exiled him to the frontier post of Vienne in the south of Gaul (see Josephus, *Antiquities* 17 §§ 342–344). There he eked out his existence on a small pension in a rude land inhabited by barbarian Gauls in animal skins, who stank of the beer and wild boar they consumed in huge quantities.

The revolt of 4 B.C.E. was crushed by Varus, the Syrian legate of the time, who marched his army through Galilee to Jerusalem, reducing Sepphoris and other strongholds of the rebellion to rubble on his way (see Josephus, *Jewish War* 2 §§ 39–75). The Temple had been the hub of the insurrection, mounted by Galileans, Pereans, and Idumeans as well as Judeans. Although Varus merely imprisoned some of the revolutionaries, he crucified two thousand of the most prominent instigators, which vindicated Rome's honor. When the dust had settled and the blood had dried after yet another revolt in 6 C.E., the emperor determined that Judea and the Temple should be ruled more directly by Rome. He created the post of a local prefect, junior to the Syrian legate, but still carrying enough authority and pomp to exceed the reasonable ambition of most people from Rome's equestrian ranks.

The desire to maintain his authority, to reveal nothing of his own anxiety, would have been evident in Pilate's tone of voice as he dismissed his attendants.

"*Ite* (Go)," he said curtly.

They bowed to him, their eyes on the floor, straightened, turned smartly, and left the room. Pilate remained seated until they departed, then he rose from his chair and walked out to the balcony overlooking the city. The Jews were engaged in their usual madness. They hauled their bloody sacrifices to their invisible god, singing songs of praise to a deity that, as far as he could tell, had done little for them. Where was Yahweh's power and might? Who really ruled this land that he had supposedly given to them? Pilate could never understand why the Jews persisted in their loyalty to a god that had so obviously been humbled before the emperor, the true *Divi filius*.

And yet he had learned the hard way not to underestimate the fealty of Israelites toward their god. In the five years since he had taken up his post he made several mistakes by underestimating the fierce loyalty of Yahweh's subjects. Pilate knew that he now had to thread his way carefully in order to survive in his appointment. He had already undertaken some actions, in tune with the anti-Semitism Sejanus had encouraged in Rome, which could be perceived as provocative and used against him. If Sejanus toppled, then the *ius gladii* ("the law of the sword"), which Pilate had wielded against his hapless Jewish charges perhaps once too often, might well be brought to bear against him.

Not all Romans shared the anti-Semitic attitude of Pilate and Sejanus. As the story of the curing of the centurion's servant suggests, there were many Romans who admired Judaism and respected its teachings. In order to trace the politics in Jerusalem in 31 C.E., which would now determine the course of Jesus' life, we need to understand a little more about the history of Rome's perplexing relationship with Judaism.

Judaism was the only foreign religion in the empire which enjoyed the status of a *religio licita*—meaning that assemblies for Jewish worship were legal throughout the Roman world. Judaism's unique status in the empire was something of an anachronism. When Rome was still vying for power with Carthage in the western Mediterranean in 161 B.C.E., it had entered into an alliance of mutual defense with the Maccabees (see 1 Maccabees 8:23–32). At opposite ends of the Mediterranean, the ambitious Roman republic and the petty kingdom of Maccabean rebels could do little for one another; they had different spheres of influence. The arrangement was decorative, an attempt at mutual legitimation. As a gesture of the alliance Rome recognized "the religion of the Jews" as a legal form of worship.

By the dawn of the Common Era, synagogues all over the empire served a population of millions of Jews and many "God-fearers" like the centurion. Judaism was attractive to reflective men and women of his kind, because it offered an alternative to the comic-book polytheism that many Greco-Roman thinkers found simplistic, crude, and irrational. The idea of one God, a single principle of creation and morality, had enormous appeal, and among religions only Judaism could claim to have discovered it. Judaism's practices often offended the aesthetic sensibilities of the Hellenists; its ritual preoccupations with blood, cutting off foreskins, and avoiding some of the most delicious meat available impressed the classical mind as useless, ugly, and barbaric. Nonetheless, its elegant, monotheist philosophy was revered.

The ambivalence toward Judaism helps to explain the success of Christianity in the Greco-Roman world during the second century and later. By being able to offer the philosophy of Judaism, with only a reduced requirement of ritual purity (absent circumcision, for example, which Hellenists abhorred as a mutilation of the human form), Christianity competed extremely well with other religions, even when it was persecuted. Still, tensions remained between the classical adoration of human beauty and the Judaic prohibition of worshipping anyone or anything except the one God.

Rome had grown from an ambitious republic to a mighty empire, with "Syria Palaestina" (territorial Israel) under its yoke and the strange deal they had made with the Jews still in place. The scale of the empire's Jewish population and respect for its faith protected Judaism's status as a *religio licita*.

Still, it galled many Romans that Jews refused to bow down to the emperor or the gods of Rome. And the weird covenant of circumcision, the refusal of Jews to work on Shabbath, and their uncivilized diet aroused Roman suspicion. A good example of the animosity many Romans felt is provided by Cicero, the great Roman orator of the first century B.C.E. He defended a client in the year 59—an administrator who had illegally prevented Jews in Asia Minor from sending gold to their Temple—on the grounds that Judaism was a "barbaric superstition" (*Pro Flacco* 66–69).

What ultimately clinched the uneasy alliance between Jews and Rome was a peculiar arrangement within the Temple in Jerusalem. Although other citizens and subjects of the Roman Empire could be required on penalty of death to offer sacrifice (incense and wine) before the image of the emperor, Rome benevolently exempted Jews from this requirement, which would have meant breaking the Jewish commandment against idolatry. In exchange for the toleration of their beliefs, Jews accepted on Mount Zion sacrificial animals for which the emperor himself had paid. Accepting a sacrifice meant endorsing the one who offered it and, in effect, praying for him, so that this offering sealed Israel's alliance with Rome (see Josephus, *Jewish War* 2 § 409). By a brilliant stroke, Rome had made the Temple into a symbol of the emperor's majesty and its own authority.[4]

E ager to ingratiate himself with Tiberius, Pilate began his tenure in office with a stunning, symbolic attempt to reinforce Rome's claim on the Temple (see Josephus, *Jewish War* 2 §§ 169–174; *Antiquities* 18 §§ 55–59). The new prefect ordered some of his troops, both cavalry and infantry, away from the port city of Caesarea where he normally resided (thirty miles north of where Tel Aviv sits today) to winter in Jerusalem. There they would monitor the influx of pilgrims for Jewish feasts and demonstrate Rome's military control over Palestine.

It was routine for the prefect's troops to march to Jerusalem for the great feasts. But on the auspicious occasion of his appointment, Pilate had commanded them to enter the sacred city with a prominent display of the image of the emperor on their shields. He wanted to assert Rome's power and demonstrate his own gratitude and subservience to the emperor. To Jews this was simply—and aggressively—blasphemous. The image of the emperor who claimed to be God's son was known to be used in Roman worship, which posed no problem to Jews as long as that silly idea was not imposed on them. Introducing the emperor's image into the vicinity of the Temple, however, amounted to calculated, blatant idolatry.

Pilate ordered his army into Jerusalem under cover of night, obviously aware his gesture would not be appreciated. But he was unprepared for the vehement response from hundreds of outraged Jews who went up to

---

4. Rome guarded their symbolic hegemony over the Temple jealously. During the years after work on the Temple and Mount Zion was completed (from 63 C.E. on), rebellious actions against the army by factions of Jewish militants grew. But Nero only appointed Vespasian to head up the *Legio X Fretensis* and restore order to Syria Palaestina after the manager of the Temple, Eleazar, refused to accept offerings from non-Jews, the emperor included, and after the rebel attack on the Syrian governor, Cestius Gallus, during his attempt to restore order. All that was tantamount to a declarion of national revolt, and the eventual result was the Roman arson of the Temple and Jerusalem in 70 C.E.

Caesarea to protest to him personally. He gathered them in the city's stadium, ostensibly to hear their suit, ordered troops to surround them, and
threatened them with death if they didn't disperse. To his astonishment,
they offered their necks to the sword, rather than submit to idolatry. Pilate relented: the imperial insignia were returned to Caesarea. There
were limits even he had to observe: Rome had no interest in promoting
insurrection, and although the public execution of rebels might be an ed-
ifying spectacle from the prefect's own point of view, the slaughter of
pious innocents could only feed the simmering threat of revolt. Pilate's
retreat—however reluctant—was wise and made good strategic sense.

Despite the appearance he gave of acquiescing to the Jews' demands, Pilate was far from through with his campaign of symbolic domination. His next metaphorical onslaught on Jerusalem was better
planned and more ruthless (Josephus, *Jewish War* 2 § § 175–177; *Antiquities* 18 § § 60–62). In order to build a huge aqueduct into the city, Pilate confiscated the necessary funds from the Temple's treasury,
presumably sending in troops to seize the money from the sacred buildings that surrounded the sanctuary itself. He doubtless knew that he
would face violent opposition in Jerusalem for this deliberate and arrogant violation of the Temple's integrity. This time, rather than avoid the
inevitable confrontation, he ordered soldiers to dress as civilians—con-
cealing clubs beneath their cloaks. He traveled to Jerusalem, pretending
to want to hear the protesters from a tribunal (a raised wooden stand,
about five feet high with steps). Perhaps three hundred Jews had gathered and were shouting their indignation at his cynical abuse of sacred
wealth. Pilate appeared to listen to them and indicated he might accede
to their demands. Then he gave his troops the prearranged signal to attack (probably by raising his hand and pointing to the crowd). Many
demonstrators and bystanders were clubbed to death or crushed by their
own stampede.

Pilate had been emboldened in these arrogant demonstrations of
Roman power over Judea during the years between 26 C.E. to 30 C.E. by
Sejanus' ascendancy. Sejanus' anti-Semitism (see Philo's *Embassy to*

Gaius 159–161) provided just the environment Pilate needed in order to achieve in 30 what he had failed to bring off in 26. His deadly order for his soldiers to club the protesters near the Temple marked the height of his violence in the holy city.

Pilate's slaughter of the protesters in Jerusalem made a vivid impact on Jesus and those around him (Luke 13:1–3):

> *Yet some were present in the same time, reporting to him concerning the Galileans whose blood Pilate had mixed with their sacrifices. He replied and said to them, Do you think that these Galileans had been sinners beyond all Galileans, because they suffered these things? No, I say to you, but unless you all repent, you will similarly perish!*

To Jesus, Pilate was just one more Roman, a constant reminder of Israel's frailty until repentance opened the way for God's Kingdom. News of Pilate's cruelty only hardened his resolve to make the climactic sacrifice for Sukkoth and alerted him to the danger he would face.

He was prepared to face danger, perhaps even death in Jerusalem, but he showed no specific awareness of the deadly combination that would shortly confront him. Herod Antipas presented a known quantity of mortal animus, and Pilate was a predictable—if merciless—agent of Rome. But no one could have guessed, least of all Jesus, that their forces would be brought to bear in an extraordinary coalition of enmity directed against him by Caiaphas, high priest of the Temple.

ELEVEN

"A Cave of Thugs"

Caiaphas has already put in an oblique, anonymous appearance under Barnabas' envious gaze at the high priest's turban during the Sukkoth sacrifice of 24 C.E. Now it is time to become better acquainted with the man who would become pivotal in determining Jesus' fate. It is necessary to understand the role of the high priest and how Caiaphas was positioned vis à vis the politics of Rome to grasp fully what awaited Jesus as he prepared for his Zecharian sacrifice. Indeed, we can appreciate the political forces that were to buffet him in a way Jesus himself could not.

Caiaphas would have been winding up his day of overseeing the Temple's operation and politicking with the most important people in Jerusalem as Pilate brooded in the Antonia over Sejanus' insecure standing in Rome. Having bathed before dinner, Pilate retired to his elegant apartments in the Antonia. He might have dined alone. Wives were not allowed along on the prefect's posting, but for Pilate that was probably no great hardship; he had privileged access to the brothel adjacent to the bathhouse inside the Antonia. His sexual proclivities are not a matter of record, but young men and women, even children, were available to him. In any event, he was a trained warrior, a hardened servant of the empire, not the kind of man to feel loneliness.

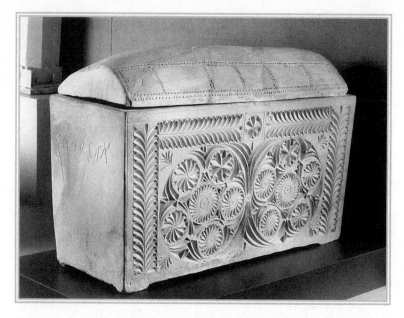

THE OSSUARY OF CAIAPHAS

Caiaphas' standing in his exalted role is marked by the care and devotion attested by his burial. In a major archeological discovery in 1990, a bulldozer took the top off a cave half a mile south of Mount Zion, uncovering a mausoleum. An adult,

Caiaphas, on the other hand—as we know from the evidence of his carefully crafted tomb, uncovered by accident in 1990—had a wife and at least four children. Some died while they were still very young, victims of disease or the food poisoning that in this pretechnological age was common among meat eaters in cities.

Caiaphas was preoccupied with the logistics of sacrifice during the stringent ritual routine of Sukkoth. His staff had swollen to handle the sacrifices streaming into the Temple. The high priest spent much of his time directly or indirectly engaged in the performance of the *zebach shelamim,* the sacrifice of sharings. Each day hundreds of beasts were inspected, tethered, and readied for slaughter. The rota of levites, junior priests, and priests did much of that tedious work, but the actual slaugh-

even a short adult, could not have stood erect inside the cave, but a pit had been dug near its entrance to allow mourners to stand while tending to their dead and praying. Corpses were laid out on a shelf, and after the flesh had decomposed, the bones were gathered and stored. Bone storage for the anonymous poor was in a pit dug in the cave's floor, while the bones of wealthier, prominent people were kept in small limestone ossuaries placed in the shafts that ran outward from the central cave like spokes.

One such ossuary had the name "Caiaphas" carved roughly into its side and back. A coin discovered in the cave is dated 42/43 C.E. (during the reign of Herod Agrippa I). If the ossuary were for Caiaphas the high priest, he would have been about 60 when he died (c. 46): and, inside the ossuary marked with Caiaphas' name, the bones of a man aged 60 years old were indeed found, along with the bones of an adult female, two infants, a small child, and a young adult. Death apparently came to them all from natural causes. The ossuary's elegant carving distinguishes it from most ossuaries of that place and period. It is carved with a pattern of five floral designs, for the most part in spirals, arranged around a central, spiraling flower. The palm design that surrounds the circles on Caiaphas' ossuary picks up a motif in the Temple's decoration. Placed in the tunnel to the south of the cave, his ossuary was in fact oriented to face the Temple. His status and his connection to the Temple are attested by this find, and the ossuary is an eloquent witness of Judaism in the first century: a vibrant religion, centered on the Temple and passionately devoted to the worship of God through sacrifice in that holy place. (Photograph courtesy Israel Antiquities Authority)

ter and the offering of the animals was handled by a highly trained permanent staff of priests.

Each animal was trussed and hung by its hind legs from a rope tied to iron rings fitted into stone pillars on the north side of the altar. Slaughtering the animals properly was crucial. The knife cut to the throat had to be quick and clean. From the severed carotid artery the animal's heart rhythmically pumped out the blood that priests caught in special vessels of bronze, silver, and gold (Tamid 3:4–5 in the Mishnah). Expert levitical butchers worked with precision and at great speed; they skinned, carved, and salted the carcass, and meted out portions to those who had offered the beast, the priests, and God himself. (Such carefully calibrated customs and procedures established the expertise for what we now know as kosher butchery.) The basics of the butchery were already laid out in the book of Leviticus, which specifies that the person who offered an animal personally killed it (1:5). By the first century, however, slaughter was almost always a priestly prerogative. The meat was laid on the altar or placed in pots. The whole process was labor intensive; in the case of an ox, twenty-four priests were required for the offering (Mishnah, Yoma 2:7). Each action was carried out according to the strict prescriptions of the priests' own traditions and the not always helpful interventions of groups such as the Pharisees.

As the offerings were brought to sacrifice, Caiaphas stood at command central on the top step of the Sanctuary, behind the west side of the altar. The Sanctuary, with its huge doors that were opened during the day, towered behind him. It was made of white stone and rose to a height of 150 feet (Josephus, *The Jewish War* 5 § § 207). The Temple was a solar shrine, oriented precisely to the east, so that on the Day of Atonement, and only on that day, the rays of the sun rising over the Judean Hills shot through the Sanctuary doors into the Holy of Holies, the empty chamber where God himself resided. The sun lit the mammoth tapestry—eighty-two and a half feet high and thirty feet wide, of indigo, scarlet, purple, and embroidered with stars—that guarded God's chamber (see Josephus, *The Jewish War* 5 § 211–214, 219). Only Caiaphas was allowed to enter this room and then only on the Day of Atonement. It had once housed the Ark of the Covenant, which the Egyptians had stolen during the reign of the Pharaoh Shishak (1 Kings 14:25–26) but since the tenth century B.C.E., vacancy had been the mark of the divine presence.

Caiaphas still felt the reverberations of sanctity and awe that had come from entering that sacred space on the Day of Atonement, prior to Sukkoth. He enjoyed the cool air coming from the cavernous Sanctuary at his back. From his post on its steps he could see the ornamented interior of the tightly enclosed Court of the Israelites, which was surrounded by a massive wall of white stone, sixty feet high (Josephus, *The Jewish War* 5 § 196). There were huge gates built into the wall, and through them Caiaphas could see portions of the Temple's enormous South Court, where Israelites and other visitors congregated, and its almost equally expansive North Court, where the cavalcade of animals was tethered, trussed, and slaughtered.

The altar itself was enormous, according to Josephus, a square structure of unhewn stones, twenty-three feet high and seventy-five feet in both length and width (*Jewish War* 5 § 225; somewhat smaller, according to the Mishnah, Middot 3:1). Its corners were decorated with large stone horns, so that looking down on it from above, as God did, it had some resemblance to the head or face of the beasts it consumed. The altar was the center of the Temple and the focus of much of Caiaphas' attention. He was the master of what we can think of as an incredibly complex barbecue pit.

Despite the altar fire's huge size, it had to be carefully managed by the priests for the different tasks of burning, cooking, and parching. Getting right the thousands of sacrifices offered at the Temple each day at Sukkoth involved not only the physical effort of hauling and slaughtering the beasts, but stamina and culinary expertise at the altar in the thick of heat and smoke.

Around the pit, priests skillfully shifted pieces of flesh with hooks and long-handled forks. With ornate, ceramic shovels they heaped frankincense on smaller glowing piles of fig-wood embers inside the altar. They roasted wheat and barley near coals at the edges of the blazing timbers. Blood, wine, and olive oil were poured on hot parts of the fire, so they whooshed up, combining with the smell of roasting meat and popping fat to create what the Torah called the *"reach nichoach,"* the aroma of pleasure, to dilate Yahweh's nostrils.

Priests twisted off the heads of sacrificial doves, the meager offerings of the poor. Blood spattered onto their vestments as they sprinkled it on the altar and then threw the bodies into the fire for the flames to consume. For the *olah,* or burnt offering (which was entirely consumed by the flames), they skewered meat on their long forks and flicked the hunks of flesh with the accuracy of archers into the hottest parts of the fire, making sure the blazing timbers of oak, pine, and broom entirely consumed both meat and fat (Tamid 2:4–5 in the Mishnah).

To God was given the sweetmeats and fat from each beast, especially the kidneys and fatty lobes extending from the liver, and the *alyah,* the fat tail, which Leviticus prescribed should be taken right off to the backbone (Leviticus 3:3–5, 9). This *touchus* was Yahweh's special delicacy. There were "wave" sacrifices and "heave" sacrifices, priestly portions of meat merely lifted in ceremonial fashion in front of the fire so that the priests could consume them later with their families at home. They conveyed these choice cuts to the extensive warehouses, which Caiaphas also managed through his staff, inside the warrenlike complex of the Temple courts. All the while the Pharisees looked on, ready to pounce at any moment if they thought correct procedure was being violated. They were known to shower hapless priests with derision and scorn, and even to pelt them with the lemons carried in the Sukkoth procession.

But when Caiaphas was in the zone, fully engaged in the sacrificial act, he hardly noticed the Pharisees yelling out their useless advice. The fire was alive, and different every day, speaking to Caiaphas in a distinct voice, disclosing to him its mystery and moods, changing with the seasons, the sacred time of the festivals. The construction of the fire and the way the priests moved around it, feeding it offerings, had its own sacred design. The pit and the choreography of sacrifice were inscribed in Caiaphas' memory and imagination in much the same way that Jesus' visionary world was constructed around the architecture of the Throne. Caiaphas could offer sacrifice as frequently as he liked (according to the Mishnah, Yoma 1:2), or delegate his routine duties through the *sagan* (his chief of staff). But whether personally or through his surrogates, he was master of the holiest place on earth.

The prestige of the highest office in Israel was incalculable, but so were its burdens. Caiaphas watched with relief as the altar fires were banked down and the various doors of the Temple shut (all under the watchful eyes of the loitering Pharisees, might the Lord strike down the most annoying of them!). His bones ached, and his face, clothes, and skin were permeated with greasy smoke and charred incense from standing in smoke for hours on end. He turned from the fire now, from the clanking of the priests with their rakes, the snap and sizzle of fat-drenched wood, the stench of soot and charcoal and grease. He looked over the Judean hills bathed in golden light by the late afternoon sun. This had been among his longest days, and he silently thanked God it was over.

He would have arisen before dawn, feeling a little bloated from his diet, persistently meat-rich since he had broken his fast after the Day of Atonement. Now, with Sukkoth in full swing, the wealthy were bringing their bounty to the altar. He had been feasting on oxen fattened all season on grain and grass, washed down with rich Cypriot wine. He relished the wine, as God commanded, but he was under no illusions. The Cypriots were among many in a long line of malcontents who could coalesce at any time to challenge the Temple's status quo. There were also the Syrians, Galileans, and tight little groups of Essenes from Judea and from as far away as Egypt, all of them now converging on the city, climbing the steps up the holy mount, pressing with their offerings toward the one point that to them was the apogee of pilgrimage and sacrifice, the one place where true offering was possible. They failed to understand that the Temple would endure and thrive only if the high priest succeeded in appeasing the Romans. What did these malcontents expect? Was the Temple not more magnificent now than it had ever been in the past, even in the days of Solomon? What was collusion with Rome when the altar was served as it should be and the sacrifices continued unabated? And the nonsense he had to endure! For many days now he had been embroiled in an endless argument about where dung did and did not belong.

When Caiaphas heard the rumors of Sejanus' tottering position in Rome, he had acted decisively, taking advantage of Pilate's relative weakness by getting him to agree to two moves that tightened Caiaphas' grip on the Temple and, therefore, on the city.

First, Caiaphas had expelled the Sanhedrin from their special room and place of honor called the Chamber of Hewn Stone, within the Court of the Israelites. The Sanhedrin, dominated by the pesky Pharisees, were the seventy-some member council of the most important Jews in the city, who advised Caiaphas and Pilate on cultic and civic matters. They were "exiled," as their own recollection of this expulsion put it, to Chanuth, the market on the Mount of Olives (according to the Babylonian Talmud in Shabbath 15a; Sanhedrin 41a; Abodah Zarah 8b). Caiaphas was now freed from having to consult constantly with other religious leaders, as custom dictated; he would act with virtual autonomy.

The Sanhedrin had plenty of room on the Mount of Olives because Caiaphas had also ordered the vendors at Chanuth, who sold the beasts and birds to be offered at the altar, to set up shop within the Great Court of the Temple. And this, his second move, was what had embroiled him in what was turning into an epic argument about dung.

The offering of animals meant dealing with their waste; any priest knew that. In the past, the custom had been to keep their excrement out of the southern portion of the Great Court (see Philo, *De specialibus legibus* 1 § 74; Josephus, *Antiquities* 5 § 224; Middot 4:6 in the Mishnah). Animals were sold in Chanuth, led up to the north side of the altar, and killed there. If they defecated on their way to the knife, the bucket brigade of levites with shovels, brooms, and purifying pails would instantly descend upon the waste, whisking it away.

There were problems with this method, however, as James during his sacrifice in the Temple in 16 C.E. and countless other pilgrims had realized. The animal bought in Chanuth might be injured on its way to the Temple or, for one reason or another, fail to meet the exacting criteria of the priest at the north gate. Besides, it was hard to know which animal was yours in the confusion of herds of bellowing beasts and swarms of shouting, gesticulating priests (many of whom were fresh on duty from the rota, and as confused as everyone else about what was going on). If the wind was blowing wrong, you were likely to be blinded by thick gales of fatty, pungent smoke in any case.

In a bold stroke, Caiaphas had found a way to assure that your offering would be accepted for sacrifice, because you would buy it in the Temple itself. You could lead the animal yourself to the officiating levites and priests, lay hands on it all you liked, and know it should be yours through each step in the sacrificial process.

But from the point of view of the Pharisees and most Jews, trade on the southern side of the Great Court was anathema. Purses were not permitted in the Temple, according to the Pharisees' teaching (in the Mishnah, see Berakhot 9:5), but in order to buy an animal in the Great Court you needed money, and that made at least part of the Temple into a marketplace, with the clanging of the big bronze and silver coins into metal receptacles, and endless, excited haggling. This appalled the Pharisees, who insisted that the act of sacrifice should be a noncommercial encounter between the people of Israel and God.

Caiaphas could see their point. But his priestly backers were solidly behind him. They applauded this bold extension of their authority over Temple operations. They benefited from the power and prestige that controlling sacrifice gave them, and from the considerable profit of managing the sale of the animals. His reform was as beneficial in practical terms as it was sacrificially elegant.

Caiaphas turned from contemplating the buttery light on the bare hills. The thought of all he was doing for his caste and his Temple gave him pleasure, despite the trouble involved; after all, Yahweh himself had commanded Israel to support its priests. He supposed that it was typical that the arguments over his actions had degenerated in recent days into the debate about dung and where it did or did not belong. Couldn't his opponents appreciate that he had restricted the vendors to the colonnades that Herod the Great had built around the Great Court on its southern side? Didn't the prospect of cloven-hoofed beasts defecating all over Herod's philo-Roman architecture appeal to them? In any case, what was the difference between animals defecating in the colonnades or on the pavement inside the north gate?

He directed his gaze toward the colonnades across the expanse of the Great Court, which he could see through the gates in the Court of the Israelites. From his perch above the altar platform he could see that it did look a bit shabby over there. Even the fanatical shoveling and scrubbing of the levites hadn't quite eradicated the barnyard appearance and smell coming from what had been a choice spot, out of the sun, for Pharisaic discussion and debate. Colonnades were much more difficult to clean than open pavement. He hadn't quite anticipated the mess that would be involved, especially as made by the birds. Still, on balance, the arrangement worked.

He walked down the steps of the Sanctuary and across the Court of the Israelites to his private room off the Sanctuary, where attendants helped him unwrap his turban. He stepped behind a curtain and peeled off his vestments, made from the finest white linen from Pelusium in Egypt (Mishnah Yoma 3:7). The attendants were attired more simply in tunics, pants, head coverings, and cinctures (Mishnah Yoma 7:5). He himself removed from its special compartment his sceptered staff for his walk home. He really didn't like anyone else touching it, especially the priests who might succeed him. It was his rod and his staff, the emblem of his power, topped by a precious stone of seven facets that symbolized his capacity to remove sin by his sacrificial actions (see Zechariah 3:4–9).

Caiaphas washed and changed into perfumed clothing. In addition to all the strain of Sukkoth, the continuing arguments about placing the vendors and sending the Sanhedrin away had exhausted him. As gambits to enhance high priestly control over the Temple, they were deft maneuvers, but they involved a degree of risk. He had not been notably inclined to gamble before, but the rumors about Sejanus had emboldened him. Still, the objections to the arrangements had been loud and vociferous, and Caiaphas was all too conscious of the soldiers staring down from the Antonia Fortress over the persistent argument he had occasioned.

The energy his people devoted to argument never ceased to amaze him. Let them lift the heave offerings and wave offerings and grill meat in front of scorching flames from dawn till dusk. Then let them see if they felt like yelling about dung! The river of sacrifice should flow through their veins as it did through his, the blood of the animals that was now like his own blood. For Caiaphas, flesh and blood, sinew and smoke, were the stuff of God. They were for him what Spirit was to Jesus. He was immersed in them, saturated by them. They were divine.

He walked through the streets with his entourage. The good people of Jerusalem greeted him respectfully, bowed to him as he strode along with the preoccupied air of a proud man bent to the service of God. He made his way to the high priest's palace to the west of the Temple, a magnificent perquisite of his appointment. The entourage bid him good night, addressing him as "My Lord High Priest." He passed through an ornate gate, walked across a stone courtyard, and entered the opulent mansion, built from the distinctive white limestone that is still used for building in Jerusalem today.

He had a personal staff of eight servants, all of whom were levites. When he entered the house, he slipped off his sandals and sat on a wooden bench. One of his staff washed his feet in a bronze bowl of warm water and dried them with a linen towel.

Dinner with his wife and surviving children was a comfort, and beautifully served by the levitical staff. He might have dined on the ox meat that was plentiful now, perhaps served up with lentils and onions, herbs and spices. There was bread, of course, and more of the rich Cypriot wine. He blessed the Lord of Israel for the provision of this supper, but he would not have seen this repast as Jesus saw meals with his disciples. Sharing food with another Israelite was a blessing, but the greatest moment of purity for Caiaphas was not celebrated by feeding one's belly. He was the peerless master of ceremonies in the spectacle in which Yahweh took the deepest delight, and he knew what it was to stand each day at the center of the purest place on earth.

The Temple's incalculable power and wealth, presided over by Caiaphas, his daily enactment of sacred rituals that kept Israel in a privileged relationship to God, have their distant, quite diminished corollaries today in the Vatican and the pope. In Judea, Caiaphas would have been revered somewhat as the pope is today by most Polish Catholics. To Jewish Galileans, Caiaphas was just another high priest, although he had been in power for thirteen years, an extraordinary achievement in itself. High priests served at the prefect's pleasure, and most served in the post only one year.

Jesus' attitude toward Caiaphas would have been ambivalent. He had an innate respect for the high priesthood and the sacrificial purpose it served, but Caiaphas' Judean background, his privileged family pedigree in Jerusalem (which had landed him the job), and his easy contact with wealthy merchants and the Roman administration undoubtedly made Jesus skeptical of the high priest's integrity. That kind of skepticism was why constant scrutiny of the high priest by the Sanhedrin had been a valued custom.

But Jesus would have been unaware of the extent of Caiaphas' collusion with Pilate, and it was the relationship between the prefect and the high priest that would land the provincial rabbi in grave danger. Nowhere is the cooperation between them clearer than in the arrangement Caiaphas had acceded to regarding the custody of his festal vestments.

Pilate had insisted that the vestments be stored not within one of the rooms adjacent to the Sanctuary but in the Antonia. As a result, on holy days, the high priest had to request his robes from this den of iniquity. This setup allowed Pilate to symbolically rub the nose of the Jews in the power of Rome. It also had an immediately practical side (as was generally the case with the Roman administration), allowing Pilate to make sure that the high priest had all the festal arrangements (especially for security) well in hand before releasing the garments (see Josephus, *Antiquities* 18 §§ 90–95). He wanted to know in advance that there was no trace of revolt, nothing anti-Roman in the great festivities of Sukkoth, Passover, and Weeks.

For many Jews, this was an affront to their autonomy of worship on Mount Zion. As Pilate's collaborator, Caiaphas had apparently simply accepted the humiliating arrangement of Roman custody of the vestments, despite the shame it naturally would have caused any high priest. Caiaphas cooperated with Pilate in order to extend the influence of the priestly class by centralizing its control of the Temple and its wealth in his own hands. By doing so, the vast building project to increase the Temple's monumental splendor, begun under Herod the Great, continued unabated. He was a uniquely successful high priest precisely because he knew better than to fight largely symbolic battles with Pilate over where his vestments were stored.

The Zecharian prophecy that Jesus was determined to fulfill had promised that never again would there be a trader or merchant near the Sanctuary. This had probably meant no more to Jesus when he had set out on his pilgrimage than the general assurance that his Galilean cohorts would not be required to purchase their offerings from vendors specifically authorized by the priests. But now, without knowing it, he was coming to Jerusalem at exactly the time that the Temple itself had been turned into a marketplace.

His camp rose before dawn, gathered their belongings, and started out for the holy city. As they approached what is now called the Damascus Gate into Jerusalem, their ranks were swelled by sympathizers and curiosity seekers. As usual, Jesus was primed for contention. He was years away from the ease of Capernaum, and many meals short of the hospitality he had enjoyed there. His paunch was gone. He was fit, lean, his face etched by sun, a harsh regime, and the rigors of his meditative practice. He felt filled with a sense of purpose and direction. The trek through Galilee and Samaria with his rambunctious, eager followers had spurred him on. He was returning to Jerusalem with exactly the kind of support he had lacked when he had been harried from the Temple in 24 C.E.

He anticipated resistance from the priests when he pressed the issue of Galileans being able to offer sacrifice on their own terms, without intermediaries. But he was fed up with them. Was it so unreasonable that Galileans wanted to know the animals that they offered were theirs, acquired either by their own sweat or honest trade? Couldn't the priests see that Israelites were sick of Chanuth, where the sharp traders routinely cheated them? And why couldn't they grasp that ordinary Jews wanted with all their hearts to be able to lay hands on their own beasts prior to slaughter?

Jesus was not the first rabbi to insist upon what he saw as the correct procedure for sacrifice. Rabbi Hillel had taught that sacrificial animals should have hands laid on them by their owners and then be given over to priests for slaughter. Worshippers offered their own property to express the direct link between God and Israel, and touching them was a statement of ownership. The followers of Rabbi Shammai, however, insisted that animals could be given directly to priests for slaughter, without the laying on of hands. The debate raged between the two rabbinic schools. The Talmud recounts an abrupt about-face by a wealthy Shammai disciple, who was so struck by the rectitude of Hillel's position that he had herders drive three thousand sheep and goats into the Temple (see the Babylonian Talmud, Besah 20a, b; Tosefta Chagigah 2.11; Jerusalem Talmud, Chagigah 2.3 and Besah 2.4). They were free for the taking. Anyone who wanted to could lay hands on the beasts before they were slaughtered.

As Jesus and his group passed under the arch of the city's gate, they were swept up by the festive parade of other pilgrims on their way to the Temple. The morning sun glowed pink on the white stone of the city's buildings. The air was crisp and clean. Throngs of people waved willow branches and palm fronds, with lemons and sprigs of myrtle tied to them, all for the Sukkoth celebration of fertility. They marched and danced along, singing psalms and giving praise to the Lord. Many pilgrims unconnected with his movement had heard of Jesus and felt a sense of joy and anticipation as they fell in with his company. They even commandeered an ass for Jesus (Matthew 21:1–9; Mark 11:1–10; Luke

19:28–38; John 12:12–16), fired with the prospect of what this Sukkoth sacrifice could mean.

That act was an evocative symbol, which further whipped up the enthusiasm of the crowds. The book of Zechariah itself promised the triumph of a just and gentle king, riding on an ass, and this Davidic rabbi fulfilled the prophecy (Zechariah 9:9). The processional march became a delirious event. The crowds shouted their expectation of the Kingdom of God, which they knew was Jesus' focal concern, and they sang out that expectation in Davidic, messianic terms (Mark 11:10):

> Blessed is the coming kingdom of our father David,
>   Hoshannah in highest heights!

His supporters threw willow branches and palm fronds in his path, piled some of their own clothes on the beast for him to sit on, and laid more of their clothing in front of him, a makeshift carpet for a peasant prophet, a threadbare king.

The procession brought him to the steps of Mount Zion. He bathed and made himself ready for the ascent. It had been fifteen years since he had climbed the steep steps with his family, and the torches flamed and hissed as he recollected they had long ago in the dark chute of the stairwell. He and his brethren sang wild songs of praise. He came off the stairs into the dazzling light, the wide open space of the Great Court ringed with its porticos sheathed in glittering gold. His eyes adjusted to light—and what he saw there appalled him.

The vendors were busy transacting business on large stone tables within the colonnades around the great Court. Tethered cattle, sheep, and goats bellowed and bleated in fright; birds fluttered, squawked, and moaned the lament of doves in their cages. In the Temple where Jesus had intended to enact the vision of Zechariah, he found a direct contradiction of Zechariah's prophecy. He felt a catastrophic collision between what he had expected to find and what was actually there. How could he and his followers take part in the final, apocalyptic sacrifice predicted by Zechariah in a Temple that had been defiled? They swept away from the holy precincts, down the steps, pushing against the crowd. He needed a place to regroup, and he found one in Bethany (Mark 11:11), where he stayed with Miriam and Martha and plotted his next move.

Zechariah clearly condemned the presence of the vendors. Jesus knew he needed to clear them from the Great Court for his vision of climactic sacrifice to be enacted. He wanted to ensure that his Galilean followers would climb Mount Zion with their *own* offerings, not merely with *mammon* with which to buy the priests' produce.

Three days after his initial visit to the Temple he returned, after walking from Bethany early in the morning with thirty male followers. By advance agreement, he met others at Zion's immersion pools. Most of his supporters, 150 to 200 men, had already taken up positions inside the Great Court. The Temple police and the priests could not have known anything was amiss, because they almost completely failed to react. Jesus' group was large, but large groups often came to the Temple at feast times and there were already about two thousand people in the Temple for the *tamid,* the morning sacrifice which would have just taken place. Jesus and his group surged up the stairs and into the southern portion of the Great Court, at the end of the Temple complex opposite from the Roman garrison. Only then did it become unmistakably plain to the Temple authorities that this eager crowd was an army of zealots.

Jesus shouted: "Is it not written that: my house shall be called a house of prayer for all the Gentiles? But you have made it a cave of thugs" (Mark 11:17; Matthew 21:13; Luke 19:46; John 2:16). It was the prearranged signal to act. His followers moved in squads. They overturned the vendors' tables, released the birds, untethered animals and drove them out the ceremonial gate on the west side of the Temple. The vendors yelled and shouted in outrage and horror. Some were pushed and dragged out of the Temple by Jesus' followers. Others were beaten, punched, and kicked. There was at least one murder of a vendor by Barabbas (Mark 15:7), one of the many violent militants who had attached themselves to Jesus. The Temple police were hopelessly outnumbered. Not even the Roman garrison reacted, blindsided by the speed with which the raid was mounted, struck at its targets, and dissolved among what soon became the confused and scattering throngs inside the Temple.

From his privileged place on the steps of the Sanctuary, Caiaphas at first was aware only of the extra noise of argument. Then came the sounds of fighting, cries of pain, outrage, and fear, the bellowing panic of animals, and the crash of stone tables on the pavement. Through the sight lines of the gates in the high wall around the Court of the Israelites, he could see something of the fracas swirling in the Great Court, but he had to wait for his staff to report on the scale of this embarrassing disaster in the midst of the celebration of Sukkoth. Sacrifice itself was interrupted for a time (Mark 11:16), and some of Jesus' levitical followers might even have ripped knives from the hands of priests to slay their own offerings.

Caiaphas knew instantly that he faced the most direct challenge to his authority in his career. He looked toward the Antonia Fortress, where the prefect he had reassured about the festive arrangements resided with his troops during major feasts. The soldiers had grown accustomed to the noise and confusion in the Temple, and were slow to appreciate the violence of the mob in the part of the Great Court furthest from their post. Caiaphas was loath to call for Pilate's help and thus to make an open admission that the situation was out of hand.

As he purified the Temple of merchants, Jesus must have felt an overwhelming sense of accomplishment. All the tension that had accumulated during the years spent on the run from Antipas went into this stormy, calculated outburst. His longstanding dream of pure sacrifice in the place that meant more to him than anywhere else on earth was now being realized. For a brief time, he was a master of the Temple. He thundered in his triumph (John 2:19), "You are destroying this Temple, and . . . I will raise it up!"

He and his followers fled before the Temple police could summon reinforcements and the garrison could deal with them; Jesus' occupying mob would have been no match against eighty trained Roman soldiers. The Galileans dispersed into the city. Jesus, with James, the Twelve, and a few others, hustled back to Bethany. They reentered the house of Miriam and Martha exhilarated: they had purified the "cave of thugs."

TWELVE

At the Tomb
of the Dead

Rabbi Jesus could no longer contain or redirect the messianic expectations he had ignited. He had provoked a rabble into a raid in the Temple more violent than the protest Hillel had encouraged, and his rioting mob was fueled by a prophetic zeal that neither Caiaphas nor Pilate could prudently ignore.

When Jesus cited Jeremiah 7:11, equating Caiaphas' arrangement in the Temple with "a cave of thugs," he implicitly invoked Jeremiah's prophecy of the Temple's destruction (see Matthew 21:13; Mark 11:17; Luke 19:46 with Jeremiah 7:1–15). That use of the prophecy could easily be distorted into the claim that Jesus wanted to see the Temple destroyed. Caiaphas and his supporters encouraged precisely that distortion in the days and weeks that followed the riot, to whip up opposition to Jesus in Jerusalem. After 70 C.E., when the Romans actually burned down the Temple, Christians also twisted Jesus' words and deeds into a prophecy of destruction. That reading is perpetuated by scholars who, unaware of the practical realities of power in the Temple and the rabbinic precedent for Jesus' actions, turn Jesus into an opponent of sacrifice altogether. But the force of Jesus' message concerned what the Temple should be, not its demolition.

After Jesus' raid in the Temple, Jerusalem held its breath, waiting for Caiaphas' response. A forbidding stillness settled over the city. Caiaphas had a police force at his disposal for security in the Temple, but it was not strong enough to control the violent reaction he might face if he tried to arrest Jesus by sending a squad into Jerusalem or its outskirts. For the moment, the high priest was forced to seethe in silence. For all the splendor of his turban, cincture, vestments, and scepter, he was impotent in the face of Jesus and his Galilean mob. Caiaphas knew he couldn't act on his own. Large numbers of Jews had opposed his moving the vendors into the Temple in the first place, and the force behind the sympathy for Jesus' occupation now appalled Caiaphas. His only recourse was to turn to Pilate. He sent a message through one of his levitical servants that he wanted to see the prefect, acutely aware of how bad he looked after the riot in the Temple. After Jesus' raid on the Temple, they met in Pilate's hearing room in the Antonia, where the priestly vestments were stored.

Pilate would have been seated in his favorite chair, surrounded by the insignia of Rome: a bust of the emperor and ornamental shields bearing a medallion of the emperor's image welded onto the bronze. What the prefect could not display in the Temple, he could flaunt within the walls of his own fortress. Decorations on the walls portrayed classical motifs of naked gods and goddesses in various postures of cavorting and intrigue. Caiaphas entered the chamber with distaste, but he was nothing if not a pragmatist. He knew what he needed to do in order to maintain the level of privilege he and his fellow priests enjoyed and—above all—to assure the security and integrity of the Temple.

The high priest stood while Pilate remained seated. *"Shelama,"* Caiaphas said in Aramaic.

"Khaire (Hail)," Pilate replied in the Koine Greek that was the language of empire. When Alexander had conquered the Mediterranean basin and the Near East in the fourth century B.C.E., he gave his world and the rulers who succeeded him a common tongue of government and culture.

Caiaphas' knowledge of Greek would have been too clumsy for diplomatic purposes; he had brought along his own interpreter, a levite fluent in Koine, and persisted in speaking Aramaic during this vital conversation. By waiting for the translation of what Pilate said, although he understood it clearly enough, Caiaphas made himself time to reflect on the best approach to each issue as it emerged.

He outlined the situation to Pilate. His Temple police had managed to arrest Barabbas and were holding him in one of the priestly mansions. Caiaphas asked Pilate to take Barabbas into Roman custody, because continuing to keep him under the guard of the Temple police could provoke an ugly confrontation between the priestly retainers and the mob that had joined in Jesus' raid. With that request, Caiaphas was also making it clear that he regarded what had happened in the Temple as going beyond incidental violence and common murder. Barabbas had acted as part of a staged revolt that posed a threat to public order and therefore to Rome's rule. Caiaphas wanted military reinforcements from the prefect's own troops for the Temple police, in case there was further insurrection. And he took the opportunity to identify the instigator of the whole problem, to request that Pilate's troops arrest Jesus for disturbing the peace of the Temple.

Pilate must have conveyed to Caiaphas that he viewed Jesus' actions as an internal problem to be settled among Jews (a position also later taken by a proconsul named Gallio when synagogue elders invited him to arrest and judge Paul; Acts 18:12–17). Pilate did agree, however, to detain Barabbas, and assigned Caiaphas two dozen troops from his ancillary forces to help police the Temple. These were not Romans but mercenaries, a ragtag mix of Jews, Syrians, and Nabateans.

Caiaphas was uneasy when he exited the Antonia. Prior to the feast of Sukkoth, he had assured Pilate of the security of Mount Zion, when he asked for the release of the high-priestly vestments from their custody in the Antonia. He had been so utterly outmaneuvered by Jesus that no explanations, no matter how skillful, could successfully allay Pilate's doubts that Caiaphas had the situation under control.

Pilate's reinforcements at least ensured that Jesus did not enter the

Temple again. His raid had made its point, but in the months afterward it did not change the way sacrifice was conducted on Mount Zion. Yet aside from reinforcing the Temple police, Pilate was content to let Caiaphas dangle. Why should he underwrite the machinations of a high priest who had misjudged his power in an attempt to extend it? Pilate needed Caiaphas but, for the moment, he had no interest in increasing the high priest's power or influence.

In the aftermath of the Temple raid, Jesus and his disciples remained near Jerusalem in the home of Miriam and Martha. The rabbi did not dare return to Mount Zion or even enter the city. He had put pressure on Caiaphas, but for the time being, the merchants remained where the high priest wanted them. The exhilaration Jesus had felt when he returned to Bethany was fading, and in its place was disappointment that his attempt to seize control of the sacrificial process had failed. As was often the case, his actions had made as many enemies as friends, and the riot in the Temple made him even more controversial in Judea than he was in Galilee.

Violence swirled around him: the police of Caiaphas were prepared to nab him if he came near the Temple; the levites and their supporters, outraged at his arrogance, were ready to pounce on him anywhere near Jerusalem, to beat and stone him if they could. The soldiers of Pilate were poised to react with force at any hint of further insurrection. And Jesus must have felt at least partially responsible for the violence committed by thugs such as Barabbas, who had turned zeal for the Kingdom into a lust for human blood.

Still, he refused to leave the vicinity of Jerusalem. He was committed to his Zecharian vision of sacrifice. Some of his disciples must have pressed him to return to the comparative safety of Galilee or Syria. By remaining where he was, he was putting himself and his followers in danger. He had reached the moment of all or nothing—and he chose all. As he carefully explained to his disciples, "Yet I have an immersion to be im-

mersed in, and how I am constrained until it is accomplished!" (Luke
12:50). He referred to the metaphorical baptism that now obsessed him:
a visionary immersion in the primordial waters that surrounded God's
Throne, the primeval deep beyond the firmament whose waters the holy
Spirit moved at the beginning of creation. He sought complete communion with God. He wanted to drown in Spirit. Zechariah had prophesied
that waters would well up from under the city and flood the earth at the
final Sukkoth (Zechariah 14:8). Fixated on this immersion, he was compelled by the exigency of his own vision to remain near the Temple until
it was accomplished. He employed the language of constraint (using the
Aramaic verb *teqeyph,* "to act with strength") in various forms (evident,
for example, in Matthew 11:12; Luke 16:16), both for what he felt and
for the force with which God's Kingdom exerted itself.

Clinging to the prospect of enacting the moment of universal sacrifice as prophesied by Zechariah, Jesus at the same time needed to keep
his distance from the Temple. In the tug of war between vision and necessity, he began in a conscious and deliberate way to demand that his
practice of sharing meals as holy feasts continue, despite the easy target
they presented for his enemies. In his mind, they took over some of the
qualities of the sacred banquet that God wanted to see offered in his
Sanctuary. The promptings of his visionary world once again created
hardship for those around him. Held in an atmosphere of persecution,
his meals became more solemn than they ever had before.

The widowed sisters Miriam and Martha, no longer young, struggled
with the demands of hospitality on their home in Bethany. They were
honor bound to provide food and shelter for Jesus and the ever-changing
contingent of disciples who depended on him. The sisters were consumed with purchasing and trading goods, housekeeping, and cooking,
assisted by some of Jesus' female followers. They must have wished,
more than once, that their rabbi's *halakah* included instructions for managing what was suddenly an unwieldy household (Luke 12:14), the center of spontaneous and joyous festivity, but also a crucible of rebellion
and apocalyptic energy.

The sisters' difficulties during the winter of 31–32 C.E. are evident in one particular story, when Martha complained that her sister spent her time listening to Jesus, rather than working (Luke 10:40–42):

> But Martha was distracted with great provision. She advanced and said, Master, doesn't it matter to you that my sister left me behind alone to provide? So speak to her, so that she will assist with me! The Master answered and said to her, Martha, Martha, you worry and are troubled with many things, but there is need of few—or one! Because Miriam chose the good share, such as will not be removed from her.

The one necessary thing, for Jesus, remained the Kingdom, and what he said about Miriam of Bethany, the Galilean relative he had known since he was a boy, defined the place of women in his movement. They, too, were disciples, not merely servants, and shared in divine Wisdom and Kingdom in these meals. Miriam was approaching the age of sixty. "The good share" that Jesus gave her was more than a part in his discussion with his followers; it was a portion of a different world, as one of the Chariot's mystic riders.

Many teachers in Jerusalem and ordinary pilgrims sympathized with Jesus' occupation of the Temple. They were as appalled as he was by Caiaphas' placement of the vendors. The disaffected gathered together with the Sanhedrin in their exile on the Mount of Olives and embroiled themselves in deep debate over the implications of Caiaphas' actions and what should be done.

Occasionally Jesus joined them. It was an easy walk from Bethany to Chanuth on the Mount of Olives, east across the Kidron Valley from the Temple, where the Pharisees and other disgruntled teachers congregated. Although going there placed him perilously close to the reach of Caiaphas' police in the Temple, Jesus was eager as ever for debate. He could no more resist the cut and thrust of religious dialectics in Jerusalem than he could in Capernaum. We can only imagine the volatility of the scene as dozens of learned and incensed Jews congregated to discuss the recent events in the holy city, figure out the correct way to live the Torah, and convince one another of the rightness of their own positions on a broad range of issues.

Rabbi Jesus was at the top of his form, taking on all comers and reveling in the controversy he provoked. Some Zadokite priests challenged him: What happens to a woman who has had several husbands by the time she dies? Whose wife is she when resurrected? *"Reqa!"*[1] Jesus replied. An empty, foolish question! In the resurrection people will be as angels, neither marrying women nor, in the case of women, being given in marriage (Mark 12:18–27; Matthew 22:23–33; Luke 20:27–38).

The priests put their case in the speculative fashion of spinning hypotheses and their possible ramifications out of the Torah, a method instanced in the Talmud, while Jesus advanced a position that derived from mystical texts and visionary experience. It's easy to miss the focus of his succinct argument's focus. The point is not just that God is all-powerful, but that as in the description of Daniel, human beings will become comparable to the angels before Yahweh's Throne. Since both femininity and masculinity are included within the divine, angelic emanation should be conceived, as Jesus sees it here, as androgynous. The image of divine androgyny also flourished in later kabbalistic writings, but Jesus pressed the image to define resurrected *humanity:* not only God but people before God's Throne were to be angelic, no longer distinguished by their sex. That was why, confronted by all the dangers he faced in Jerusalem, he determined that his women followers should face them, too. A place in

---

1. This was a term Jesus taught should not be used against a person (see Matthew 5:22), but his intemperate outbursts against *questions* he considered stupid, no matter what their source, show that he had no scruple when it came to naming theological pedantry for what it was. In any case, some of his sayings suggest he broke his own rule when it came to the attitudes of some people (see Luke 12:20; 24:25; Matthew 7:26; 25:1–13).

his vision of the divine Chariot—and therefore the risks the vision entailed—belonged to all his disciples.

The battle of wits between Jesus and the priests drew a crowd.
Chanuth was a derelict area now that the vendors were ensconced in the
Great Court. The ground was bare and there was little shade. From the
midst of the crowd a clever Pharisee yelled: what about the taxes we owe
Caesar, should we pay them, or not?

The Gospels portray this question as a trap, an attempt to get Jesus
to side with a call to arms, because a refusal to pay taxes was tantamount
to revolt against Rome.[2] Had they succeeded he could have been denounced to the prefect as a rebel, more than an apolitical cultic upstart
(Mark 12:13–17; Matthew 22:15–22; Luke 20:20–26). No doubt, as
Mark indicates, there were Pharisees present who sympathized with
Herod Antipas and their Roman rulers as relatively benign despots who
let them worship as they pleased. But Pharisaism itself was riven by the
question whether to take up arms against foreign rule (and Jewish officials such as Herod Antipas who disregarded the Torah). This was at base
a genuine, heartfelt question: did entering the Chariot with Jesus neces-
sarily mean a refusal of Caesar's tax, the certain prospect of Rome's coun-
termeasures, and, therefore, military revolution?

That setting is what makes Jesus' response pointed rather than a tru-
ism (Mark 12:17; Matthew 22:21; Luke 20:25):

Caesar's repay to Caesar, and God's to God!

Rome's coin, Rome's economy, Rome's goods could indeed be traded, and
all its duties and taxes paid. But Jesus' teaching had nothing to do with

---

2. When Rome had sent in her first prefect to replace Archelaus in 6 c.e., a Galilean in-
surgent named Judas had organized a revolt against the official attempt to take a census
and collect taxes on the grounds that God alone was Israel's master (see Josephus, *Jewish War* 2 §§ 117–118, 433; 7 § 253; *Antiquities* 18 §§ 4–10, 23–25; 20 § 102; Acts
5:37).

submitting to Rome as an end in itself. Instead, Jesus urged his followers to enter into commercial transactions for the purpose of acquiring for
God what belonged to God: the sacrifices that, correctly accomplished,
would eradicate every vestige of Roman power.

While Jesus was matching wits with the mavens on the Mount of
Olives, events in Rome had altered the political landscape
around him in ways he himself could not begin to fathom. Tiberius sent
another letter from Capri, which he ordered read in Rome before the
Senate with Sejanus present. Any worry Sejanus felt was overcome by recent rumors that Tiberius was about to promote him, making him second
in command to the emperor himself. The Senate assembled on October
18 (31 C.E.) in the temple of Apollo on the Palatine, and listened to the
sort of long, rambling missive Tiberius had acquired the habit of sending.
But the message became increasingly pointed in its criticism of Sejanus
and at last accused him of treason. As the letter was read, Sejanus'
colleagues edged away from him, as though the fate awaiting him were
contagious.

At the end of the reading of the imperial letter, the *Vigiles* (local police) circled the prefect with swords drawn, bound him, and marched
him to the Mamertine dungeon. A crowd had gathered in the street, and
they screamed in hatred as Sejanus was bullied past them. They demanded a terrible harvest for his years of oppression. Tiberius had
thrown his subjects a scapegoat, someone to attack for all their dissatis-
faction and hardship. They ran wild, smashing the statues that Sejanus
had erected to himself, and the forces of order in Rome did nothing to
stop them. In his confinement, Sejanus might have hoped for a sentence
of exile, rather than death, although everyone knew the Senate would act
quickly, before Sejanus got any bright ideas of what to do with the nine
thousand crack troops of the Praetorian Guard under his command.

By the end of that same day, the Senate ordered Sejanus strangled,
even for Rome a gruesome form of execution. The executioner and ac-

companying soldiers burst into Sejanus' chamber, unexpected and unannounced. They seized and held him. The executioner wound a leather garrot around Sejanus' neck, yanked its crossed ends, and crushed his windpipe. Sejanus' back arched and his limbs flailed and twitched, his eyes protuberant in horror. His mouth strained open as he tried to suck air into his heaving lungs. His tongue protruded at a ghastly angle as his face turned blue. Legs and arms gave a final, futile jerk; he was dead. The soldiers pulled the corpse into the street. The waiting crowd descended upon it and tore it to pieces.

Pilate learned of these events from traders and Roman functionaries recently arrived from Rome itself. The arrest of a high official on the charge of treason was enough to strike fear into anybody's heart. But the gruesome tale went on and on. Sejanus' uncle and son were also killed, as well as many of his friends and collaborators. His divorced wife, Apicata, committed suicide. Even his two young children were executed, the girl gang-raped by soldiers before she was dispatched. Livilla, to whom Sejanus was engaged, found little mercy, although she was a member of the imperial household. Her own mother, in a demonstration of fealty to the emperor, starved her daughter to death. The emperor's whims were as capricious as his power was boundless; *"Divi filius,"* Pilate thought. A well-known Jewish proverb, quoted both by Jesus (Matthew 26:52) and the Targum of Isaiah (50:11), said those who live by the sword die by it. That applied especially to those who served the empire.

Pilate knew that the Senate would stumble over itself to fill the vacuum that Sejanus' removal created. They perennially bemoaned the influence they had lost when the oligarchical Republic they governed had become an empire in 31 B.C.E., ruled by the brute fact of Augustus' concentrated military power. They couldn't quite get it through their heads that the empire would crumble if it was ruled by an effete gaggle of nobles, overly impressed with their own oratory. Hard and fast decisions had to be made to keep tribute flowing in and malcontents from Gaul to Judea in check. Yet the Senate would no doubt try to reverse Sejanus' practices and introduce a kinder and gentler approach to imperial policy.

Pilate was known to be a hard-liner in his dealings with the Jews, in keeping with Sejanus' attitudes. He was afraid that his association with Sejanus and his policies could lose him more than his position unless he could win the favor of his Jewish subjects.

As he ruminated over Sejanus' death, Pilate's thoughts turned to Caiaphas. A strong working relationship with the high priest was now imperative, like it or not. Caiaphas would have known that, and he pressed Pilate on the matter of Jesus' arrest. After Sejanus' death, Pilate gave this Galilean rabbi the dubious benefit of his callous attention. Jesus had initially registered on the prefect's radar as an annoying but essentially harmless lunatic. Now Pilate wanted to appease Caiaphas and show Rome that he controlled Judea without deliberately antagonizing local leaders as he had in the past. Terror and humiliation were still his tactics, but he had to learn to find the right targets.

Pilate had little choice but to make common cause with Caiaphas. In his redefinition of a vitally important alliance, he showed himself a consummate politician. Yet he bided his time. He would not allow himself to appear weak in the sight of the people he ruled. The city was winding down for the winter in any case; the prefect was not going to act unless it was necessary, and then only when action was most clearly to his own benefit.

As if Jesus wasn't already in enough danger from the prefect and high priest, his old foe Antipas was also taking a keen interest in events in Rome and the tightening of the alliance between Pilate and Caiaphas. After all, many of Antipas' Galilean subjects had been killed in Jerusalem in 30 C.E., when Pilate ordered his troops to club the crowd that protested his confiscation of funds from the Temple. Antipas felt Pilate owed him a favor after the prefect's ruthless action, and this was a propitious moment to collect it. More important, he wanted to show himself both in command of his own territory and cooperative with other agents of Rome in the uncertain circumstances after Sejanus' execution. Might he use his Roman colleague and priestly coreligionist to rid himself of Jesus at long last and solidify his position? Unless Antipas, Caiaphas, and

Pilate together showed that they could effectively rule their Jewish subjects, each of them was in danger being stripped of his title, position, and power. Sejanus, once an example of how far you could rise by pleasing Tiberius, was now an object lesson in what it meant to fall out of his favor.

The emerging agenda that united the interests of the high priest, the prefect, and the tetrarch eluded Jesus as much as the recently changed complexities of power in Rome. Politically, he was completely out of his depth.

Despite his naivete, Jesus knew that he courted danger as he shuttled between Bethany and Chanuth, evading Caiaphas and Pilate as he had once evaded Antipas. All the moving and the constant danger took a toll on his followers, as Jesus well knew. They had to be ready to give up wealth and family (Mark 10:13–31; Matthew 19:13–30; Luke 18:15–30), to ruin their lives if necessary for the message of the all-consuming Kingdom, to bear the Romans' cross if it came to that (Mark 8:34–38; Matthew 16:24–27; Luke 9:23–26). Even these travails were a small price to pay for the glorious fulfillment of becoming a rider of the Chariot in the world of vision. Jesus' demands were not, as the later Church made them, quasi-Stoic commendations of austerity or simplistic promises of reward later for suffering now. Jesus framed his teaching to make hardship the gateway to vision. The practice of the Chariot was not only for times of tranquility and leisure. As in the case of the book of Daniel, resistance intensified one's appreciation of God's presence and the sustaining strength of his angelic court.

Every person was made in God's own image and likeness, because God created everyone that way (Genesis 1:26–27). In his concentration on "the one like the person," Jesus incorporated into his *kabbalah* the Danielic insight that humanity is represented before God's Throne. But then Jesus pursued this insight further: every person possessed the angelic likeness of "the one like the person" and mirrored some of the truth of the divine Chariot. God's Throne was there, shining through the eyes of a neighbor, even if that neighbor hated you (Matthew 5:43–48; Luke 6:32–36):

> You have heard that it was said, You shall love your neighbor and you shall hate your enemy. Yet I say to you, Love your enemies, and pray for those who persecute you, so you might become descendants of your father in heaven. Because he makes his sun dawn upon evil people and good people, and makes rain upon just and unjust. For if you love those who love you, what reward have you? Do not even the customs-agents do the same? And if you greet only your fellows, what do you do that goes beyond? Do not even the Gentiles do the same? You, then, shall be perfect, as your heavenly father is perfect.

While arguing at Chanuth, he had come to the realization that the love one owed the Throne was exactly what one owed one's neighbor (Mark 12:28–34; Matthew 22:34–40; Luke 10:25–28). Love of God (Deuteronomy 6:5) and love of neighbor (Leviticus 19:18) were basic principles embedded in the Torah. Jesus' discovery was that the two were indivisible: love of God *was* love of neighbor, and vice versa.

Every neighbor belonged to the Chariot, accompanied by all the angels of Israel's God through the ages. That is the basis of Jesus' distinctive and challenging ethic of love in the midst of persecution—a love that reaches out past the fear of reprisal from the agents of Rome, an Antipas, a Pilate, or a Caiaphas. Love for a neighbor—even a neighbor who hated Jesus—was joined in his meditative experience with the love he felt coming from his *Abba*. He linked a loving heart to the transformed society Zechariah had predicted, Israel and the nations joined and numinous with compassion. His words point the way to the transcendence that individual suffering can achieve, a transcendence that for him was always linked to the communal body of all those who take on the meaning and the practice of sacrifice. Jesus, like Buddha, saw that we are all intimately connected—what we do to others we do to ourselves, in actions rich with future consequences.

E vents in Bethany brought a new crisis: a disciple named Eleazar (Lazarus in the Hellenized form of his name), the brother of Miriam and Martha, died (John 11:1–44). John's Gospel relishes and embroiders the symbolism of the scene, yet strong elements of Jesus' actual practice flicker through John's symbolic picture. Bethany was clearly Jesus' center during this period, but he was away at the time of Lazarus' death; he feared stoning at the hands of his opponents (John 11:7–9). For John, these opponents are "the Jews" (as if Jesus' closest friends, disciples, and supporters were not also Jewish!). In this Gospel, Judaism and Christianity are different and mutually antagonistic religions, set at persistent enmity. Nevertheless, reference to the threat of stoning makes plain the political situation that Jesus faced. In Bethany he did not fear the official action of Pilate or even of Caiaphas (since Jesus was well outside the Temple); what he worried about was quick, summary killing at the hands of thugs who were loyal to the high priest.

At their brother's death, Martha and Miriam were inconsolable. Martha rebuked Jesus for being away, and Miriam flatly refused to leave the house to see him as he approached Bethany (John 11:17–21). The description of his pain over Lazarus' death includes the shortest verse in the Bible, "Jesus wept" (John 11:35). Never was he more grieved: "he censured himself in the spirit and shook himself" (John 11:33, 38). Those present were disturbed by his seemingly uncontrolled emotion.

Recent research has revealed the existence of a previously unknown document, called *Midrash Hashkem,* a compilation of Talmudic mysticism that details a basic principle of kabbalistic magic. Starting from a statement in the book of Psalms that "The Lord is your shadow on your right hand" (Psalm 121:5), this midrash speaks of how God reveals himself in human feelings:

At the Tomb of the Dead

What is "your shadow"? If you laugh to it, it laughs to you; if you weep to it, it weeps with you . . .

In the depth of prayerful vision, one is face to face with the Throne. And God's deepest passions mirror the emotions on the seer's own face. The affinity between the divine image and the human image, the foundation of the Chariot discipline, means that people influence God, just as God influences people.

Jesus had raised the daughter of Jairus in Gennesaret from seeming death, as well as the widow's son in Nain. Now he stood before a cave that had been fashioned into a tomb, the burial place of his friend, four days dead. Martha had come out to meet him there, and eventually Miriam appeared, too (John 11:28–29). Other mourners looked on with incredulity at the depth of Jesus' grief and his powerlessness to prevent this sudden death (John 11:36–37).

Lazarus had been dead for a day beyond the traditional three days that mourners might visit a loved one's corpse to be sure that he or she had truly passed from life. But Jesus believed that he was "sleeping" (John 11:11). As in the case of all the instances in the Gospels where Jesus is said to raise the dead, it is evident that from his own point of view he was reviving a person who had been prepared for burial but was still alive.

Within the tomb, Lazarus was lying on a stone shelf, wrapped in cloth and anointed with scented oil, his face covered with a separate linen. Outside, Jesus ordered the stone that covered the door of the cave rolled off, despite the objections of Martha that after four days the stench of death would be unbearable (John 11:39). Jesus persisted. As he visualized God in the Chariot, his pain stood face to face with God's pain, and he knew that "if you weep to it, it weeps with you." Through a choked sob he screamed, "Eleazar, come on outside!" (John 11:43). At this moment Jesus seemed beside himself, as out of control as he had been years before during his exorcisms in Nazareth.

Then, a hush. Jesus' breath rasped. The mourners' sobs subsided. The still spring air seemed to magnify these little sounds, each a relief after Jesus' shrieking. From within the burial cave came different sounds: rock scratching on rock, pebbles brushed away by a foot, and then Lazarus appeared, wrapped in his white burial sheet, his face white, a ghostly image staggering out into the sunlight and warm air.

"Loose him [from his graveclothes] and let him depart," Jesus commanded (John 11:44).

Legends about Lazarus have abounded in the history of the Church and in literature. According to one of them, he went on to write the Gospel according to John. I do not subscribe to that often revived theory, but I do think that in Lazarus we have a definite case of Jesus' miraculous capacity to discover life in people whom others had given up for dead.

Jesus fled after he raised Lazarus (John 11:54). He had risked exposure to his enemies even in returning to Bethany during the highly public occasion of mourning. One of his followers, nicknamed "the Twin" (*Toma* in Aramaic) because he would not be separated from his rabbi, urged the others to join Jesus in Bethany with him, so at least they would die together (John 11:16). The resuscitation of his friend put Jesus all the more directly in harm's way.

The months of disputing on Chanuth had raised the level of opposition among some Pharisees, and priestly retainers loyal to Caiaphas sought by any means they could to eliminate the high priest's greatest nuisance. Moreover, Jesus had become a readily recognizable public figure in Jerusalem and its vicinity, the perfect target for any violent group that wanted to prove its loyalty to Rome and the high priest. Jesus was also an easy mark for zealots like the imprisoned Barabbas who wanted to show that they, unlike Jesus, were capable of leading a violent revolt all the way through to its bloody conclusion. Never had one of his healings been as dramatic and public as the raising of Lazarus; news of Jesus' actions at the tomb of the dead reached Caiaphas and his entourage

At the Tomb of the Dead

(John 11:45–53). It gave them another card to play against Jesus with Pilate. In this act, Jesus gave every appearance of being the kind of false prophet Rome feared, capable of leading an insurrection.

Yet winter passed without incident. The three rulers wanted to act in concert with one another, and also in agreement with the aristocratic council in Jerusalem, the Sanhedrin. The advice of these seventy men did not have to be followed, but in the prevailing delicate situation, it was only wise to accept their counsel and seek their consent in dealing with the troublesome rabbi from Galilee. Pilate would demonstrate that he had departed from the high-handed practices of Sejanus; Caiaphas would make amends for banishing the Sanhedrin from the Temple; Antipas would show himself a loyal Jew and a ruler worthy of Rome's confidence.

Pressure on both Caiaphas and Pilate mounted as the Passover of 32 C.E. approached. Thousands of devout Jews would stream into the city, and Jesus was in a perfect position to storm the Temple again and lead a revolt. Caiaphas had to assure his control over the holy precincts for the celebration of Passover to proceed. Pilate had every interest in supporting him fully now and permitting the festivities to go ahead, provided public safety and the honor of Rome could be assured. Both goals could be met, and Herod Antipas pleased, if Jesus were simply arrested as a threat to public and cultic order. But how could members of the Sanhedrin be convinced to tolerate such an action? That crucially important support finally came not as a result of changes in Rome or Jerusalem or Tiberias, but in response to news of the shocking innovation that Rabbi Jesus was introducing into his fellowship at meals. He had come far, but in political terms was about to overplay his hand.

247

THIRTEEN

King of the Jews

Caiaphas knew he had to convince Pilate to act *before* the feast of Passover (see Matthew 26:5; Mark 14:2). To wait any longer would have been foolish. The influx of pilgrims, the chaos and expectation accompanying the feast of Israel's liberation, would work to Jesus' advantage, not that of the authorities. The forces of violence and repression were gripping the land again, strengthening an empire that fed itself on revolt. Rome's strategy, when faced with insurrection, was to ratchet its power by imposing its will on its subjects militarily, and demanding more tribute to support the armies of occupation. Caiaphas had to persuade Pilate to cooperate with him by arresting Jesus before Passover, as a security precaution. Delay might easily cost Caiaphas his high priesthood and Israel its Temple.

The Gospels' technique of compacting episodes tightly together is never stronger than when they relate the events leading up to Jesus' capture, and what awaited him at Pilate's hands. They reflect the liturgical practice in Christianity, still pervasive today, of commemorating a single "Passion Week" around Passover, framed by Palm Sunday, when Jesus entered Jerusalem, and his resurrection on Easter. Collapsing all the events of Jesus' final few months into a few days muddles them, and the particular context of each is all but lost.[1] By extricating what the Gospels relate about Jesus' execution and its causes from Christianity's liturgical calendar, and placing that information in the context of Jewish sacrificial worship and Roman politics, we can discern the succession of events that Jesus set in motion. And for the first time, the reasons for the terrifying outcome of those events become clear.

John's Gospel is correct in asserting that by early spring Jesus was dodging into wilderness areas around Jerusalem, aware that Caiaphas' sympathizers were after him (John 11:54–57). He sought out the support of people in the small villages around Jerusalem. When he once did dare to return to Bethany, he avoided the home of Miriam and Martha, and feasted at the house of Simon, a "leper" whom Jesus had restored to health (Mark 14:3–9; Matthew 26:6–13; John 12:1–8):

> *There came a woman who had an alabaster of genuine, expensive perfumed ointment. Smashing the alabaster, she poured it over his head. But some were angry among themselves, This waste of the ointment happened for what? Because this ointment could have been sold for more than three hundred denarii and given to the poor! And they were censuring her. But Yeshua said, Leave her: why are you making problems for her? She has done a fine deed with me. Because you always have the poor with yourselves, and whenever you want, you can always do them good, but me you do not always have. She acted with what she had; she undertook to myrrh my body for*

---

1. Passover had always involved arrangements long in advance. The tax of the half-shekel for the Temple was collected a month before the holiday outside Jerusalem, ten days later in Jerusalem itself (in Mishnah, see Sheqalim 1:3); pilgrims needed to arrange for accommodation in an increasingly crowded city; the lamb had to be selected four days before the holy day itself (Exodus 12:3). So the picture in the Gospels that Jesus zipped into Jerusalem on the first day of the feast itself, and that everything was instantly ready for his Seder with his disciples is implausible, another example of their telescoping technique in the interest of a liturgical Passion Week (Matthew 26:17–19; Mark 14:12–16; Luke 22:7–13). Jesus was arrested in Jerusalem before Passover. The stark truth of how Jesus fell victim to political realities he barely comprehended is closely woven into the texts.

burial. Amen I say to you, wherever the message is announced in the whole world, what she did will also be spoken of in memory of her.

The disciples were annoyed not only because the woman had wasted three hundred denarii when they were all nearly destitute, but because she had openly embraced Jesus as the messiah, the anointed one, calling attention to him when simple prudence demanded a low profile.

The rabbi, however, had a different interpretation of the woman's act: she was foretelling his death. "She undertook to myrrh my body for burial," he said, referring to the practice in Judaism of anointing a corpse for its interment. Moreover, whenever his message was announced, he said, the apostles were to mention this woman in particular (Mark 14:9; Matthew 26:13). She knew better than any of them who Jesus was, and what the cost of his being the messiah would be. She had every reason to know: she was seven-demoned Miriam of Magdala, who had followed her love from Galilee to Jerusalem and Bethany. It was she who saw most clearly that his flame was in danger of being extinguished precisely because it burned so bright and could burn in no other way.

As Passover approached, Jesus and his disciples continued to take semiprivate meals together, often behind closed doors in rooms lit with oil lamps. The nature of these meals had changed, however; they had acquired a revolutionary new meaning when Jesus spoke of sharing his "blood" and his "flesh." In his passion to convey the reality of the Chariot and bring his disciples with him to the Throne, Jesus crafted his holy feasts into the prototype of what is now called Eucharist, Mass, or Holy Communion. This new meaning made his meals into the primary technique of his mystical practice, but they were also deeply divisive. Not only did they alienate a large proportion of his popular following in Jerusalem, they also turned some of his closest disciples against him and sealed his fate with the Sanhedrin.

Stunned by what Jesus was doing in this new version of his holy feasts, some of his disciples even began to collude with Caiaphas, perhaps hoping that their defection, together with official pressure, would force Jesus away from Jerusalem. But he would not go. During the winter of 31–32 C.E., as gray skies darkened the holy city and cold rain fell on the stark Judean hills, Jesus endowed his meals with a disturbing significance that would underlie the fundamental rite of a new religion.

Before exploring what Jesus was actually doing when he offered his blood and flesh to the disciples, it's necessary to understand how the Church has traditionally conceived of the Eucharist. Only then can we appreciate Rabbi Jesus' own *halakhah* of blood and flesh in its initial, Judaic context.

In the celebration of Mass all over the world today, Christians arise from their knees holy, pure, and free of sin after they have eaten Christ's flesh and drunk his blood. Powerful though this theology is, its way of looking at the Eucharist owes more to the thought of the Hellenistic world of the Gospels than to Rabbi Jesus' revolutionary teaching.

After Jesus' death, his teaching of the Eucharist fell on fertile soil in the Greco-Roman world. In the pagan cults that were called Mysteries (because they were secret initiatory rites that brought the divine to earth), worshippers vicariously enacted the death and rebirth of a god, such as the fertility deity Dionysius. Each spring, Dionysius sacrificed himself and then was reborn so the land could once again produce crops, and the worshippers were deified by imitating Dionysius.

Another god, Mithra, was particularly popular among Roman soldiers. In his cult, the initiate maintained a regime of fasting for weeks, immersing himself repeatedly. At the proper time, he joined in a performance that reenacted on the earth what was happening in the divine realm, as the god Mithra triumphed over and slaughtered the cosmic bull. The ceremonial performance took place at night, complete with elaborate costumes, dance, carousing, and feasting. At its climax, the initiate descended into a deep pit with an iron grate overhead. A bull was lead onto the grate, and its throat was cut; blood pumped out, showering the initiate with the power of life. He emerged from the pit, and his fellow worshippers cried out that he was *Renatus in aeternum* ("Reborn into eternity").

To Hellenistic Christians of the Gospel period, Jesus was a new god of the Mysteries, who gave himself so that they might be reborn to eternal life by distributing his own flesh and blood in the meals held in his name. After all, in these last meals he had proclaimed that bread and wine really were his body and his blood. For the vast majority of Gentile, Greek-speaking Christians, that could only mean that Jesus was referring to himself: bread and wine were symbols of him personally and became his body and blood when believers consumed them.

The only serious question for later Christian orthodoxy was how the transformation took place. Did the bread and wine literally become Jesus' body and blood, or was the ritual a metaphor or symbol? This question ignited wars among churches from the sixteenth-century Reformation to the genocide of the Huguenots, which was virtually completed during the eighteenth century. To this day, divisions over Eucharistic teaching thwart efforts at serious ecumenical discussion. Yet the various denominations have all agreed with the Hellenistic interpretation that the meaning of Christ's "body" and "blood" is autobiographical, that Jesus was talking about himself. In their desperation to find some common ground in Eucharistic doctrine, theologians and scholars of religion have persisted in their belief that the Last Supper began a religion of Mystery in which the god gave himself to be eaten, and historians have advanced the idea that Jesus started a new sect of Judaism by telling his followers to eat bread and drink wine as if they were his personal flesh and blood.

I just do not find these assertions plausible. What Jew would tell another to drink blood, even symbolic blood? The Mishnah makes the implausibility of such a thought explicit. It imagines the most heinous defect possible on the part of a priest involved in sacrifice:[2]

If he slaughters in order to eat from its flesh and to drink from its blood.

---

2. The specific slaughter in mind is that of the red heifer (Parah 4:3), whose ashes mixed in water produced a potent agent of purification. By contrasting the purity of the rite with the impure thought of the priest, the Mishnah makes its hypothesis all the more vivid.

People had no right at all to blood; here even the *thought* of drinking it was sacrilegious. To imagine drinking human blood and eating human flesh could only make the blasphemy worse.

So if the flesh and blood Jesus was talking about were his, the "Last Supper" can only be understood as a deliberate break from Judaism. Indeed, scholars either have seen Jesus as deliberately breaking from Judaism, or have portrayed his followers as doing so in his name and inventing the "Last Supper" themselves. Both theories find adherents today. The lines are still drawn between those who see Jesus as a Jewish renegade and treat the Gospels as literal history, and those who believe that the Gospels are Hellenistic fairy tales, which justified faith in their new Dionysius by inventing a fanciful rationale for what Jesus did.

But the Gospels were no fairy tales and Jesus was no apostate. His personal, longstanding practice of the feast of the divine Kingdom gives us the context we need in order to understand and appreciate his final meals in their original, Judaic setting. He promoted neither symbolic cannibalism nor a rejection of Judaism. These meals were Jesus' last, desperate gesture to insist that his own meals were better sacrifices than what was offered in Caiaphas' corrupt Temple.

The Eucharist's Jewish meaning came to me only in early 1990, after years of working with Aramaic sources and with anthropological studies of sacrifice. I had reconstructed much of Jesus' teaching in Aramaic from the Greek of the Gospels, and had come to appreciate the essential conflict between Caiaphas' prerogatives as high priest and Jesus' vision.

At the same time, my reading of anthropologists such as Mary Douglas and E. E. Evans Pritchard helped me articulate what I had personally experienced in the liturgy of the Eucharist as well as while eating with friends: the deep connection between simply sharing food with others and sacrifice was finally driven home to me. Just as meals bring human families and communities together, so the sacred offering of food by human beings expresses and strengthens their solidarity with the divine. A new thought struck me, straightforward but visceral: when Jesus spoke of his "blood" and "flesh," he did not refer to himself personally at all. He meant his meal really had become a sacrifice. When Israelites shared wine and bread in celebration of their own purity and the presence of the Kingdom, God delighted in that more than in the blood and flesh on the altar in the Temple.

In an instant (although after twenty years of study), all I learned from the church of my youth, and from my advanced studies was turned upside down. Jesus was not talking the language of a new religion or a personal cult; he was insisting on God's approval of his own vision of sacrifice in the Temple. And with that, I at last began to comprehend the sequence of events in the last, tragic chapter of Jesus' life.

The winter rains relented, spring came, and Jesus still had not been arrested. Caiaphas was hamstrung as the Sanhedrin debated the nuances of whether Jesus' raid in the Temple was justifiable. He could not simply be dispatched as a cultic criminal. He had not attempted to denigrate the sanctity of Mount Zion; his intention was to "raise it up" and reestablish purity within its precincts. Other rabbis of this period also engaged in physical demonstrations when they wanted to insist on their own brand of purity in sacrifice. Rabbi Jesus' raid was extreme, but not without precedent.

Why did the Sanhedrin finally agree to arrest Jesus? The Eucharist provides the key. Members of the Council, like many other devout Jews in Jerusalem, were offended by the scandalous new element in Jesus' practice. Jesus said over the wine, "This is my blood," and over the bread, "This is my flesh" (Matthew 26:26, 28; Mark 14:22, 24; Luke 22:17–20; 1 Corinthians 10:16–17; 11:24–25; Justin, *Apology* I.66.3; *Didache* 9:1–5). Referring to blood first, and then flesh (the original order reflected in *Didache* 9:1–5; 1 Corinthians 10:16–17; Luke 22:17–20), he followed the sequence of sacrifice. He asserted that this "blood," symbolized by the wine, was equivalent to actual blood poured into the sacred fire. "This bread is my flesh," he said—the replacement of butchered meat offered on the altar with horns.

His words can have had only one meaning. He cannot have meant: "Here are my personal body and blood"—that interpretation makes sense only after Jesus' movement distinguished itself from Judaism. The radical meaning of his words was that wine and bread replaced sacrifice in the Temple, and that was a direct challenge to established ritual practice in Israel. In the absence of a Temple that permitted his view of purity to be practiced, Jesus proclaimed wine his blood of sacrifice and bread his flesh of sacrifice. In Aramaic, a language redolent in Jesus' time with the concerns of Judaism, "blood" (*dema*) and "flesh" (*bisra*, which may also be rendered as "body") regularly carry such sacrificial meanings.

Judas sought an opportunity to inform the priests when Jesus would be close enough to the Temple so that their police could seize him (Matthew 26:14–16; Mark 14:10–11; Luke 22:3–6; John 13:26–30). He was not by any means the only disciple who was disaffected. When Jesus had made his meals into an altar that rivaled the Temple's, many disciples deserted him (John 6:60–71).

Judas' opportunity came when despite the risks involved, Jesus made preparations to stay in Jerusalem prior to Passover and for the feast itself. He sent some of his delegates into the city to meet a man carrying a clay vessel on his head filled with water. That was an unusual sight, because carrying water outside the Temple was women's work. It was a signal; the man had agreed to make himself known to the disciples in this way, as part of his arrangement to host Jesus clandestinely (Mark 14:13–15; Luke 22:10–12; Matthew 26:18). He showed the disciples an upper room, large and hidden from Jesus' enemies, for the joyous meals that anticipated the great feast of Passover. The man they met was Barnabas, the only person of wealth Jesus had ever known (see *Praise of Barnabas* 13.209–237).[3]

---

3. Through Jesus' new rite, Barnabas had finally arrived as a levite. He would never carry water within the Temple, one of the functions of the levites who could serve there. But he did signal his own understanding of Jesus' sacrificial meals by carrying the vessel to signal where the Last Supper would be held.

Passover's approach corresponded to the stirrings of spring: the prospect of the yearling lamb offered in sacrifice, of barley harvested and offered, of the earth ready to yield after the winter. Barnabas' house was crowded with disciples. Meals there were sumptuous; Jesus and some of the Twelve reclined on couches, others were almost as comfortable on the carpeted floor. Many disciples, both male and female, gathered for the glimpse Jesus offered of God's promise in the midst of danger. The Renaissance paintings of "the Last Supper," showing a group of men only sitting solemnly at a table, give a misleading impression.

The weeks before Passover were a festive time, and Jesus' meals, even during this period of danger and persecution were more rowdy than reverent. Sheep were plentiful and fairly cheap at market, because flocks had been culled prior to the selection of yearlings as paschal lambs. Mutton from older animals was stewed with onions and herbs, and the taste of the flesh in the disciples' mouths was sweet with the seasonal recollection of exodus from bondage.

But the last meal in Barnabas' house was troubled, for Jesus persisted in calling the wine and bread his sacrificial "blood" and "flesh." Moreover, his own pessimism, near to despair, hung like a cloud over the meal. On the way into the city, his disciples had remarked on how beautiful and lavish the Temple was, and he had said that the whole thing would one day be destroyed (Mark 13:1–2; Matthew 24:1–2; Luke 21:5–6). He spoke of how much he had wanted to keep the Passover itself with his disciples, but he also acknowledged that this would probably be impossible (Luke 22:15).

Yet the imminence of Passover meant the themes of that feast dominated their conversation. The warmth of spring and the satisfaction of eating good meat were fused with the remembrance not only of Israel's liberation, but of the glorious Throne of the Lord that Moses had encountered on Sinai during his meal there (Exodus 24:9–11). The Chariot was all that mattered in Jesus' mind now, and his meals were its realization, the blood and flesh of a sacrifice in which God took deep pleasure. One of the classic texts of the Chariot (Chagigah, 14b in the Talmud) speaks of the rabbis' disciples joining the angels in the banqueting halls of heaven. Jesus' meals had also become angelic banquets, his "blood" and "flesh" a communion with the divine on earth that took the place of the Temple. Yet he also lamented—paraphrasing the Psalmic complaint (Psalm 41:9)—that even some of his companions had turned against him (Luke 22:21–23; Matthew 26:25–29; Mark 14:18–21). Jesus knew, as they did, that it would take only a word to bring him down.

He knew why that word would be spoken and even told Judas to do whatever it was he had to do quickly (John 13:27). Judas, his character so often distorted by our own feelings about Jesus, was neither jealous of his rabbi nor frustrated by Jesus' lack of political zeal. Jesus forced Judas to choose between his loyalty to the Temple or his commitment to the Chariot, and Judas chose the Temple.

Judas' motives have been perennially misunderstood, because it has been assumed that he somehow knew about the agreement among Caiaphas, Pilate, and Antipas to work with one another. In fact, there is no reason to believe that he understood the intricacies of power politics in Jerusalem any better than Jesus did. Given his limited knowledge, it seems clear to me that Judas did not deliver Jesus to the high priest because he wanted to see him killed. If he had wanted his rabbi's death, he would have engineered a quick capture by a nameless crowd. A push over a parapet followed by stoning would have been the easiest way to kill him; that was how Jesus' brother James died thirty years later (see Josephus, *Antiquities* 20 § 200; Eusebius, *Ecclesiastical History* 2.23.1–18). Instead, Judas turned Jesus over to Caiaphas and his police, who did not themselves have the legal authority to execute anyone.

It is much more likely that Judas' immediate aim was to have Jesus expelled from Jerusalem by a force that could seize him but was not empowered to kill him. Perhaps Judas longed for the relative simplicity of the days in Galilee, and for the old feasts of the divine Kingdom that had not turned blasphemous by denigrating sacrifice on Mount Zion.

Jesus feared violence from Caiaphas, and even more from the levitical thugs who formed youth gangs driven by family loyalty and religious zeal. These hoods would have been all too happy to support their high priest with an impromptu stoning. But Jesus could scarcely have expected that the high priest was in a position to arrange his execution by the Romans.

After his meal in Barnabas' house, he walked with a number of disciples to a place called Gethsemane ("Oil Press") on the Mount of Olives, just outside Jerusalem's walls (Mark 14:32–42; Matthew 26:36–46; Luke 22:39–46). He met a small group of his sympathizers there, for this was near to where he had taught and disputed with Pharisees and Zadokites. He climbed up out of the Kidron Valley, a steep incline of rough, stony paths, low walls, olive orchards, and a few scraggly broom trees. He and his group walked carefully in the darkness, talking quietly among themselves, passing Chanuth, desolate of its customary vendors, and empty of the daytime gatherings of Pharisees, councilors, and religious debaters.

The city loomed above him, the torches on the mount making the Temple stone glow in the dark with a trace of rose hue. He could see a few dimly lit windows in houses; the wealthier mansions west of the Temple were more brightly lit. The fire from the sacrificial altar smoldered with cinders, fat, and bone, sending a faint plume of smoke into the dark sky. Beyond the city's walls was the moonscape of the Judean wilderness. But in Gethsemane the hills were fragrant with spring: olives and figs had begun to flower; the delicate scent of almond and quince was in the air. John's Gospel calls the place a garden (John 18:1), but it was more like a rough park, a reminder of Galilee.

Jesus had come to Gethsemane for solace and quiet conversation with his disciples and his God. What he found in the midst of his prayer was instead deep struggle. He prayed to his *Abba* for "this cup," as he called it, to pass from him (Mark 14:32–42). With his pronouncements about the wine and bread that he offered at his own altar, he had put himself in opposition to the Temple establishment, and he felt exposed and alone. Could there not be, even now, both Temple *and* Chariot, both holy feast of intimate fellowship *and* the kind of sacrifice on Zion that he and every Galilean with him would embrace?

His arrest came quickly and violently, before he found answers to those questions. A group made up of both Temple police and Roman soldiers stormed into Chanuth (Mark 14:43–52; Matthew 26:47–56; Luke 22:47–53; John 18:2–11). The presence of the soldiers was the first indication to the disciples—Judas included—that they confronted the forces not only of Caiaphas but of Pilate as well. Yet there was no time for thought; Judas went ahead with his plan, committed to an agreement with the high priest. The militia roughed up many of the disciples, stripping one and leaving him to flee naked; but some of the disciples were armed with their pilgrims' staffs and even a few weapons; they struck back at their aggressors until Jesus stopped them. He wanted no repetition of the deadly violence he had seen during his raid on the Temple. Judas kissed his rabbi for the last time, to designate him for the militia, as the texts say, but also—as the texts do not say—because he still loved him. Later, when Judas discovered that he had delivered his master not to the high priest but to the Romans and their most humiliating form of execution, he killed himself (Matthew 27:3–10; Acts 1:18–20).

Confronted with an overwhelming force, and disappointed that he had been handed over by one of his own, Jesus still could not resist mocking this dramatic display of power (Mark 14:48–49; Matthew 26:55; Luke 22:52–53):

Have you come out with swords and clubs to apprehend me as a thug? I was with you daily in the sacred space teaching, and you did not seize me.

He taunted the guards, because he saw them as Caiaphas' representatives, even with their Roman reinforcements. For all their arms, they were powerless to kill him; he had escaped them at the occupation of the Temple, and Roman law could have no interest in him now. Or so he thought.

Caiaphas, while the arrest was taking place, was with members of the Sanhedrin, seeking assurance that the council would back his denunciation of Jesus to Pilate as the source of an illegal movement of violent opposition centered in the Temple. The Gospels give the impression that Jesus appeared at a formal Jewish trial, but all the evidence, along with common sense, suggests that he had no real hearing. A formal session of the Sanhedrin would have had to take place during the day with at least twenty-three members convened to hear a specific charge supported by witnesses (see Sanhedrin 1:4–5; 4:1–5:5; 7:5 in the Mishnah). None of those conditions is met by what the Gospels say (Matthew 26:57–75; Mark 14:53–72; Luke 22:54–71; John 18:12–27). Rather, during the night Jesus was shuttled between the homes of Caiaphas and Annas, Caiaphas' predecessor in the high priesthood. Some of the Sanhedrin had been present during the disputes at Chanuth after Jesus' occupation of the Temple and they objected to what they saw as his arrogant attitude. Caiaphas sought to enlist their support. He wanted his denunciation of Jesus to appear to be made jointly with at least some of the members of the Sanhedrin, and not just as the product of a personal vendetta.

At first, he focused on the charge that Jesus had prophesied the destruction of the Temple. But so had Jeremiah (see Jeremiah 7), and later in the first century, another Jesus (Yeshua ben Ananias) had prophesied the fall of Jerusalem (see Josephus, *Jewish War* 6 § 300–309); neither of them incurred the death penalty. Such prophecies were no capital offense and, in any case, witnesses could not even agree on what exactly Jesus had said during the hectic day of the Temple raid and in the months that followed (Matthew 26:59–61; Mark 14:56–59).

Caiaphas finally prevailed by focusing on a more controversial and fundamental question. Having been well informed by Judas about Jesus' Eucharists, he asked: are you teaching that your feasts replace Temple sacrifice because you are God's own son? Jesus' answer was unequivocal (Mark 14:61–64; Matthew 26:63–66; Luke 22:66–71):

I am, and you will see the one like the person sitting at the right of the power and coming with the clouds of the heaven!

Silence at this point might have saved his life, just as a little discretion in Nazareth or Capernaum years earlier could have allowed him to live through maturity with the respect accorded a rabbi and sage. But not even the high priest's impressive display of prestige and influence was equal to Rabbi Jesus' obstinacy.

Caiaphas was triumphant. There was no further need of interrogation, because this was a curse from Jesus' own lips. He proclaimed that the authority delegated to him by the angel before God's Throne was greater than the authority that the high priests held in the Temple, an authority mandated by the Torah.[4]

By ripping his own garments (Mark 14:63; Matthew 26:65), Caiaphas conformed to a practice reflected in the Mishnah, that judges tear their clothing and never sew it back again, when they render the finding of blasphemy that must be punished (Sanhedrin 7:5). Key members of the council in the ad hoc meeting joined him. According to the theology of first-century Judaism, if you attacked any divinely sanctioned institution you were denigrating the God of Israel and exposed yourself to divine retribution, either directly or through the decisions of Israel's courts. The power of speech could insult God and inflame his divine wrath.

On the night of the arrest, Jesus had told Simon Peter that he would deny even knowing Jesus, but that this experience of failure would be a

---

4. Within the Judaism of this time, "cursing" God (traditionally translated "blasphemy") or one of the institutions God established (such as the Temple or the Law) was punishable, even by death (see Sanhedrin 7:1–11 in the Mishnah; Josephus, *Antiquities* 3 § 307; *Against Apion* 1 §§ 59, 223, 279). Here Jesus, true to his teaching of the Chariot, invoked "the one like the person," the angel in the heavenly court, as his authorization of a new, messianic *halakhah* in the Temple.

crucible where he would be purged to serve others (Luke 22:31–34; Mark 14:27–31; Matthew 26:31–35):

> *Shimon, Shimon, look: Satan sought you out to sift you all like wheat, but I petitioned concerning you, so that your faith would not give out. And you, when you have turned: harden your fellows. But he said to him, Master, I am ready with you to proceed even unto prison, even unto death! Yet he said, I say to you, Rock: a cock will not sound today until you three times deny knowing me.*

To a *talmid* who was indeed ready to die with his rabbi, a skilled fisherman who had been prepared to leave behind his family and comfortable house in Capernaum to join a messianic band on the run in Syria, these forbidding words gave no comfort. They seemed to endorse the despair of what Peter actually did that night. He stayed as close as he dared to the house of the high priest (Matthew 26:69–75; Mark 14:66–72; Luke 22:54–62; John 18:25–27), but he repeatedly denied his connection with Jesus when a nosy serving maid recognized his Galilean accent and accused him of being a disciple.

When the day dawned, Caiaphas made his way to see Pilate in the Antonia Fortress, wearing his turban, bearing his scepter, surrounded by his entourage and the members of the council who had been most distressed by Jesus' blasphemy. The prefect received them in his hearing room, with its emblems of Rome's might and his own authority. Pilate could not have been pleased to be summoned early in the day, but Caiaphas and his cohorts were eager to act before the Shabbath, which would commence at sunset that same day.

Pilate's personal guards and his most senior centurions would have been present. They must have noticed the prefect's growing satisfaction. By his agreeing to execute this nuisance, Caiaphas would remain in Pilate's debt, and post-Sejanan Rome would be impressed that he was able to act in tandem with the local Jewish authorities. Besides, a public crucifixion would be an ideal spectacle, the perfect display of Pilate's undiminished power. The Gospels make Pilate into a troubled, ethically minded magistrate at this point, who personally interrogated Jesus to determine his guilt or innocence, but in all probability Pilate condemned Jesus *in absentia.*[5]

Pilate exploited the situation for all it was worth. He knew that Jesus came from Galilee, and in the wake of his slaughter of the Galilean pilgrims in 30 c.e., he wished to appease Antipas. That had been a double affront to Antipas: his own subjects had been killed, and he was liable to the charge that he should have controlled them better in the first place. Antipas was in Jerusalem for the Passover, staying in the family palace. Having married his brother's wife and decapitated a respected rabbi, he did whatever he could to burnish his eroded reputation as a practicing Jew.

Pilate sent Jesus in chains to Antipas early Friday morning, an act of cunning grace—as if he were thoughtfully seeking the advice of the petty ruler of Galilee and Perea for what was already a forgone conclusion. The gambit worked. Finally, Antipas had Jesus where he wanted him. He enjoyed this moment of glory, goading the rabbi, daring him to demonstrate one of his legendary signs (Luke 23:6–11). The interrogation was lengthy, probably covering all the insults—real and imagined—that Jesus had heaped on Antipas since his days with John the Baptist. Antipas' soldiers beat him, and in a spirit of cynical mockery they dressed him up as a king before returning him to Pilate.

From that time, Pilate and Antipas were no longer at odds; condemning Jesus confirmed the working relationship between them in the

---

5. After all, this Galilean was not a Roman citizen (who could claim a formal hearing), but a provincial troublemaker whose death would serve the ends of Rome and Pilate's own career. Written during the decades when Christians no longer enjoyed protection as practitioners of Judaism, a *religio licita,* the Gospels were designed to model Christian behavior under the threat of persecution. They urged an appeal to the nobler side of Roman judges, and therefore cast Pilate in the role of a diligent, careful, almost compassionate official (Matthew 27:1–26; Mark 15:1–15; Luke 23:1–25; John 18:28–40). Likewise, they exaggerated the formality of Caiaphas' consultation with the Sanhedrin, as if it were principally responsible for Jesus' death.

new order of the empire (Luke 23:12). Antipas was placated: at long last he was rid of John's most prominent disciple, the man who had mocked his best efforts to capture him in Galilee. By sending Jesus back to Pilate in a monarch's robes, he returned the prisoner as a messianic and royal pretender, a threat to Roman hegemony. The gesture signified that the prisoner could be crucified as "King of the Jews."

Pilate could not resist toying with the priests one last time. He offered to release Jesus: "Do you want me to discharge to you 'the King of the Jews'?" (Mark 15:9; Matthew 27:17; Luke 23:14). There was Barabbas, after all, still being held for murder, as well as other criminals to be crucified at the same time in a demonstration of Roman power prior to Passover. Perhaps Barabbas should be killed instead of Jesus? These were games of cat and mouse, which Pilate played to demonstrate that he was not acting against the wishes of the high priests (Matthew 27:15–26; Mark 15:6–15; Luke 23:17–25; John 18:39–40). The Gospels portray crowds of Jews demanding Jesus' death from a reluctant Pilate. In Matthew, the prefect literally washes his hands of responsibility and "all the people replied and said, His blood is upon us and upon our children!" (Matthew 27:24–25).[6] That portrayal suited Christian communities in the Hellenistic world. They wanted to ingratiate themselves with their Roman rulers, and to charge antagonistic synagogue leaders with instigating every conceivable form of violence against them. But the realities of power in Rome and Jerusalem, as well as Pilate's own temperament,

---

6. Only Matthew has Pilate wash his hands at this point (Matthew 27:24). That is a nice, theatrical touch, which seems in keeping with Pilate's penchant for the dramatic. But if Pilate was dramatic, Matthew's Gospel sometimes verges on the operatic. Instead of having the high priests meeting with Pilate, Matthew portrays Jews as nationally responsible for Jesus' death, after Pilate washed his hands (Matthew 27:25).

The desire to remove blame from the Romans for the crucifixion that only they could have been responsible for is understandable. After all, the earliest Christians had to live under the hegemony of officials like Pilate. Crucifixion, however, was the method of humiliating death that these men jealously guarded for Rome's glory alone. The attempt to exculpate them produced the myth of Jewish "blood guilt," and the countless cruelties of Christian anti-Semitism.

make the theory of general Jewish guilt for the death of Jesus completely implausible in historical terms.

Beneath Pilate's hearing room, in the lowest level of the Antonia, Jesus was ridiculed, beaten, and flogged by the Roman soldiers in their quarters before he was crucified (Matthew 27:27–31; Mark 15:16–20; John 19:1–3). They stripped off the garments in which Antipas' soldiers had sardonically garbed him. The garrison could take virtually any liberty with this "King of the Jews" who had dishonored Rome. As long as he was alive for the crucifixion itself, he was a legitimate target for their sport. There was no limit in Roman law, as there was in Jewish practice, to the number of times the leather whip, tipped with metal scourges, could bite into his flesh. The whip lashed into Jesus, cutting into his back to the bone. It flayed his ribs, shoulders, elbows. His cries were drowned by the soldiers' jeers as they shouted made-up titles for this "king" and bent their knees in a parody of bows before the mock messiah.

Dumb with pain and loss of blood, he was still alive. Rome's honor required a living victim for crucifixion, the most exemplary method of execution, deliberately more cruel than decapitation or burning. Jesus' pilgrim's cloak was pressed onto his bleeding shoulders, and he was pushed and punched out of the Antonia, forced, along with those to be executed at the same time, to carry the *patibulum,* the rough, seventy-pound crossbeam that would be affixed to a vertical stake.

He was marched east from the Antonia in the morning, at about eight o'clock.[7] The disciples had made themselves scarce. The city would have been filling up with pilgrims for the Passover feast, and in the wide street north of the Temple people made way for the victim and the unwieldy

---

7. Pilate at this stage was in no position to inflame local feeling against his administration. Had he authorized a route through the city for the execution of the bleeding victim, he would have faced problems. That fact, and the probable location of Joseph of Arimathea's tomb (discussed in the next chapter) makes the traditional *Via Dolorosa* in Jerusalem very unlikely in historical terms. If one of the main city gates was used to lead Jesus out, it would probably have been the Benjamin Gate just to the north of the Temple, but I have surmised that the Antonia afforded a direct route out of the city.

beam he carried on his shoulders. The crowds pressed back against the stone walls of buildings, muttering to themselves and whispering to one another. Rabbi Jesus staggered past them, his wounds bleeding. The Sheep Gate was on his right and the pools of Bethesda on his left as he faltered outside the city's walls and started downhill into the glaring white stone and dust of the Kidron Valley. He collapsed. The Romans commandeered Simon, a Jew from Cyrene in North Africa, to carry Jesus' *patibulum* (Matthew 27:32; Mark 15:21; Luke 23:26). The Romans dragged the criminal to his feet and pushed him along, up Kidron's eastern slope.

At a site called Golgotha, which means "Skull's Place" in Aramaic, the soldiers stripped Jesus naked at "the third hour," in the estimate of Mark 15:25, nine o'clock. Judaism placed a premium on modesty; nudity added indignity and humiliation to the shame of public execution. The soldiers laid him on his back, held him down, and with a heavy oak mallet nailed him through the wrists to the *patibulum*. He and his crossbeam were hoisted onto one of the thick vertical posts sunk deep into the ground on Golgotha, permanent gibbets that gave the place its name. The post and beam met at a notch and were lashed together with a thick flax rope. Contrary to many images of the crucifixion, this post was squat. Jesus did not tower over his tormentors; he was not set against the sky. Part of the point of crucifixion was that the tormented victim should dangle just above the ground. The soldiers roped Jesus around his weakened, sagging torso; that kept his body erect against the cross so his weight did not rip his wrists away from the nails in the crossbeam. Then they nailed him with a long iron spike through the tops of his feet to the vertical post. He was doubtless in deep shock from pain and loss of blood as he watched the soldiers cast lots (Matthew 27:33–35; Mark 15:22–24; Luke 23:33–35; John 19:23–24) for his bloody cloak, tunic, and sandals.

An onlooker offered Jesus a wine-soaked sponge attached to a reed to kill his pain, one of a few kind people amidst the throng Rome encouraged to watch its crucifixions and to learn fear. The last human voices he heard were jeers. "Save yourself," "Misery for the one demolishing the

JAVELIN POINT

This four-inch-long point came from a javelin (pilum) left at Masada. The javelins used by the Roman legionary infantrymen consisted of a long, four-sided, pyramidal iron head with a four-sided shank set into a wooden shaft. The javelin was generally a little more than six feet in length. At the beginning of a battle, infantrymen hurled their javelins at the enemy before they closed in for combat with their swords. Carried by soldiers marching in and around Jerusalem, these weapons exhibited Rome's capacity for physical coercion. (Photograph courtesy of the Institute of Archaeology of the Hebrew University of Jerusalem)

Temple," "Let's see if Eliyah comes to take him down" (Mark 15:23, 27–37; Matthew 27:34, 38–50; Luke 23:35–46). Even some of those being crucified alongside him managed to rouse themselves from their own suffering and rally the energy to ridicule Jesus (Matthew 27:44; Mark 15:32; Luke 23:39–43). Those of his followers who dared to watch until the end, most of them women, looked on from a distance (Matthew 27:55; Mark 15:40; Luke 23:49). The last distinct words of Jesus started a recitation of Psalm 22 in Aramaic (Mark 15:34; Matthew 27:46):

> And during the ninth hour Yeshua bellowed in a loud voice, Eloi, Eloi, lemma sabakhthani, which is translated: My God, my God, why have you forsaken me?

Then he was too weak to speak clearly (Matthew 27:50; Mark 15:37; Luke 23:46), and he died with an incoherent scream.

Death by crucifixion could sometimes take a day or two. Shock or dehydration might be the cause of death, but usually the victim lost the ability to support his weight by his arms; his thorax closed and he gradually suffocated. Pilate was surprised that Jesus had died in only six hours, bleeding from the wound of a javelin a soldier had thrust into him (Mark 15:44; John 19:34). The prefect must have been relieved. The derisive title suggested by Herod Antipas, "King of the Jews," had in fact been inscribed over the victim's head on the cross (Mark 15:26; Matthew 27:37; Luke 23:38; John 19:19).[8] If this "King" died weakly, so much the better. A good day's politics had been done, and everything had gone off satisfactorily, without any irritating repercussions.

---

8. From Pilate's point of view, this was a successful but routine execution. He did not interrogate Jesus, as the Gospels report (Mark 15:2–5; Matthew 27:11–14; Luke 23:3; John 18:33–38), and could not have done so directly for the simple reason he did not speak Aramaic, any more than most Romans of his class, but only Greek and Latin. The scene of his wife's dream (found only in Matthew 27:19) is unlikely, since prefects of his rank did not have the privilege of being accompanied by their spouses on foreign assignment.

FOURTEEN

❧

The *Kabbalah* of Crucifixion

The corpse of a man who had been executed could not remain exposed, even for a night: Moses' Torah insisted that the body should be rapidly interred to avoid defiling the land (Deuteronomy 21:22–23). Joseph from Aramithea, a Sanhedrin rabbi, requested Jesus' body from Pilate and arranged for its burial (Mark 15:42–46; Matthew 27:57–60; Luke 23:50–54; John 19:38–42). In John's Gospel, another rabbi, Nicodemus, lends a hand with the arrangements, and that seems plausible: Nicodemus had joined in discussion and debate with Rabbi Jesus in Jerusalem that winter, intrigued by his teaching (John 3:1–13; 19:39–40).

The task of bathing Jesus before swathing him in a fine linen burial cloth was gruesome. Two of Jesus' female disciples had little choice but to prepare the corpse, the men having been in hiding since the arrest at Gethsemane. Miriam of Magdala touched her love's body for the last time to wash it clean of blood and filth. She was joined by another, older woman, also named Miriam, the mother of two disciples (Mark 15:40, 47). Together they wound the linen loosely enough so the wrapping would not be soaked in blood. Joseph gave them money to buy burial ointment, olive oil scented with myrrh and aloes (John 19:39). They were to return after Shabbath to apply the oil and wind the sheet more tightly once the blood and lymphatic fluid had congealed.

A straightforward reading of the Gospels' portrait of the burial has been challenged by revisionist scholars, who theorize that Jesus died in a mass crucifixion: the body was thrown into a common, shallow trench, to become carrion for vultures and scavenging dogs. This makes for vivid drama but implausible history. Pilate, after all, had been forced in the face of Jewish opposition to withdraw his military shields from public view in the city when he first acceded to power. What likelihood was there, especially after Sejanus' death, that he would get away with flagrantly exposing the corpse of an executed Jew beyond the interval permitted by the Torah, and encouraging its mutilation by scavengers just outside Jerusalem?

Revisionism can be productive. But it can also become more intent on explaining away traditional beliefs than on coming to grips with the evidence at hand, and I think this is a case in point. It is worth explaining why I go along with much of the Gospels' account of Jesus' burial, because doing so will help us grapple with the vexed question of what happened three days after his crucifixion.

Time and again, the Gospels reveal the tendency of the first Christians to shift the blame for Jesus' death away from Pilate and onto the Sanhedrin. Yet when it comes to taking on the weighty responsibility of burying Jesus, we find members of that same council taking the lead, while most of Jesus' disciples had beaten a hasty and ignominious retreat. Joseph's and Nicodemus' public act cost them: they donated mortuary dressing and ointment as well as use of the cave. They also contracted uncleanness for seven days after the burial. On each of those seven days they would have had to explain to curious colleagues where and why they had come into contact with a corpse, a powerful source of impurity.

Joseph's act went beyond a mere display of ordinary decency. He ensured that Jesus was interred in one of the caves he had recently dug for himself and his family. The significance of this gesture is plain: there were those within the council who had not agreed with Caiaphas' con-

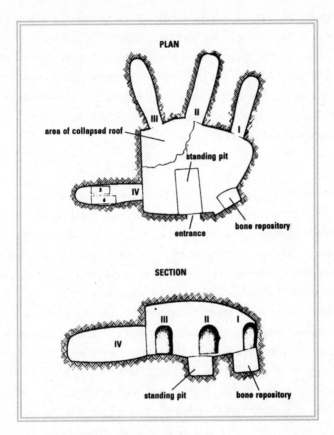

BURIAL PLAN

Viewing the Caiaphas tomb from above and in cross-section shows its layout. This would have been the kind of tomb in which Joseph of Aramithea interred Jesus. Entering through a collapsed portion of the roof, excavators found four ossuaries in the center of the chamber and noted four 6-foot-deep by 1.5-foot-wide arched niches (I–IV on plan) carved into the cave's soft limestone walls. Known as loculi (singular loculus, kokh and kokhim in Hebrew), these niches were an architectural tip-off that the cave had probably been used for Jewish burials. (Illustration courtesy of Biblical Archaeological Review) demnation of Jesus to Pilate. Adding insult to injury, Joseph's newly hewn cave was probably not far from the site of Caiaphas' own family mausoleum on the hillside south of the Temple. Scores of burial caves from the first century of the kind that Joseph prepared for Jesus are visible there today.[1] The irony is poignant: the bodies of the two antagonists, the high priest and the renegade rabbi who had so bitterly clashed, ended up interred in the same cemetery.

The memory of Jesus might have faded away among the forgotten people of history, but for the force of the vision that he had instilled in the minds of his disciples. Like Buddha, he was a superb teacher, capable of imparting the inner energy as well as the outer form of the religious wisdom he had discovered. The disciples' mystical practice of the Chariot only intensified after Jesus' death, and to their own astonishment and the incredulity of many of their contemporaries, they saw him alive again. They immediately knew that their experience of Jesus' resurrection was different from the resuscitation of Lazarus, whom Jesus had restored to life in the walking, talking body familiar to his family and friends. The resurrected Jesus, as the disciples instantly grasped, had profoundly changed; indeed, at times, they didn't even recognize him. He appeared to them in vision, alive in the glory of the Throne, not restored to the world in the way Lazarus had been.

The first of his disciples to have this visionary experience were the .

---

1. The probable location of Jesus' grave contradicts over fifteen hundred years of pious geography. During the fourth century, the Emperor Constantine ordered the destruction of a temple to Venus outside Jerusalem, and the alleged burial cave of Christ was found beneath (see Eusebuis, *Life of Constantine* 3.25–50). "The Church of the Holy Sepulcher" was accordingly built, just outside the walls of the Byzantine city. Christians venerate the site to this day, and different denominations compete fiercely for control of the space inside, but there is no evidence of a first-century cemetery there. In any case, the site was *within* the walls of the city at the time Jesus died: exactly where Jews would not have put a cemetery.

two Miriams, who returned to his tomb with a companion after the Shabbath to anoint him. Mark 16:1–8 describes the scene:

> *And when Shabbath elapsed, Miriam Magdalene and Miriam of Yaaqov and Shalome bought spices so they could go rub him with oil. And very early on the first of the Shabbath they come upon the tomb when the sun dawned. And they were saying to one another, Who will roll the stone away from the door of the tomb for us? They looked up and observed that the stone had been rolled off, because it was exceedingly big. They went into the tomb and saw a young man sitting on the right, a white robe wrapped around, and they were completely astounded. But he says to them, Don't be completely astounded. You seek Yeshua the crucified Nazirite. He is raised; he is not here. Look—the place where they laid him. But depart, tell his students and Rock that he goes before you into Galil; you will see him there, just as he said to you. They went out and fled from the tomb, because trembling and frenzy had them. And they said nothing to any one; they were afraid, because—*

Such is the stunning, enigmatic ending of Mark's Gospel in its original form. (A longer ending was patched on in later manuscripts, but it is an obvious pastiche from the other Gospels.) When the women turned from the tomb of Jesus, directed away from any search for Jesus' corpse by their vision of the white-robed youth, the question of what became of his physical body was left open forever.[2] They fled from the spot, trembling, in a frenzy. Why does the text go out of its way to emphasize their fear?

As we have seen, visions of the Chariot were associated with both ecstasy and fear, the "trembling and frenzy" of which Mark speaks. The stone had moved away from the tomb's entrance, seemingly of its own vo-

---

2. The later Gospels embellish this scene (Matthew 28:1–15; Luke 24:1–12; John 20:1–10) to depict Jesus' resurrection in physical terms, making it a resuscitation comparable to that of Lazarus.

lition. The angelic young man clothed in white signaled that the women had entered the trance world of the *Merkavah,* or Chariot. When he said Jesus was not to be found there, or in the majestic rhetoric of Luke, "Why do you seek the living among the dead?" (Luke 24:5), the event we call the resurrection was born.

The circumstances that generated the resurrection narratives of the Gospels will always elude our complete understanding. But it seems clear to me that after the Transfiguration, Jesus' disciples began to see their rabbi as part of the heavenly pantheon around the Throne, standing at God's side along with Moses and Elijah. In a sense, he had been raised while he was still with them. His mystical ascent began on Mount Hermon before his death.

The fear and pressure of the events leading to Jesus' crucifixion, and the grim suffering that their rabbi experienced on the cross, intensified his followers' experience of his angelic persona and sharpened their vision of the spirit world where they, like he, increasingly dwelled. The horror of the crucifixion magnified their transformed consciousness and gave it a common point of focus: as they met together, meditated, and prayed, their journey into the world of the Chariot brought them face to face with Rabbi Jesus. Their visionary trances were collective, and sometimes even on a mass scale. The disciples were gripped by a disciplined form of religious hysteria, and the fear, trembling, and frenzy that seized the women at the mouth of their rabbi's tomb describes the condition of many of those who experienced Jesus as raised from the dead.

J esus was no stranger to the hope of resurrection. The concept of being raised from the dead was certainly not an invention of the early Church, imposed at the end of the Gospels after the fact, as some kind of final proof that Jesus was truly divine. The resurrection was an intrinsic part of the Jewish teaching that Jesus passed on to his *talmidim,* especially at the end of his life.

The promise of resurrection is unequivocally stated only in one of the

Hebrew Bible's latest works, and it is articulated without specifying *how* "many of those who sleep in earth's dust shall awake" (Daniel 12:2). The hope was sufficiently inchoate to allow the Zadokites to argue that the Torah did not require belief in resurrection, but sufficiently emphatic to allow some Pharisees to insist that one was raised from the dead in the *same body* in which one had died. Rabbinic literature records that one rabbi from the early second century, Joshua ben Chananiah, performed experiments on the tiny coccyx at the base of the spine, submitting it to fire and smashing it to prove that it was indestructible; in his theory, it was the germ capable of surviving any form of death and destruction, from which God would regenerate the body whole again (Leviticus Rabbah 18.1). Physical regeneration was a contested issue in ancient Judaism, insisted on by some, denied by others. Modern Judaism is frequently portrayed as this-worldly, disallowing the possibility of any such thing as bodily resurrection, but its ancient counterpart was quite different.

After the Transfiguration, when Jesus had taken his place alongside Moses and Elijah by the divine Throne, resurrection had figured prominently in his *kabbalah*. By his last winter in Jerusalem, his teaching on the resurrection had emerged as distinctive and mature. He asserted to priestly Zadokites on Chanuth that resurrected humanity was angelic (following Mark 12:24–27, compare Matthew 22:29–32; Luke 20:34–38):

> *Stated Yeshua to them, For this are you not deceived, knowing neither the writings nor the miracle of God? Because when the dead arise they neither marry nor are they given in marriage, but are like angels in the heavens. But concerning the dead—that they are raised—have you not read in the book of Mosheh in the passage about the thorn-bush?—how God talked to him saying, I am Avraham's God and Yitzchak's God and Yaaqov's God? He is not God of the dead—but of the living. You are much deceived!*

By directly comparing those who are resurrected with angels, Jesus engaged in a theological debate with both Zadokites and Pharisees. Against the Zadokites, he found the resurrection hope *within the Torah itself,* in its reference to the enduring lives of the patriarchs. Against the Pharisees, he rejected a physical conception of being raised again, when he compared the resurrected patriarchs to angels. He seems both to affirm and deny resurrection in the same breath: those who are raised in God's sight are alive, but they are raised to an angelic status that transcends even the intimate relationship of marriage. It has never ceased to amaze me that discussions of the resurrection often begin as if Jesus had stated unequivocally that the dead *are* raised physically, in exactly the same bodies they had at death. That is just what he went out of his way to deny in his carefully crafted teaching.

B ut what does it mean to be resurrected "like angels in the heavens"? And how, in Jesus' mind, does it happen? To answer these questions we must confront the last element of Jesus' esoteric teaching—his *kabbalah* of crucifixion. On the way to Mount Hermon, Jesus rebuked poor Peter—that much-abused apostle—for failing to understand this most difficult part of his rabbi's science of approaching the Throne (Mark 8:31–33; Matthew 16:21–23; Luke 9:21–22):

> *And he began to teach them that: The one like the person must suffer a lot and be condemned by the elders and the high priests and the letterers and be killed and after three days arise. And he was speaking the word frankly; Rock took him aside and began to scold him. But he turned back and saw his students, scolded Rock and says, Depart after me, Satan, because you do not think God's way, but humanity's.*

This is obviously an instance where the Gospels impute to Jesus more advance knowledge about the specifics of his death than he really had. But it authentically conveys his deep sense that all of us (here he uses the Aramaic phrase "one like a person" to designate ordinary human beings) must remain aware of our frail, suffering nature in the midst of the vision of the Throne and its angels. One of the pitfalls of any spiritual discipline is that the practitioner might exalt his own importance, claiming to be as infallible and powerful as the divine world he trains himself to see. Forgetting our mortality betrays God, and we run the risk of supplanting God's majesty with our own arrogance. That, to Jesus, was the way of Satan. He insisted his disciples understand that the approach to the Chariot required suffering, and the conscious acceptance of suffering. He rebuked Peter for mistaking the glory of God for the glorification of Jesus and his followers, in the manner of all too many religious teachers who confuse divine majesty with their own exaltation.

Jesus understood that his final pilgrimage to Jerusalem courted danger. Suffering was not to be avoided, but embraced as a prophetic sign that God's Kingdom was making its way into a world that resisted transformation. He spoke of how encountering persecution could link a disciple all the more intimately with the one like the person beside the Throne (Mark 8:35–38; Matthew 16:25–27; Luke 9:24–26):

For whoever wishes to save one's own life, will ruin it, but whoever will ruin one's life for me and the message will save it. For what's the profit for a person to gain the whole world and to forfeit one's life? Because what should a person give for redemption of one's life? For whoever is ashamed of me and my words in this adulterous and sinful generation, the one like the person will be ashamed of also, when he comes in the glory of his father with the holy angels.

Rabbi Jesus pushed, bullied, cajoled, berated, threatened, wheedled, whined, and otherwise made himself a nuisance until his disciples came to think of their lives not as the happenstance of pleasure and pain, but as a prophetic vocation. Each of them was to seek the life beyond this life. In God's presence alone the sum of one's sojourn on earth was measured. He offered an answer to the question posed in Ecclesiastes: "Who knows whether the spirit of people goes up above, and whether the spirit of beasts goes down under the earth?" (3:21). The direction of one's spirit, he taught, was no mere matter of happenstance; it was within one's power to influence.

For this rabbi, whether you realized the Spirit of God within you or not was no abstract issue; it was a matter of life and death. He saw we are all poised on the razor's edge between our divine potential and the abyss of Gehenna. The struggle truly to be in the image of God was something you worked out in your life, in the choices you made, the strength of your convictions, the purity that could only come from your heart. It is not what goes into a person but what comes out of a person that defiles one, he had said. And what proceeds from a person is either all or nothing. "Because what should a person give for redemption of one's life?" In his final months his parables penetrated into the core of what it means to be alive and human. The disciples learned that putting their lives in jeopardy, for all the risk involved, enabled them to stand before the heavenly Chariot with the one like the person.

During their final stay in Jerusalem, he repeated the promise to his loyal Twelve that, despite their lack of power in this world, they would sit on thrones, judging the tribes of Israel (Matthew 19:28; Luke 22:28–30). The last would be first; the first, last. Yet he also complained about the Twelve. They argued among themselves about which one of them would be preeminent (Matthew 18:1–5; 19:13–15; Mark 9:33–37; 10:13–16; Luke 9:46–48; 18:15–17), effectively excluding themselves from the Kingdom that was for the humble and meek, for children, not for the power-hungry and proud.

Jesus' *kabbalah* of crucifixion instilled the constant awareness that no one was powerful before God. What were twelve thrones compared to the Chariot? One faced *Abba* with a child's vulnerability. When Jesus in his humility rejected the stratagem of a victorious messiah during the Satanic temptations on Mount Hermon, he also insisted that his followers learn the same humility. It is not modesty or self-deprecation, but the recognition that one is limited, weak, in need of nurture and forgiveness in the presence of the creator of all things. Jesus' *kabbalah* did not treat pain as a virtue in itself, but turned the endemically human experience of suffering into a means of discovering divine power in the midst of our own weakness.

He promised his followers the reward of a prophet: the vision of God (Matthew 10:40–42; 13:16–17). But that reward required payment (Matthew 23:34–36; Luke 11:49–51). He reminded them that the prophets of Israel had suffered, and suffered for the sake of their vision. Isaiah was a much-abused servant (Isaiah 53). Jeremiah was put in stocks by the Temple priests (Jeremiah 20:1–2). Ezekiel's prophecy left him bereft and ridiculed (Ezekiel 24:15–27). Persecution, even painful death, was the prophet's badge of honor. By the first century, oral and written traditions circulated widely that detailed how many of Judaism's prophets had died. Martyrdom—the act of serving as a "witness" (*martus* in Greek, *ed* in Hebrew)—was viewed as part of the prophetic vocation. "Abraham carrying the wood was like a man carrying his cross." That comparison from a Rabbinic *midrash* (interpretation) links the Roman mode of execution to the first great patriarch's willingness to sacrifice his only child to God on Mount Moriah (Genesis Rabbah 66.3). The suffering required to follow God's will, no matter what the cost, expressed the heart of the prophetic conviction.

R abbi Jesus insisted that his followers be ready to suffer as he did, if they truly wanted to serve God and walk along the path he walked, to angelic status and everlasting life (Matthew 10:37–38; Luke 14:26–27):

> *The one who loves father or mother more than me is not worthy of me, and the one who loves son or daughter more than me is not worthy of me, and whoever does not take his cross and follow behind me, is not worthy of me.*

Jesus' teaching about suffering came to be so fused with the final events leading up to his death that the Gospels present his crucifixion, step by step, as divinely ordained. But what was providential in Jesus' execution was not that it was predetermined, but that it became the vehicle for an unconquerable vision. The "cross" he expected to carry, and expected each of his followers to carry, did not refer to the particular sequence of events that brought him to his death. Rather, it symbolized the potential of suffering to serve as the gateway to vision.

In losing his life he saved it, consummated his angelic identity, was resurrected, and took his place by the Throne with Moses and Elijah at God's side. He was consciously, even obstinately, moving toward this point as Caiaphas baited him after his arrest in Gethsemane.

"Are you the messiah, the son of the blessed?" the high priest asked.

Instead of any demurral or silence, there came the words, "I am, and you will see the one like the person sitting at the right of the power and coming with the clouds of the heaven." Jesus' reply sealed his fate. He ended his life by remaining faithful to what he knew to be the reality of his vision. The final choice he made, after which he had no choices to make, reached deep into the visionary world that had long sustained him.

In the Jewish theology of martyrdom that saw Jesus through his last hours, suffering endured for truth is taken into the majesty of that truth; the witness's persona shines with the glory he attests. Rabbi Aqiba died in 135 C.E. under Roman torture with the ancient words on his lips, "Hear, Israel, the Lord our God is one" (Deuteronomy 6:4). The Talmud depicts both of his agony and of his prophetic reward (Berakhot 61b):

> He held on to the word, "One," until his soul expired as he said the word "one." An echo from heaven came forth and said, "Happy are you, Rabbi Aqiba, that your soul expired with the word 'one.'" The serving angels said before the Holy One, blessed be he, "Is this Torah and that the reward . . . ?" He said to them, "Their portion is in life." An echo went forth and proclaimed, "Happy are you, R. Aqiba, for you are selected for the life of the world to come."

The principle of prophetic martyrdom neither began nor ended with Rabbi Jesus.

In his case, the one like the person was his companion through the torture that preceded his death: the beatings and baitings, the scourge of a whip, the iron spikes that were driven through his wrists and feet, the soldier's lance in his side. The one like the person beckoned him to his final transformation. He was changing again in his progression from *mamzer* to *talmid,* to rabbi, to messianic exorcist, to *chasid,* to prophet, and now to angel. The apocalyptic sacrifice of Zechariah was unfinished, incomplete. But in the end he had accomplished something more profound. He had opened a way from this world to the realm of God for all who chose to take up their daily crosses and follow him.

In his final hours, he had cried out with his heartbreaking plea (taken from Psalm 22): "My God, my God, why have you forsaken me?" (Matthew 27:46; Mark 15:34). But people also remembered his saying, "Amen I say to you, today you will be with me in the paradise!" (Luke 23:43), and "Father, into your hands I commend my spirit!" (Luke 23:46).

Whatever his agonies on the cross, his thoughts remained with the Throne and "paradise" (Luke 23:43), the garden within which, according to Jewish theology, those who had access to the Chariot rejoiced (see Chagigah 12b in the Talmud). The same psalm that Jesus began to recite on the cross culminates in an anticipation of all people, in a transformed world, offering sacrifice in God's Kingdom (Psalm 22:27–28). It was with that transformative power of the mystical garden in view, the paradise that once held Adam and Eve and now awaited the enlightened just, that Jesus breathed out the last of his spirit with what some Gospels portray as a wordless shout (Matthew 27:50; Mark 15:37) and which Luke and John wisely interpret as the return of Jesus' spirit to its source (Luke 23:46; John 19:30).

The progression of visions of Jesus after his death followed the pattern suggested by the white-robed angel the two Miriams and their companion encountered when they came with their balm to the mouth of Jesus' tomb on the morning after Shabbath. "You seek Yeshua the crucified Nazirite. He is raised; he is not here . . . depart, tell his students and Rock that he goes before you into Galil; you will see him there." After the crucifixion, Peter had retreated to Galilee, away from the danger of persecution, much as Jesus had done after the death of John the Baptist. In Galilee, Peter's visionary practice took a new and provocative turn. He was fishing all night on the Sea of Galilee, catching nothing, with six other disciples. In the morning a figure appeared on the shore, telling them where to cast their net. They didn't recognize him, even though he had the same know-it-all manner that Jesus displayed in Capernaum, and they did draw in a great catch. Peter stripped down and swam to where the man stood on the shore; the others followed by boat. The stranger made a breakfast for them of bread and fish. "Tend my sheep," "shepherd my sheep," he repeated to them, and disappeared, and they knew the stranger was their rabbi (John 21:1–24).

After this incident, the Twelve reassembled and returned to Jerusalem in time for the great feast of the Pentecost, the wheat harvest, which occurred seven weeks after Passover. They were circumspect and went into the Temple anonymously, not as followers of Jesus. In their experience of their resurrected Lord, as they gathered privately in their festal meals, they felt themselves vindicated, reenergized (Luke 24:36–52; Acts 1:12–2:42; John 20:19–31). In their understanding, the risen Jesus poured out on his disciples the same Spirit he had been immersed in since his time with John. They remained near Mount Zion, where Jesus had promised the Zecharian apocalypse would begin.

In Jerusalem, they had many experiences of the resurrected Jesus, and the New Testament records that five hundred other followers in Galilee also saw the rabbi raised from the dead.[3] These accounts perplex readers of the Gospels. If this is supposed to be the same Jesus the disciples knew, why is he sometimes physically unrecognizable? How can he appear in distant places nearly simultaneously, and both walk through doors and snack on fish? Why does he insist that Miriam of Magdala

3. So 1 Corinthians 15:6, which—with many other scholars—I would associate with Matthew 28:16–20 (and not limit that appearance to the eleven apostles).

keep her hands off him, but invite Thomas to finger his wounds? As long as we fail to grasp that the resurrection was an angelic, nonmaterial event, these accounts will continue to confound us.[4]

James lay low after his brother's death; he did not join Peter and the Twelve in their resumption of fishing by the Sea of Galilee. Instead, he went back to Nazareth to tend his fields and be with his wife, his mother, and Jesus' other siblings. It must have been with grim despair that family and friends in the little hamlet struggled to accept what had happened in Jerusalem.

James had heard of the angel by the tomb, the stranger's commissioning of the apostles over bread and fish, and the appearance of Jesus in Jerusalem to Peter's circle and to the five hundred in Galilee. He himself went back to Jerusalem soon after Pentecost in the summer of 32 C.E. to join Peter and the others who were reporting that Jesus was alive. He worshipped with them in the Temple, devoted to the vision of the Zecharian transformation that Jesus had foretold. He probably stayed with Miriam and Martha in Bethany, practicing the *kabbalah* Jesus had taught him. And then he, too, began to have visions of Jesus as risen from the dead.

Because the New Testament itself does not record James' experience of his brother's resurrection, Jerome—the brilliant scholar and saint of the fifth century—cites the second-century Gospel According to the Hebrews alongside the New Testament to refer to James' resurrection experience (Jerome, *Liber de Viris Illustribus* 2). In the report of this precious document, after Jesus' death James begins fasting to purify himself, but then Jesus appears to him and tells him to eat, "because the one like the person is risen from the dead."

Peter and James had different experiences of Jesus' resurrection, which resulted in differing understandings of their rabbi's true identity.

---

4. The stories alluded to are, in the order cited: Luke 24:13–35; John 20:19–23; Luke 24:36–43; John 20:17; John 20:27.

For Peter, the Spirit that had once been active in Jesus alone, as God's son, was poured out on his followers, commissioning them to forgive and heal on his behalf. But for James, Jesus specifically became the same one like the person in heaven, envisaged by Ezekiel and Daniel, of whom Jesus himself had so often spoken.

The importance of Peter within the early church, particularly as a source of faith in Jesus' resurrection, has lead to the understandable but careless conclusion that Simon Peter's vision is the only real source of the belief that Jesus was raised from the dead. But it was James who took over Jesus' movement in Jerusalem. James—always more an ascetic than his famously carousing brother—practiced Nazirite vows of purity in a dedication to worship in the Temple that made him a paragon among Jews as a whole, not only in the little movement that came to be called Christianity.

Hegesippus, a second-century historian, recounts that James "Drank no wine or strong drink, nor did he eat flesh; no razor went upon his head; he did not anoint himself with oil, and he did not go to the baths . . . he used to enter alone into the Temple, and be found kneeling and praying for forgiveness for the people, so his knees grew hard like a camel's."[5] It was James with his camel's knees who promoted worship in the Temple and regulated the life of the Christian community in the holy city before he was killed by the high priest Ananus in 62 C.E. for proclaiming that Jesus was both the one like the person and the gateway into heaven.

The oldest text to mention the resurrection, written long before the Gospels, is Paul's first letter to the Corinthians, written around 56 C.E. The twelve delegates, the five hundred "brethren" of Jesus, James,

---

5. Hegesippus is quoted in Eusebius' *Ecclesiastical History* 2.23, a source from the fourth century. James' death is also recounted by Josephus in *Antiquities* 20 § § 200–203.

other apostles, and Paul himself, are listed along with Peter as having experiences of the risen Jesus (1 Corinthians 15:5–8).

Paul's own resurrection vision occurred in 32 when he was a young zealot in Jerusalem—still named Saul—on a mission from Caiaphas to denounce Jesus' followers in Damascus both in synagogues and to Roman officials. On route, Saul was surrounded by light and a heavenly echo such as Aqiba heard, which identified itself as Jesus of Nazareth (Acts 9:1–20; 22:3–21; 26:9–20). This was in no sense a physical encounter with Jesus; there is not even an indication that Saul had ever met Jesus personally prior to his crucifixion. But it is an appearance very similar to what Peter and his companions experienced, complete with prophetic commissioning and the symbolism of the holy Spirit in the surrounding light.

Saul turned around and, after a retreat into solitude for three years, went back to Jerusalem: he knew exactly where to have his vision explained to him. He spoke about it only to Peter and James (Galatians 1:18–20). He understood that his experience was more visionary than physical, as he carefully says in a passage of straightforward Greek that has been perennially mistranslated: God, wrote Paul (as he came to call himself), "took pleasure to uncover his son *in* me" (Galatians 1:16). Rather than representing what Paul said, word for word, even translations that claim to be literal falsely objectify Paul's experience, and speak of when God was pleased "to reveal his son *to* me." By distorting the meaning of a single preposition, traditional Christianity has falsified its premier apostle's own visionary experience of what he explicitly (1 Corinthians 15:8) understood to be the resurrected Jesus.

In Jerusalem, Peter and his circle were a constant annoyance to Caiaphas, who tried time and again to persuade the Sanhedrin to denounce them to Pilate. But the disciples never again mounted the kind of raid on the Temple Jesus attempted, and they had learned to practice their rabbi's blasphemous meals in private. Except for short periods of incarceration on charges that did not stick, Caiaphas' efforts failed (see Acts 3:1–4:31; 5:12–42), and he apparently did not even try to denounce James.

Caiaphas could never count on the council's support again after Jesus' execution, and he had to rely on his authority as high priest to create what difficulties he could for Jesus' disciples. His office gave him access to literate assistants and the capacity to communicate by letter with cities outside Israel; priestly correspondence between Jerusalem and Antioch, for example, has been a topic of recent inquiry in New Testament scholarship. Caiaphas' last, feeble maneuver was to seek to identify those who claimed to see Jesus as still alive and pouring God's Spirit out from the divine Throne, in the hope of making trouble for them with the Roman officials and Jewish leaders of the cities in which they resided.

At times, it must have seemed to the high priest that supernatural forces were working against him. During this period, the Babylonian Talmud records (in Yoma 39b) that portents of the Temple's demise startled the Jewish population of Jerusalem. Within the Sanctuary, the torches of the menorah nearest the holy of holies persistently went out, as if the divine presence itself had weakened in its earthly abode. The majestic doors that shut in front of the Sanctuary at night spontaneously opened, prompting the fear that God had truly grown impatient with the place. Finally, the Talmud reports, even the ritual of the Day of Atonement (Yom Kippur) presaged evil. As was customary, the high priest took two goats, and determined by lot which would be a scapegoat (to be driven into the wilderness) and which would be a sacrifice in the Temple (to remove the sin of Israel). Year after year, the lot that selected the animal for sacrifice in the Temple came up in Caiaphas' *left* hand, a bad omen for Israel as a whole, because the left was equated with the sinister throughout the ancient world.

Within this complex of bad omens, Caiaphas had to face other portents that seemed connected with Jesus' execution in the disciples' minds. The huge tapestry hanging in front of the holy of holies was torn in two (Matthew 27:51; Mark 15:38; Luke 23:45). It was as if the Temple itself rebelled against Caiaphas' reforms and the execution of Jesus by the Romans.

Pilate, it turns out, was only momentarily reformed by the death of Sejanus. He was soon up to his vicious tricks again. He had many Samaritans killed with their prophetic leader on Mount Gerizim for inciting what Pilate anticipated was going to be insurrection (Josephus, *Antiquities* 18 §§ 85–87). Both Caiaphas and Pilate were dismissed in 37 C.E. by Vitellius, the Roman legate in Syria who also had the high priest's vestments moved out of the Antonia, back to their proper place in one of the side chambers of the Court of the Israelites (Josephus, *Antiquities* 18 §§ 88–95). Pilate, we can surmise, retired to Italy;[6] Caiaphas would have become an ordinary member of the Sanhedrin.

Jesus' other nemesis, Herod Antipas, committed political suicide when, urged on by his ever-ambitious wife, Herodias, he angled to be granted the title of "king" of Galilee and Perea. Herodias persuaded Antipas to travel to Rome in 39 C.E. to meet with the emperor to discuss the matter. When they arrived in the eternal city, Caligula, who had succeeded Tiberius as emperor, had Antipas banished to Spain on charges trumped up by Herod Agrippa, Herodias' own brother (Josephus, *Jewish War* 2 §§ 181–183; *Antiquities* 18 §§ 240–256). So Antipas was finally undone by the ambition of the woman John the Baptist had said it was against God's will that he marry, and by the endless intrigue of Herod the Great's troublesome progeny.

Fueled by ambition or heroism, guided by cunning or folly, human events on the public stage inscribe history like a tapestry with varying patterns of hope and fear, eruptions of violence, forces that erect and deconstruct great institutions and civilizations. Within that tapestry of

6. A later tradition, attested by Eusebius (*Ecclesiastical History* 2.7) claims Pilate committed suicide, but that assertion is an early example of a long line of wishful thinking. See Ann Wroe, *Pontius Pilate: A Biography* (New York: Random House, 2000).

meaning, the resurrection is both the most elemental and the most difficult to grasp of all Gospel teachings. And yet the confidence that God raises life from the dust of death, for all the various ways it is presented in the New Testament and in later theology, is the genetic chain informing and sustaining the entire organism of Christianity.

Jesus' conception of the transformation from a physical to an angelic state was inextricably rooted in a Semitic understanding of what makes for human life and personality. Greek philosophy sometimes referred to soul (*psukhe,* meaning "breath") as something apart from the physical body, but Hebrew *nephesh,* meaning both life and breath, coordinated body and breathing within a single, living whole. *Nephesh* was linked categorically to the view that God was Spirit (*ruach*), the almighty force of wind breathing life into all creation. Jesus' understanding was that human beings, in the course of their lives, could shape their innermost breath—the pulse of their being as well as their cognitive awareness of the Chariot—to correspond to the overpowering creativity of divine Spirit. They became angelic, and that was the substance of their resurrection. Jesus focuses us on the essence of our humanity, and allows us into his parallel universe, imbued with the justice and glory of God.

As I have struggled to see how this highly specific focus can be realized, terminally ill patients whom I have counseled as they approached their own deaths have taught me a great deal. Some of them have been Christian, some of them not; all, in my experience, were both searching and confused. Yet they showed me that dying could affirm their humanity, and they have instructed me in the sense of Jesus' message. They have recounted stories of friendships from thirty years before, the longings of old relationships, the rewards and regrets of lives richer and more diverse than any narrator could or should relate. "All my bones are out of joint," is the way the psalmist refers to the dissolution of who we are physically (Psalm 22:14), and that disjointed agony of a little Golgotha—with or without medical relief—awaits us all in one way or another.

At the close of our lives, we linger for a time in that limbo where physical being fades and any life that remains must either be in spirit or relinquish any claim to be real. The pain of those struggling weeks or minutes is more metaphysical than medical, as anyone who has attended a deathbed will know.

Fear sometimes makes us wish for a quiet and sudden end, even for a violent termination, rather than confront that moment which is as inexorable and unyielding as eternity itself. But those of us who have experienced the human cost of taking a life—by means as crude as murder or as self-effacing (and self-justifying) as denying medical care—can attest that trying to evade the instant when we truly and completely lose ourselves only compounds pain with delusion.

Standing by the graves of the people I bury, recollecting the ancient wisdom that ashes return to ashes and dust to dust, I'm viscerally aware of bewildered faces around me, bodies cramped with grief, loss, and fear, the aching awareness that a person has passed beyond our reach. Here we know that we, too, are broken, as completely as it was once shown to me in Dubrovnik we all are. But Spirit does not die.

Death summons us to join the *ruach* pouring down through fissures in the firmament, from angelic openings that Jesus' vision trains us to discern. Our spirit merges with the wind that rushes over the land, connecting with the sapphire Throne that Israel's seers saw towering in heaven above the emblems of ancient sacrifice—a dark plume of smoke, redolent of fat and frankincense and blood. The sacrifice of our own lives frees Spirit to fly across the heavens in a Chariot moving at the speed of lightning, there at the beginning and as it will be at the end. It is in all places at once, constantly sustaining and renewing creation.

There is no one way to die, any more than there is a unique wisdom of what dying means, or a single cross we all have to bear. Jesus' *kabbalah* of crucifixion, the discovery of who we are in the midst of our pain, offers the vision that death's change is not simply degradation and despair. It is not the end of us, but the end of who we think we are. To lose one's life is to save it, Jesus said. Death is our hardest lesson, but it is also the gateway into the true, divine source of human identity.

Epilogue

Remarkable though his success had been in conveying to his disciples his visionary discipline of the divine Chariot and his hope that God's Kingdom was at hand, Rabbi Jesus never accomplished the Galilean reformation of the Temple that he so passionately desired and dramatically attempted. The first century of the Common Era came and went with little to show for the transformative vision for which he had died. His movement did not reform Judaism, and Christianity's influence in the Greco-Roman world remained marginal.

The name "Christian" was not even used commonly before the year 45; it was coined in the Hellenistic city of Antioch to mock the ridiculous, deluded congregations of domestic servants and former slaves who worshipped Jesus as Messiah, the *Khristos* who would come from heaven to rule in a world where the first would be last and the last first. They stood with hands and eyes uplifted, waiting for him to descend with all the splendor of a Greek god or a Roman statesman. Christians came to the wide notice of the Roman Empire only in 64 C.E., when Nero accused them of setting fire to Rome and encouraged the sadistic pogrom of torture and crucifixion that ensued. Not until the second century did Christianity begin to be taken seriously; it competed in the marketplace of ideas with other popular philosophies such as Stoicism, Platonism, the Dionysian and Mithraic Mysteries—and Judaism.

A failure on the world stage in his own time, Rabbi Jesus also fell short of making a lasting mark within Judaism. Dead at thirty, he had not yet framed his *mishnah,* the formally crafted public teaching that a rabbi typically transmitted to his students by around the age of forty. Nonetheless, he generated a new religion. He never articulated a doctrinal norm or a confessional requirement, but the events of his life, his public teaching, and his *kabbalah* gave rise to distinctive, emotionally resonant rituals such as baptism, prayer, anointing the sick, and the Eucharist. Jesus taught others to see as he saw, to share his vision of God, so that even after his death he appeared to his disciples as alive, a human presence within the swirling energy of the Throne.

That vision persists among those who hope that the pure of heart will indeed see God, become intimate with him, stand at his side through eternity as Jesus does with Moses and Elijah. The descendants of Adam may yet be restored to their lost paradise. We cannot physically mount the Temple steps with Jesus to realize his hope of a Sukkoth that will transform the world. No building anywhere could accommodate his followers today, nor could he or any teacher reach them all with his healing touch. In any case, the Temple he revered was demolished as surely as his own body was broken. Yet he remains a measure of how much we dare to see and feel the divine in our lives.

The joining of our lives to God was what was awakened in me in Dubrovnik. I intuited that our suffering, pain, and disappointment, as well as our joy, pleasure, friendships, and the love we feel for one another can enable us to realize who we are in God's presence. Jesus' force resides in his vulnerability not only on the cross but throughout his life. He entices each of us to meet him in that dangerous place where an awareness of our own weakness and fragility shatters the self and blossoms into an image of God within us. That is the gift that his biography and death have left us, and it is what makes Rabbi Jesus the treasure of the Church and the unique possession of no institution, no person on earth.

Epilogue

Nearly two millennia of Christianity have seen Jesus' vision interpreted, with its emphases constantly shifting, its proper application within human lives debated and disputed. Yet even while the centrality of the vision has been preserved, a vital truth of how Jesus taught it and crafted a discipline for its realization has been ignored.

The rabbi from Nazareth never claimed he was unique. His *Abba* was the *Abba* of all. His teaching, purifying, exorcism, healing, prayers, signs, meals, and sacrifices were not for himself alone, nor were they intended to demonstrate his personal power or bring him adulation for his attributes or accomplishments. All his work was undertaken to open the gate of heaven so that Israel might enter before the Throne of God.

Far too much theology has been preoccupied with closing that gate. By exalting Jesus as the only human being to sit on the right hand of God, many theologians have denied heaven to others. They remind me of Jesus' complaint about some Pharisees, who used the key of knowledge to shut God's Kingdom to those of lesser learning (Matthew 23:13; Luke 11:52).

Jesus' own message was not for the fainthearted or the cynical. He spoke to all those willing to open their eyes to see and their ears to hear, to refine their senses and attune their minds and hearts to the divine Kingdom in their midst. Now, as Rabbi Jesus' movement enters its third millennium, its great goal has yet to be achieved: to share Jesus' vision with all humanity, that it may enter through the gates of heaven and be transformed by the energy of God.

Notes

Foreword

The works I have in mind are Samuel Sandmel, *We Jews and Jesus* (New York; Oxford University Press, 1965); Asher Finkel, *The Pharisees and the Teacher of Nazareth. A Study of Their Background, Their Halachic and Midrashic Teachings, the Similarities and Differences*: Arbeiten zur Geschichte des antiken Judentums und des Urchristentums 4 (Leiden: Brill, 1964); W. D. Davies, *The Setting of the Sermon on the Mount* (Cambridge: Cambridge University Press, 1963).

   The contribution of "The Jesus Seminar" is by now famously controversial, to some extent because the organization has dared to state in public what academics have been talking about for many decades. As a Fellow of the Seminar, I have been stimulated and helped by its discussion and debate. But its published findings are based simply on how the Fellows who happen to have attended particular meetings voted on a variety of topics. Any biography concocted by polling is, at the end of the day, reminiscent of the adage that a giraffe is a horse put together by a committee. See Robert W. Funk, Roy W. Hoover and The Jesus Seminar, *The Five Gospels. The Search for the Authentic Words of Jesus* (San Francisco: HarperSanFrancisco, 1997); Robert W. Funk and The Jesus Seminar, *The Acts of Jesus. The Search for the Authentic Deeds of Jesus* (San Francisco: HarperSanFrancisco, 1998).

Chapter One: A Mamzer *from Nazareth*

Archaeological work, especially in combination with anthropological analysis, has laid much more emphasis on the distinctive culture of Jewish Galilee than was the case even a decade ago, when a more homogenized, Hellenistic character was imputed to the entire region. See Richard A. Horsley, *Archaeology, History, and Society in Galilee: The Social Context of Jesus and the Rabbis* (Valley Forge, Pa.: Trinity Press International, 1996), which is especially critical of the work of John Dominic Crossan. Yet while Crossan's social model of Galilee now seems to need revision, the fact remains that he did allow for the distinctive identity of Jews there in his *The Historical Jesus. The Life of a Mediterranean Jewish Peasant* (San Francisco: Harper, 1991).

I was put on the trail of a Galilean Bethlehem by Adolf Neubauer, *La Géographie du Talmud* (Paris, 1868) 189–191, discussed in Chilton, *God in Strength. Jesus' Announcement of the Kingdom*: Studien zum Neuen Testament und seiner Umwelt 1 (Freistadt: Plöchl, 1979), reprinted in "The Biblical Seminar" (Sheffield: JSOT, 1987) 311–313. For a recent, critical treatment of Bethlehem of Galilee in relation to other Jewish settlements, see James F. Strange, "First Century Galilee from Archaeology and from the Texts," *Archaeology and the Galilee. Texts and Contexts in the Graeco-Roman and Byzantine Periods*: South Florida Studies in the History of Judaism 143 (Atlanta: Scholars Press, 1997) 39–48.

Bauckham's article (cited in note 4) and the article by John P. Meier that he responds to, are both classics. Here, in a Catholic journal, a Protestant scholar (Bauckham) defends the notion that Joseph had been married previously, which holds the door open for the possibility that

Mary was a virgin at the time of Jesus' birth, while a Catholic scholar and a priest (Meier) insists that if Jesus' older siblings are called his brothers, they were the children of the same parents, Joseph and Mary. That is a fine example of the openness of much scholarship at the moment, and I especially admire Meier's courage in laying out his position, which he spells out further in his monumental *A Marginal Jew: Rethinking the Historical Jesus* (New York: Doubleday, 1991). Still, I think Bauckham has the benefit of the evidence as well as the argument in this case, although that does not by any means make the *almah* Mary a "virgin" in the Victorian sense.

Jesus' status as a *mamzer* (or a related caste) has been suggested on the assumption his mother had been raped during a siege of Sepphoris in 4 B.C.E.; see, for example, Marianne Sawicki, *Crossing Galilee. Architectures of Contact in the Occupied Land of Jesus* (Harrisburg: Trinity Press International, 2000) 171–173. That argument seems to me to require too much supposition about Mary's alleged involvement with that city, when we only see her associated with village life in the Gospels. In addition, the category of *mamzer* was applied generally to such cases only at a later period; see Shaye J. D. Cohen, *The Beginnings of Jewishness. Boundaries, Varieties, Uncertainties* (Berkeley: University of California Press, 1999).

Chapter Two: Pilgrimage to Jerusalem

Work on the geographical, physical, and archaeological *realia* of Judea, Galilee, and Samaria during this period has developed richly in recent years. Accessible resources include: John Rogerson, *Atlas of the Bible* (Oxford: Equinox, 1987); W. Harold Mare, *The Archaeology of the Jerusalem Area* (Grand Rapids: Baker, 1987); John J. Rousseau and Rami Arav, *Jesus and His World. An Archaeological and Cultural Dictionary* (Minneapolis: Fortress, 1995); *Ancient Synagogues: Historical Analysis and Archaeological Discovery* (edited by Dan Urman and Paul V. M. Flesher; Leiden: E. J. Brill, 1995); K. C. Hanson and Douglas E. Oakman, *Palestine in the Time of Jesus. Social Structure and Social Conflicts* (Minneapolis: Fortress, 1998); Leen and Kathleen Ritmeyer, *Secrets of Jerusalem's Temple Mount* (Washington: Biblical Archaeology Society, 1998). The anthropology of Israel's sacrifice is investigated in Chilton, *The Temple of Jesus. His Sacrificial Program Within a Cultural History of Sacrifice* (University Park: The Pennsylvania State University Press, 1992). Mary Douglas's classic work, one of my points of departure and the incentive for much recent work, is *Purity and Danger. An Analysis of Concepts of Pollution and Taboo* (New York: Praeger, 1966).

Chapter Three: The Talmid of John

John the Baptist is explicitly called "rabbi" in John 3:26. Jesus himself is addressed that way more than by any other single designation (Matthew 26:25, 49; Mark 9:5; 10:51; 11:21; 14:45; John 1:38, 49; 3:2; 4:31; 6:25; 9:2; 11:8). Despite that fact, it is routinely objected by scholars that Jesus was not a rabbi, but "a prophet (eschatological or otherwise);" so Casimir Bernas in *Theological Studies* 46 (1985) 129–130. Later in his life, we shall see that Jesus was indeed called a prophet, but never as persistently as he was called rabbi. In any case, the one address by no means excludes the other. That the term was current in Jesus' time is plain from Daniel 2:48; 4:6; 5:11 and Mishnah Avoth 1:6, 16, as well as from inscriptions; for those, see J. P. Kane, "Ossuary Inscriptions of Jerusalem," *Journal of Semitic Studies* 23 (1978) 268–282. But Bernas is definitely right to raise the issue, because being called "rabbi" did not involve an institutional qualification until a much later period, well after the destruction of the Temple. Crossan, whose work is cited above, has compared Jesus to the popular philosophers of the Mediterranean world, especially the Cynics. That comparison is helpful, although it seems clear that a Jewish teacher whose wisdom was valued would have been called "rabbi."

In her excellent study, which firmly grounds John in the practice of purity, Joan E. Taylor lays the foundation for a critical understanding of immersion and John himself; see *The Immerser: John the Baptist Within Second Temple Judaism:* Studying the Historical Jesus 2 (Grand Rapids: Eerdmans, 1997). On the argument between John and Jesus and its outcome, see Chilton, *Jesus' Baptism and Jesus' Healing. His Personal Practice of Spirituality* (Harrisburg: Trinity Press International, 1998). Influenced by such studies, Jesus' focus on purity becomes a major theme in Paula Fredricksen's *Jesus of Nazareth* (New York: Knopf, 1999). In an influential book, E. P. Sanders has argued that Jesus dropped the requirement of repentance altogether; see *Jesus and Judaism* (London and Philadelphia: SCM and Fortress, 1985). I have disagreed with him, because the persistent reference to repentance by Jesus is manifest in the Gospels and early Christian literature; see "Jesus and the Repentance of E. P. Sanders," *Tyndale Bulletin* 39 (1988) 1–18. But Sanders put scholarship on the right track by urging us to identify the evident difference between John and Jesus. Purification, in the light of more recent research, seems to have been the crucial issue.

The bird that hovered over the face of the waters in Genesis 1:2 was identified as a dove in the Rabbinic tradition of the Babylonian Talmud written in the fifth century C.E. It speaks of a rabbi of the second century, Simon ben Zoma, who saw the holy spirit as a dove in the midst of the primeval waters in his vision of the heavenly firmament during a trance (Chagigah 15a). Obviously, a direct connection with the scene of Jesus' immersion in the Gospels can't be made on the basis of such a late reference, but a fragment from Qumran that is undoubtedly pre-Christian also attests the association of spirit and dove. See Dale C. Allison, "The Baptism of Jesus and a New Dead Sea Scroll," *Biblical Archaeology Review* 18.2 (1992) 58–60.

The entire prayer of Jesus is translated back into Aramaic and explained in Chilton, *Jesus' Prayer and Jesus' Eucharist. His Personal Practice of Spirituality* (Valley Forge: Trinity Press International, 1997). The basis of that work is the Greek Gospels, and the Aramaic language attested at Qumran, evidencing the Judaic conceptions most precious to Jesus:

Abba, yitqadash shemakh, tetey malkhutakh:
Hav li yoma lakhma dateh,
Ushebaq li yat chobati, veal taeleyni lenisyona.

Chapter Four: The Prodigal Returns

The long and continuing history of the Samaritans is beautifully introduced in Reinhard Pummer, *The Samaritans* (Iconography of Religions
23.5; Brill: Leiden, 1987). The contribution of Jacob Neusner to the
study of Rabbinic Judaism and its predecessors is without parallel. By
way of introduction to his method and thought, I have especially profited
from the following books: *From Politics to Piety: The Emergence of Pharisaic Judaism* (New York: Ktav, 1979), *Judaism: The Evidence of Mishnah*
(Chicago: University of Chicago Press, 1981); *Rabbinic Judaism: The
Documentary History of the Formative Age* (Bethesda: CDL Press, 1994);
and his monumental *The Theology of the Oral Torah. Revealing the Justice
of God* (Montreal: McGill-Queen's University Press, 1999).

In a recent academic monograph, Professor Neusner and I have in-
quired into the definition of earliest Christianity as a form of Judaism; see
Judaism in the New Testament. Practices and Beliefs (London and New
York: Routledge, 1995). In all such inquiry, it needs to be kept in mind
that the written composition of Rabbinic literature (including the Targumim) postdates the time of Jesus by several centuries. That fact has been
used by some scholars of the New Testament to claim that Rabbinic
sources should not be used in exegesit at all. I have to say I find that an
odd argument. Exegetes routinely refer to later Roman historians, such as
Tacitus and Dio Cassius, to later Hellenistic authors, such as Philostratus
and Athanaeus, to later Christian writers, such as Justin Martyr and Eusebius, and to later Gnostic sources, such as the "Trimorphic Protonnoia"
and "On the Origin of the World," all in order to understand the New Testament better. (I choose those examples, by the way, because they are
widely cited, and involve a time lag after Jesus comparable to the delay in

the production of the Mishnah, the Talmud, and the Targumim.) In cases other than Rabbinic Judaism, the technique of extrapolating backward from literary evidence is accepted. Once, Jewish sources were excluded from consideration by Christian theologians for doctrinal reasons, and now it seems a kind of chronological fundamentalism is being inflicted upon them alone by some modern (and proudly postmodern) interpreters. In any case, no one would seriously argue that Rabbinic sources were simply made up by authors on the spot at the time of written composition. By means of both oral and written transmission, their heritage reaches back behind the period of the New Testament. In principle, we are dealing here with a situation reminiscent of the textual study of the Gospels themselves, which do not appear in complete manuscripts until the fourth century C.E. Naturally, critical care is necessary to sort out earlier and later material in all ancient literature, but that is the normal task of scholarship.

Chapter Five: The Spirit Chaser

The place of Hillel in the principle of purity Jesus developed was signaled in Jacob Neusner's article, "First Cleanse the Inside: Halakhic Background of a Controversial Saying," *New Testament Studies* 22 (1976) 486–495. I make it a practice to translate all ancient texts afresh, but my starting point in the case of Mishnah is his *The Mishnah. A New Translation* (New Haven: Yale University Press, 1988).

The regulations for Nazirites are spelled out in Numbers 6 and in the Mishnaic tractate Nazir. Jesus' personal practice was remarkably *unlike* that of actual Nazirites; for example they were supposed to abstain completely from wine during the period of their vow. After the death of Jesus, however, his brother James took up the formal practice of Nazirite vows and applied the term to Jesus himself. For the formative influence of James at that time, see *James the Just and Christian Origins: Supplements to Novum Testamentum* 98 (edited by B. D. Chilton and C. A. Evans; Leiden: Brill, 1999).

For a full discussion of the Old Syriac text and its importance for the understanding of Luke 4, see Chilton, *God in Strength* (cited in the notes to chapter 1), 157–177. A discussion of Jesus' connection to targumic traditions of the book of Isaiah is available in Chilton, *A Galilean Rabbi and His Bible. Jesus' Use of the Interpreted Scripture of His Time* (Wilmington: Glazier, 1984) also published with the subtitle, *Jesus' Own Interpretation of Isaiah* (London: SPCK, 1984). For targumic translations, see Chilton, *The Isaiah Targum. Introduction, Translation, Apparatus, and Notes:* The Aramaic Bible 11 (Wilmington: Glazier and Edinburgh: Clark, 1987) and Kevin J. Cathcart and Robert P. Gordon, *The Targum of the Minor Prophets:* The Aramaic Bible 14 (Wilmington: Glazier and Edinburgh: Clark, 1989). As in those editions, font changes indicate departures of the Targum from the Hebrew text. During the first century, one very famous rabbi, named Eliezer ben Hyrcanus, referred to his biblical discussion with a Christian heretic in Galilee (Avodah Zarah 16b–17a in the Babylonian Talmud). Galilee was a major source of teaching concerning the Kingdom of God, and Jesus was a remembered master of that teaching.

Chapter Six: Chasid *in the Holy City*

The actual name of the pool near the Temple is confused in the textual tradition of John 5, but Bethesda (from "place of poured waters" in Aramaic) and Bethzatha (from "bubbling over place" in Hebrew) are the best attested designations. The Aramaic form is found in the Copper Scroll from Qumran (3Q15.xi.12). The relationship to the Hebrew name Bethzatha has confused commentators, but that is easily related to the root *zeyd,* which means to boil up. Credit for proceeding on the basis of the Copper Scroll, now a commonly accepted idea, goes to John Allegro, *The Treasure of the Copper Scroll* (Garden City: Doubleday, 1960) 165–167.

Material regarding the *chasidim* has been conveniently gathered together by Geza Vermes in *Jesus the Jew. A Historian's Reading of the Gospels* (Philadelphia: Fortress, 1986) 72–80, on the basis of the earlier work of George Foot Moore, *Judaism in the First Centuries of the Christian Era* (Cambridge: Harvard University Press, 1927) I:377–378. For the dating of Chaninah, I take the Gamaliel in the story to be the first famous rabbi of the name Gamaliel, who was also the master of the apostle Paul (see Acts 5:34; 22:3). Jesus' particular link between his exorcistic, healing practice and the Kingdom of God is explored in Chilton, *Pure Kingdom. Jesus' Vision of God:* Studying the Historical Jesus 1 (Eerdmans: Grand Rapids and London: SPCK, 1996).

For an excellent discussion of the sources in regard to Barnabas, see Bernd Kollmann, *Joseph Barnabas. Leben und Wirkungsgeschichte:* Stuttgarter Bibelstudien 175 (Stuttgart: Katholisches Bibelwerk, 1998). Conventionally, scholarship has accorded priority to the first three Gospels in historical work on Jesus, putting progressively less credence in works of late date. John's Gospel, for example, is routinely dismissed as a source, on the grounds of its obviously homiletic purpose, comparatively late date, and greater distance from the culture of Galilee and Judea. In a recent book, Maurice Casey has supported that dismissal; see *Is John's Gospel True?* (London: Routledge, 1996). But the complex development of that Gospel over time has been amply demonstrated by Raymond Brown in his commentary. Its earliest sources, he argues convincingly, are comparable to the Synoptic tradition in value, although independent; see *The Gospel According to John:* The Anchor Bible 29–29A (Garden City: Doubleday, 1966, 1970). Given the way in which much early Christian and Judaic literature developed within communities in phases, rather than by the work of single authors who took responsibility for everything they wrote, it is unrealistic simply to write such texts off completely as fiction. It is clear that when materials in John and other sources can be shown to be early on literary grounds, and to accord with and complement what we may deduce from the Synoptic Gospels, it should be used with caution. That is just the method I follow here in assessing such material. For that reason, for example, Jesus' assertion in the

Gospel according to Thomas (saying 82), "Who is near to me is near to the fire; who is far from me is far from the kingdom," seems to me authentic, although it is found in a fourth-century Coptic text that renders an earlier Syriac tradition.

Chapter Seven: Capernaum's Prophet

Crossan's concept of the "unbrokered kingdom" is masterfully presented in his *Jesus. A Revolutionary Biography* (San Francisco: HarperSanFrancisco, 1994) 196. Elisabeth Schüssler Fiorenza offers a careful and innovative assessment of the importance of Jesus within the study of gender in *Jesus. Miriam's Child & Sophia's Prophet* (New York: Continuum, 1994).

The social description and analysis of Galilee during this period has been a deep concern in recent scholarship. See Bruce J. Malina and Richard L. Rohrbaugh, *Social-Science Commentary on the Synoptic Gospels* (Minneapolis: Fortress, 1992) and the seminal works of Sean Freyne, *Galilee, Jesus and the Gospels* (Philadelphia: Fortress, 1988) and Richard A. Horsley, *Jesus and the Spiral of Violence. Popular Jewish Resistance in Roman Palestine* (San Francisco: Harper & Row, 1987). On the difficulty of estimating population, see Horsley's *Archaeology, History, and Society in Galilee* (cited in the notes to chapter 1), 44–45. Josephus would seem to imply a Galilean population of three million (*Jewish War* 3 § 43; *Life* 235), but that is widely agreed to be an impossible exaggeration; see F. F. Bruce, *New Testament History* (London: Pickering & Inglis, 1982) 36.

Chapter Eight: Beyond the Pale

Knowledge of early Judaism and its variety has been vastly enriched during the last century by the publication of ancient, noncanonical sources.

Many of them are conveniently presented in *The Old Testament Pseude-pigrapha* (ed. J. H. Charlesworth; Garden City: Doubleday, 1983, 1985). See also Matthew Black, *The Book of Enoch or I Enoch:* Studia in Veteris Testamenti Pseudepigraphia 7 (Leiden: Brill, 1985). The importance of vision within apocalyptic literature is stressed by John J. Collins, *Daniel:* Hermeneia (Minneapolis: Fortress, 1993). For the motif of the visionary entry into paradise, see especially Christopher Rowland, *The Open Heaven. A Study of Apocalyptic in Judaism and Early Christianity* (New York: Crossroad, 1982) and John J. Collins, *The Apocalyptic Imagination. An Introduction to the Jewish Matrix of Christianity* (New York: Crossroad, 1984). Collins cautions that "The language of the apocalypses is not descriptive, referential newspaper language, but the *expressive* language of poetry" (p. 214). While allowing for the symbolic aspects of visionary language, I would also want to account for its frequent claim to convey a higher reality. It is of particular interest that as noted above, Simon ben Zoma's trance in Chagigah 15a involves his vision of the Spirit of God "like a dove which hovers over her young;" he is described as "deranged" or "beside himself" (as Jesus is in Mark 3:21), because the vision becomes more real to him than the presence of a colleague. Much of the literature described as "apocalyptic" (owing to its similarity to the Revelation of John, also known as the Apocalypse) engages in precise predictions of the sequence and dating of events leading up to and including the end.

Chapter Nine: Three Huts

The source called "Q" has been a topic of much debate for well over a century; see David Catchpole, *The Quest for Q* (Edinburgh: Clark, 1993); *The Shape of Q*, ed. J. S. Kloppenborg (Minneapolis: Fortress, 1994); Chilton, *Profiles of a Rabbi:* Brown Judaic Studies 177 (Atlanta: Scholars Press, 1989). On numerical symbolism within ancient Judaism, see Jöram Friberg, "Numbers and Counting," in the *Anchor Bible Dictio-*

nary, ed. D. N. Freedman and others (New York: Doubleday, 1992) 4:1139–1146. For the tractate on mourning (called Ebel Rabbati or Semachoth), see Dov Zlotnick, *The Tractate "Mourning"* (New Haven: Yale University Press, 1966).

Time and again, their colleagues have pilloried scholars who have identified the political dimension of Jesus' thought. The greatest of them was S.G.F. Brandon, who brilliantly placed Jesus in the context of Galilean insurrections in the Temple. See *Jesus and the Zealots. A Study of the Political Factor in Primitive Christianity* (Manchester: Manchester University Press, 1967). By contrast, many scholars seem simply to assume that Jesus was a pacifist, and that his contemporaries saw him as such. See, for example, E. P. Sanders's description of what Jesus did in the Temple in *Jesus and Judaism* (Philadelphia: Fortress, 1985) 61–76. He blandly remarks that, single-handed, "Jesus overturned some tables as a demonstrative act" (p. 70), as if the merchants and the police would calmly have looked on. On Judas the Galilean and the strains within Judaism he represented, see Richard Horsley and John S. Hanson, *Bandits, Prophets, and Messiahs* (San Francisco: Harper & Row, 1985); Martin Hengel, *The Zealots,* trans. D. Smith (Edinburgh: Clark, 1997).

Chapter Ten: The Sword of Rome

The unfortunate history of Sejanus is discussed in the ancient histories of Dio Cassius, Suetonius, and Tacitus, supported by other sources; see Barbara Levick, *Tiberius the Politician:* Aspects of Greek and Roman Life (London: Thames and Hudson, 1976); Charles Merivale, *History of the Romans Under the Empire* 5 (London: Longmans, Green, and Co., 1903); Robin Seager, *Tiberius* (Berkeley: University of California Press, 1972); David Shotter, *Tiberius Caesar:* Lancaster Pamphlets (London and New York: Routledge, 1992). For the relevance to Jesus of Sejanus' rise to power and eventual fall, see also Harold W. Hoehner, *Herod Antipas. A Contemporary of Jesus Christ* (Grand Rapids: Zondervan, 1980). A panoramic view of the political situation in which Caiaphas, Jesus, and Pilate all found themselves is provided by David Kennedy and Martin Goodman in their articles on Syria and Judea in *The Cambridge Ancient History* X (Cambridge: Cambridge University Press, 1996) 703–736, 737–781.

Chapter Eleven: "A Cave of Thugs"

See "Caiaphas," *The Anchor Bible Dictionary,* ed. D. N. Freedman and others; (New York: Doubleday, 1992) I:803–806, and the article on the other famous high priest in the New Testament, "Annas," I:257–258; Victor Eppstein, "The Historicity of the Gospel Account of the Cleansing of the Temple," *Zeitschrift für die neutestamentliche Wissenschaft* 55 (1964) 42–58. On the ossuary of Caiaphas, see Zvi Greenhut, "Burial Cave of the Caiaphas Family," *Biblical Archaeology Review* 18.5 (1992) 29–36, 76, and in the same issue Pieter W. van der Horst's survey of "Jewish Funerary Inscriptions," 46–48, 54–57. My reading of the ossuary itself is slightly different from that of Ronny Reich of the Israeli Antiquities Authority, and leads to my finding that one form of the name is Aramaic, and the other Hebrew. See Reich, "Caiaphas Name Inscribed on Bone Boxes," *Biblical Archaeology Review* 18.5 (1992) 38–44, 76. For further background, see Joachim Jeremias, *Jerusalem in the Time of Jesus,* trans. F. H. and C. H. Cave (London: SCM, 1969); E. P. Sanders, *Judaism. Practice and Belief 63 B.C.E.–66 C.E.* (London and Philadelphia: SCM and Trinity Press International, 1992).

For a full discussion of the half-shekel tax, see Chilton, "A Coin of Three Realms: Matthew 17:24–27," *The Bible in Three Dimensions. Essays in Celebration of Forty Years of Biblical Studies in the University of Sheffield:* Journal for the Study of the Old Testament, Supplement 87, ed. D.J.A. Clines, S. E. Fowl, S. E. Porter (Sheffield: JSOT, 1990) 269–282.

Chapter Twelve: At the Tomb of the Dead

For *Midrash Hashkem*'s bibliography, see H. L. Strack and G. Stemberger, *Introduction to the Talmud and Midrash,* trans. M. Bockmuehl (Edinburgh: Clark, 1991) 340. Scholarship in regard to the origins of the Kabbalah has been very active. My own work has greatly benefited from the contributions of Ithamar Gruenwald, *Apocalyptic and Merkavah Mysticism* (Leiden: Brill, 1980); Gershom Scholem, *Origins of the Kabbalah,* trans. Allan Arkush (Princeton: Jewish Publication Society and Princeton University Press, 1987); Moshe Idel, *Kabbalah. New Perspectives* (New Haven and London: Yale University Press, 1988); David Halperin, *The Faces of the Chariot. Early Jewish Responses to Ezekiel's Vision:* Texte und Studien zum Antiken Judentum 16 (Tübingen: Mohr, 1988); Peter Schäfer, *The Hidden and Manifest God. Some Major Themes in Early Jewish Mysticism:* SUNY Series in Judaica: Hermeneutics, Mysticism, and Religion, trans. Aubrey Pomerance (Albany: State University of New York Press, 1992); Elliot R. Wolfson, *Circle in the Square. Studies in the Use of Gender in Kabbalistic Symbolism* (Albany: State University of New York Press, 1995). In all such studies, however, it is vital to keep in mind an observation of Cecil Roth's that appears in his brief article in the *Encyclopedia Judaica* 10 (Jerusalem: Keter, 1972) 653–654: "Today the term Kabbalah is used for the mystic and esoteric doctrine of Judaism (see previous entry). The mystical connotation is unknown in the Talmud."

The remark is all the more telling when it is borne in mind that the "previous entry" is a magisterial treatment of Jewish mysticism from the twelfth century onward by none other than Gershom Scholem, then acknowledged (and still acknowledged by many scholars today) as the master of the entire field. What Roth called our attention to, with the power of his editorship of the *Encyclopedia Judaica,* is that the literary and specialist usage of the term *kabbalah* today is too limited to allow us to understand its ancient usage, where it refers to a tradition carefully received. Indeed, the verb *qabal* means to receive (as in the case of an oral tradition). Paul uses just this language to speak of what he "received" from the apostles before him: the tradition of Jesus' resurrection (1 Corinthians 15:3).

Chapter Thirteen: King of the Jews

A full study of the development of the various texts relating the Eucharist in the New Testament is available in Chilton, *A Feast of Meanings. Eucharistic Theologies from Jesus Through Johannine Circles*: Supplements to *Novum Testamentum* 72 (Leiden: Brill, 1994). Treatment of the Judaic meals that are the foundation of Christian practice is also available there, but a quick review of the materials is available in two fine articles: "Grace" by Cecil Roth in the *Encyclopedia Judaica* 7 (Jerusalem: Keter, 1972) 838–841, and "Chaver, Chaverim" in the same volume, 1489–1492. (The latter appears with a dot beneath the initial "h," rather than "ch," as has become the academic fashion.) The article "Kiddush" is beautifully developed and illustrated by Aaron Rothkoff in *Encyclopedia Judaica* 10 (Jerusalem: Keter, 1972) 974–977, and there is an extraordinary conspectus of the issues involved available in Kaufman Kohler, "Benedictions," *The Jewish Encyclopedia* 3 (New York: Funk and Wagnalls, 1910) 8–12. The study of Mithraism is still served well by the classic work of Franz Cumont, *The Mysteries of Mithra,* trans. T. S. McCormack (New York: Dover, 1956), although the field is in considerable ferment; see David Ulansey, *The Origins of the Mithraic Mysteries. Cosmology and Salvation in the Ancient World* (New York: Oxford University Press, 1989).

Chapter Fourteen: The Kabbalah of Crucifixion

Arimathea is mentioned by Josephus (*Antiquities* 13 § 127), and may have been the birthplace of the prophet Samuel (*Antiquities* 5 § 342); that might help to explain Joseph's enthusiasm for a prophetic figure such as Jesus.

Notes

Acts 23:8 asserts that the "Sadducees" (that is, the Zadokites) deny resurrection altogether, and that is also the judgment of Josephus. I have argued that despite these unequivocal statements (or rather, precisely because they are so unequivocal), we should be cautious about what the Zadokites denied; see *The Temple of Jesus*, 82 (cited in the notes to chapter 2). The Sadducees' position is attributed to them only by unsympathetic observers, such as Josephus (*War* 2 §§ 165–166) and various Christians (Mark 12:18–27; Matthew 22:23–33; Luke 20:27–38; Acts 23:6–8). The emphasis of the Zadokites was in all probability just what was promised in the Torah: prosperity here and now (not only in the resurrection) in exchange for faithful sacrifice. As a still valuable (although dated) description of ancient Judaism, see George Foot Moore, *Judaism in the First Centuries of the Christian Era* (Cambridge: Harvard University Press, 1962). Professor Moule's brief but classic article explores "Neglected Features in the Problem of 'the Son of Man,'" *Essays in New Testament Interpretation* (Cambridge: Cambridge University Press, 1982) 75–90. For Jesus' characteristic attitude toward Scripture, see Chilton, *A Galilean Rabbi and His Bible* (cited in the notes to chapter 5), and the use of this model in Freyne, *Galilee, Jesus and the Gospels* (cited in the notes to chapter 7), 204–5, 253, 256.

John Dominic Crossan, "The Dogs Beneath the Cross," *Jesus. A Revolutionary Biography* (San Francisco: HarperSanFrancisco: 1994) 123–158 adapts Alfred Loisy's theory, now translated in *The Birth of the Christian Religion*, trans. L. P. Jacks (New Hyde Park: University Books, 1962) 89–91.

My own approach to the resurrection of Jesus has been stimulated by Marianne Sawicki's *Seeing the Lord. Resurrection and Early Christian Practices* (Minneapolis: Fortress, 1994), although a visionary analysis is already represented in the work of a scholar who was later to become Archbishop of Canterbury, A. Michael Ramsay: *The Resurrection of Christ* (Philadelphia: Westminster, 1946). The philosophical challenges of speaking of resurrection at all are elegantly surveyed in Richard R. Niebuhr, *Resurrection and Historical Reason* (New York: Scribner's,

1957), and recent discussion, enriched by an awareness of cultural anthropology, has demonstrated what a complex category "body" can be in this context; see Caroline Walker Bynum, *The Resurrection of the Body in Western Christianity, 200–1336:* Lectures on the History of Religions 15 (New York: Columbia University Press, 1995). Gerd Luedemann's *The Resurrection of Jesus,* trans. J. Bowden (Minneapolis: Fortress, 1994) represents the modern attempt to grapple with the issue exegetically, while the world of quantum physics is opening up possibilities of description that I very much hope will be pursued; see Paul Davies, *Other Worlds* (New York: Simon and Schuster, 1982).

For a translation of the Gospel According to the Hebrews, see E. Hennecke, *New Testament Apocrypha,* ed. W. Schneemelcher, trans. R. McL. Wilson (London: SCM, 1963) 165. The Latin text is available in Joannis Martianaie, *Sancti Eusebii Hieronymi* 2: Patrologiae Latinae 23 (Paris: Garnier, 1883) 641–644. For contacts between Jerusalem and Antioch, see Wayne A. Meeks and Robert L. Wilkins, *Jews and Christians in Antioch in the First Four Centuries of the Common Era* (Atlanta: Scholars Press, 1978).

Acknowledgments

By dedicating this book to those who have taught me, I am admitting to a debt that I cannot repay. My teachers have been senior academics, personal tutors, and advisers, the eyes of attentive men, women, and children who have heard me out (and read my work) as I have attempted for almost three decades to discern the biography behind the icon which is Jesus. I cannot even name them all, although they know who they are. What they have shown me is that there is life inside the texts and evidence, which we can feel anew if only we pay attention, not merely to what they say but to where they come from and how they reflect the experience of those who followed Jesus at the dawn of Christianity.

Putting my scholarship into this story has involved departing from the conventions of the academy, but that is necessary if Jesus is to be a life in our thinking as well as an image. That departure has been a part of my own thinking for some time, but it would never have come to text without the active suggestion and prodding and quiet, wise insistence of my personal editor, Kenneth Wapner. He has been to me both rabbi and *meturgeman,* and if this book is as accessible as we intend, that is his contribution more than anyone's. A fellowship from the Pew Charitable Trusts freed me from other responsibilities in order to undertake this project.

Acknowledgments

Ken made the introduction to my agent, Gail E. Ross, whose confidence and advocacy saw me through the fascinating meetings I enjoyed with many editors and publishers. Each of the interviews provided the intensity one associates with a graduate seminar, with perhaps a bit more vim (and just about everyone had done the reading!). That world was new to me, and Gail is the best guide I could have hoped for. In crafting the proposal itself, Howard Yoon provided invaluable editorial advice.

The manuscript itself benefited enormously from the comments of many of my colleagues. Jacob Neusner, now also of Bard College and Bard's Institute of Advanced Theology, gave the work a detailed reading, and helped me to shape the conception of the book. Ithamar Gruenwald's extraordinary learning, especially in the fields of Jewish mysticism and Gnosticism, was brought to bear at formative moments. Marianne Sawicki offered the resources of her expertise in cognitive archaeology. In addition, careful scrutiny by many colleagues and friends—including Frederick H. Borsch, John Dominic Crossan, Craig Evans, Harry Kelly, Bernhard Lang, Jack Miles, John W. Rogerson, John Shelby Spong, and Michelle Syverson—influenced the presentation.

My editors at Doubleday Broadway, principally Eric Major and Andrew Corbin, have been both supportive and unrelenting in their dedication to the concept that animates *Rabbi Jesus*. In the early going, Mark Fretz also made seminal suggestions, and Siobhan Dunn has made sense of my proposals for illustrations.

The illustrations themselves were made available to me through the good offices (and considerable work of providing contact information) by the Biblical Archaeology Society, which also authorized my use of images from *Biblical Archaeology Review*. My thanks go especially to Hershel Shanks, Steven Feldman, and Lyn Taecker. Discussion with those who provided the illustrations went well beyond simply giving permissions, and I am grateful for my conversations with Yael Barschak and Yitzhak Magen of the Israel Antiquities Authority, Claudio Bottini of the Studium Biblicum Franciscanum, Mark Fretz at Doubleday, Bella Gershovich of The Israel Museum, Amihai Mazar of the Hebrew University's Institute of Archaeology, Zev Radovan, Leen Ritmeyer, and James F. Strange.

Why do authors feel the need to say that faults in their efforts are their own? I suppose the habit betrays the inverse vanity of going one's own way in a sea of wise advice. If so, few navigators have enjoyed the quality of counsel that has guided me in plotting the course I have charted here.

General Index

(Page numbers in italics refer to illustrations)

General Index

Houses
  Galilean, 75, 86
  in Jerusalem, *114–15*
  "Peter's House," *86, 127*
Humility, 278
Hunger, 135–36

Immersion, Jewish practice of, 27, 30,
    44–46, 48
Immersion pools. *See* Baths, purifying
Inferences, xxi
Isaiah, 149, 279
Israel, map of, *66*
Italy, 74n

Jairus, 178
  daughter, 179
James (brother of Jesus)
  authority in the congregation, 15–16, 284
  at Joseph's funeral, 21–22
  as a Nazirite, 284, 299
  relationship with Jesus, 42, 72, 78, 95,
    202, 283
  sacrificing in the Temple, 25–26, 202n
  timeline, xv, xvi
James (son of Halphayah), 175
James (son of Zebedee)
  called by Jesus, 125, 142
  close disciple of Jesus, 179, 190, 191,
    192
  death of, 129
  as Jesus' delegate, 174
Jannaeus, Alexander, 121
Javelins, 267, 268
Jeremiah, 149, 279
Jericho, 40
Jerome, 283
Jerusalem, xiii, xiv, xv, xvi, 34–35, *38–39, 114*
Jesus
  Characteristics
    authority, 118–19
    bipolar tendency, 104
    as the bread of life, 36
    clothing, 75, 179, 179n
    compassion, 35–36, 135–36
    as a compromiser, 70
    as David's son, 200–201
    as deranged, 95
    forgiving sins, 110
    as Galilean firebrand, 119–20, 180

    Galilean traits, 104
    irregular birth of, 5–8, 12–13
    as lamb of God, 57, 58
    as light of the world, 122
    mamzer, 15–16, 295
    as Messiah, 100–2, 188–89
    as militant prophet, 189, 199–200
    physical characteristics, 47, 104, 138,
      183, 193, 225
    as a prophet, 54–55
    as a prophet and revolutionary, 151
    as a rabbi, 109–10, 296
    sexuality, 145
    as Son of God, 17–18, 58n, 191–92
    speech accent, 43
    supernatural control, 111
    xenophobia, 181
  Events (in chronological order)
    birth of, xv, 6
    circumcision, 3, 4, 9–10, 10–12
    childhood, 16–17, 18
    apprentice to Joseph, 20
    excluded from Joseph's funeral, 21, 22
    pilgrimage to Jerusalem, 23–40
    at the Temple, 32
    adolescence and young adulthood,
      33–34
    exploring Jerusalem, 34–37
    searching for John the Baptist, 37, 40
    approaching John the Baptist, 41–43
    learning about Spirit, 53–54
    Spirit descending upon as dove, 55–58
    accepting hospitality, 59–60
    returning to Galilee, 64–73
    meeting the Samaritan woman, 67–69
    of marriageable age, 72–73
    teaching in Nazareth, 73–74
    working as a journeyman, 74–76
    practicing festive celebration, 76–78
    conflict with Pharisees, 85–87
    exorcisms, 92–93, 94–95, 96–97,
      147–48, 168–71
    in Capernaum, 95–97
    paraphrasing Isaiah in the synagogue,
      98–101
    in Jerusalem for Sukkoth, 103–6
    healing lame man at Bethesda, 108–9
    rabbi to Cypriots, 114–15
    calling disciples in Capernaum, 125,
      128
    healing in Capernaum, 130, 131–32
    popularity in Capernaum, 131

General Index

retreating to wilderness, 132–33
receiving foot washing from sinful
 woman, 133–34
public speaker in Capernaum, 134–35
crisscrossing Galilee and Syria, 150
calming the storm, 154–56
asleep in boat, 160
at Bethsaida, 161–64
healing the centurion's servant, 165–66
in Decapolis, 168–71
avoiding Roman cities, 171
sending twelve disciples as delegates,
 174–79
touched by unclean woman, 179
healing Jairus' daughter, 179
at wedding in Kana, 183–85
retreating to wilderness, 185–86
feeding thousands, 186–89
Transfiguration, 191–94, 274
tempted by Satan, 194
considering military conquest, 194
walking on water, 195
restoring the widow's dead son, 200
focusing on sacrifice, 202
preparing to face danger, 212
purifying the Temple, 225–30
festal entry in Jerusalem, 226–27
refusing to leave the vicinity of
 Jerusalem, 234–35
seeking immersion in God, 235
debating at Chanuth, 236–39, 242–43
reviving Lazarus, 244–46
anointed during a meal for burial, 249–50
at Gethsemane, 258
arrest of, 258–60
interrogations of, 260–61
beaten and crucified, 265–68
burial, 269–70
resurrection, 272–76, 273n, 281–85
legacy, 290–92
Relationships (*see also* Disciples of Jesus)
 Caiaphas, 224, 258
 Gentiles, 166
 John the Baptist, 33–34, 37, 40,
  41–43, 49, 58–60, 63, 69–70
 mother (*see* Mary)
 non-Jews, 166, 181–82
 outcasts, 136
 siblings, 23, 72, 78, 166, 168, 295 (*see
  also* James)
Teaching/views
 apocalypse, 199

banquets, wealthy Jewish, 80, 82
Chariot, 52–53, 55, 161–62, 163,
 242–43, 289
crucifixion, 276–81
debt, 79–80
and Galilean oral traditions, 20
hardship as gateway to vision, 242, 243
healing on Shabbath, 117–18
and Judaism, xix, 148, 291
kabbalah, 192–93
Kingdom of God, 18, 22, 84, 197–98
Last Supper, 250–56
love, 134, 243
marriage in heaven, 237
money, 78–79
nonresistance, 46
parables in Nazareth, 93–94
people made in God's image, 242–43
piety, displays of, 138–40
prayers, 22, 59, 76–77, 195
purity, 59–60, 68–69, 70, 85–90, 96,
 136–37
repentance, 48–49
repentance and forgiveness, 49–50
resurrection, 275–76
rituals, 44–46
status, 83–84
style of employing Scripture, 101
taxes, 201–2, 238–39
Temple, 231
Torah, 140–42
Zechariah's influence on, 105–6,
 198–200, 225–28
Jesus (Yeshua ben Ananias), 260
Jesus Seminar, xix, 293
Joanna, 144
John (disciple of Jesus)
 apocryphal stories concerning, 129, 129n
 called by Jesus, 125, 142
 closeness to Jesus, 179, 190, 191, 192
 delegate of Jesus, 174
John Hyrcanus, xiv
John the Baptist
 Chariot mysticism, 50, 52
 condemning Herod's marriage, 61
 death of, 61–62, 64n
 described by Josephus, 43–44
 as Elijah, 188
 fame, 72
 as guru, 53
 mishnah of, 49
 program of immersion, 44, 45, 47–48

General Index

as prophet, 54–55
on purity, 65
as rabbi, 296
relationship with Jesus, 33–34, 37, 40,
    41–43, 49–50, 58–60
on repentance, 48
on Spirit, 53–54
timeline, xv
See also Disciples of John the Baptist
Jordan River Valley, 40, 64
Joseph (father to Jesus)
  children from first marriage, 14
  death of, 20–22, 20n
  first marriage, 6n, 295
  occupation, 6, 6n
  paternity of Jesus, 5, 15
  possessions, 14
  residing in Nazareth, 13–14
  role in Jesus' circumcision, 9
Joseph Barnabas. *See* Barnabas (Joseph)
Joseph of Aramithea, 269, 270
Josephus, 43–44, 202n
Joses, 23, 72, 78
Joshua, 4
Joshua ben Chananiah, 275
Journeyworkers' feasts, 74–75, 76
Judah of Karioth. *See* Judas Iscariot
Judaism
  and Christianity, xxi, 21, 171, 193–94,
    252–53
  and Jesus, xix, 148, 291
  and Roman Empire, 207–12
Judas (Galilean revolutionary), 238n
Judas (son of Hezekiah), 90, 186
Judas Iscariot, 142, 175, 255, 257, 259
Judas Maccabeus, xiv
Judas "the Twin," 142, 246
Judeans, 4, 15, 105, 206
Julian of Norwich, 37
Julius Caesar, xiv
Jung, Carl, 146

Kabbalah, 175, 306–7
Kana, 64, 182–83
Kidron Valley, 258
King, Martin Luther, Jr., 46
Kingdom of God
  belonging to Israel, 137
  end of history and, 116, 198–99
  Galilean hope, 5, 19
  Jesus' teachings on, 18, 21–22, 84, 197–98

nearness of, 37
Kleopas, 175
Koine Greek, 62, 232

Last Supper, 252–57
Latifundium, 79
Lazarus, 244–46
Legion (of demons), 169–71
Leper, cleansing of, 87–90
Levi (Matthew), 142, 175
Levites, 112
Lineage, importance of, 14–16
Livia-Julia, 161
Livilla, 240
Logical reconstruction, xxi
Lord's Prayer, 22, 59, 59n, 77, 195
Love, 134, 243

Maccabees, xiv, 119, 159, 208
Machaerus, 61, 62, 63
Madman, Jesus exorcising, 168–70
Magdala, 78, 80
Mammon, 78
Mamzer caste, 12–13, 14–15, 81
Mantras, 52
Map of Israel, 66
Marriage, 72–73, 182–84
  in heaven, 237
Martha, 25, 235–36, 244, 245
Martyrdom, 279, 280
Mary (mother of Jesus)
  children, 23, 72, 78, 166, 168, 295 (*see
    also* James)
  familiarity with Jesus' teachings, 42
  household duties, 18, 75
  importance of Jesus' circumcision to, 12
  participation in Joseph's funeral, 21–22
  relationship with Jesus, 72, 103
  seclusion after Jesus' birth, 11–12
  virginity, 5–8, 295
Mass, 250–56
Matthew (Levi), 142, 175
Mediterranean Sea, 74n
Meier, John P., 294–95
Messiah, 100–2
Mind and body, 111
Miriam. *See* Mary (mother of Jesus)
Miriam (disciples' mother), 269
Miriam (sister of Martha), 25, 235–36, 244,
  245

General Index

Miriam of Magdala
  anointing Jesus, 249–50
  demons of, 144–45, 146
  and Jesus' resurrection, 273–74, 282–83
  preparing Jesus for burial, 269
  relationship with Jesus, 145
Miriam of Yaaqov, 273
Mishnah, 49, 175
Mithra, 251
Money, 78
Moon, 56
Moses, 55, 152n, 191, 192
Mount Gerizim, 65, 67
Mount Hermon, 190–91, 194
Mount Lebanon. *See* Mount Hermon
Muhammad, 55
Musicians, professional, 82
Mustard plant parable, 18
Mystery cults, 251

Nadab, 191
Nathanael, 58n, 64, 67, 68, 69, 71, 175
Nazareth, 71
Nazirites, 284, 299
Nebuchadnezzar, 15
Nephesh, 288
Nero, 210n, 290
Neusner, Jacob, 298
Nicodemus, 120, 269, 270
Nonresistance, 46
Numerological traditions, 187n

Octavian (Augustus), xiv, 153, 153n
Oil, 133n
Olive oil, 133
"One like the person," 157–58, 160,
    171–72, 183
Original sin, 48
Ossuary of Caiaphas, *214*
Outcasts, 136

Palatial Mansion, *114*–15
Palimpsest, 158
Paradise, 164
Paralysis, 108–9, 111, 131–32
Passion Week, 248–49, 249n
Passover, 23–24, 249n, 255–56
Paul (Saul), xv, xvi, 284–85
Pentecost, feast of, 23–24, 282

Persians, 15
Pesach. *See* Passover
Peter. *See* Simon Peter
"Peter's House," 86, 127
Pharisees
  on foreign rule, 238
  immersion pools, 30, 45
  overseeing Temple sacrifices, 218, 220–21
  power of, 121
  on purity, 84–87, 89–90
  regulations, 116–18
  on resurrection, 275
  in the Sanhedrin, 219–20
Philip (disciple)
  hometown, 64, 128, 131, 153
  with Jesus, 71
  as Jesus' delegate, 175
  with the Samaritan woman, 67, 68, 69
Philip (Herod Philip), xiv, 161, 190
Pilate. *See* Pontius Pilate
Pilgrimages, 23–24
Politics and religion, 19
Pompey, xiv, 106
Pontius Pilate
  authorizing way to Golgotha, 265n
  characteristics, 204
  collaborating with Caiaphas and Antipas,
      241–42, 262–64
  death of, 287n
  fall from power, 287
  interrogation of Jesus, 268n
  on Jesus' death, 268, 270
  portrayal in Gospels, 263n, 264n
  reinforcing Rome's claim on the Temple,
      210–12, 224
  slaughtering Samaritan rebels, 152
  timeline, xv
  warrior-bureaucrat, 205, 206, 207, 213
Pool of Bethesda, 107–9, 107n, 300
Poverty, 135–36
Priestly residence, *114*
Pritchard, E. E. Evans, 253
Prodigal son parable, 63, 71–72
Prophets, 151–53
Prostitution, 136n
Psalms, 84
Ptolemies, xiv
Purity
  of Galileans, 77
  of Israel, 185
  Jesus' view of, 59–60, 68–69, 85–90, 134,
      136–37

General Index

Spirit, 53–58, 68, 145, 288, 297
  See also Wisdom
Stars, 56
Stephen, xv
Stoning, xv, 102
Strange, James F., 97
Strangulation, 239–40
Suffering, 276–81
Sukkoth festival
  future ultimate, 198
  Galileans and, 23–24
  huts, 104–5
  and Jesus' festal entry, 226–27
  sacrifices and offerings, 105, 107,
    214–15, 217
Sun, 56
Susanna, 144
Swine, 170
Sychar, 67
Synagogues, 96, *97, 126,* 165n, 208
Syria, 185
Syriac Christianity, 129
Syrians, 81, 219
Syro-Phoenician woman, 181

Tabernacles, feast of. *See* Sukkoth festival
Talmidim, 43
Talmud, 17, 74
Tamid, 105
Tammuz, 81
Targums, xviii, 4–5
Tax collectors, 81, 136n
Taxes, 201–2, 238–39
Taylor, Joan E., 296–97
Teeth, 11
Temple
  altar, xiv, 32, 216, 217
  baths, 27, 30
  building of, xiii, 65
  Caiaphas's control of, 224
  clubbing near, 212
  description and activities, 26–32, 216–19
  destruction of, xvi, 193, 210n
  freedom of worship, 209
  guards, 27
  illustration, *28–29, 38–39*
  and the imperial insignia, 210
  Jesus purifies the, 225–30
  magnificence of, 24
  portents of demise, 286
  taxes, 201–2

treasury confiscated by Pilate, 211
  See also Sacrifices and offerings
Thaddeus, 175
Theudas, 152
Thomas, 175, 282
Throne of God. *See* Chariot (Throne of God) mysticism
Tiberias, 91
Tiberius (Emperor), 91, 205, 239
Timeline, xiii-xv
Titus, xvi
Torah, 140–42
Trachonitis, 189
Transfiguration, 191–94, 274
Trinity, 172, 191–92
Turban envy, 112

Uncleanness, 170
  See also Purity
Unclean spirits, 90
  See also Exorcisms

Varus, 91, 206
Vespasian, 210n
Via Dolorosa, 265n
Virgin birth, 5–8
Vitellius, 287

Weddings, 182–84, 182n
Weeks, feast of. *See* Pentecost
Weiss, Johannes, 54n
Wilderness retreats, 132–33, 185–86
Wisdom, 145–46
  See also Spirit
Women
  as disciples, 144, 236, 237–38
  dress of non-Jews, 27
  seclusion of, 12
  treatment by Jesus, 184

Yeshua, 4
Yom Kippur. *See* Day of Atonement

Zadokites, 45, 84, 112, 237, 275, 308
Zedekiah, 15
Zeus, xiv

Sources Index

SCRIPTURE

Sources Index

27:50...267, 281
27:51...286
27:55...267
27:57–60...269
28:1–15...273n
28:16–20...282n
Mark
1:4...48
1:6...47
1:8...53
1:9–11...55
1:15...125
1:16–20...125, 131
1:17...125
1:21–28...97
1:29–31...130
1:31...130
1:35...131
1:35–37...132
1:36, 39...131
1:40...89
1:40–45...87
1:41–44...89
2:1–12...132
2:13–17, 18–22...142
2:23–26...200–1
3:1–19...93n
3:6...180
3:16–17...175
3:13–19...143
3:17, 18–19...142
3:20–21...93, 94, 95
3:20–30...147
3:21...303
3:23–29...147
3:31–35...166
4:1–9...135
4:24...52
4:26–29...94
4:35–41...154–55
4:37–41...156
5:1–13...168–70
5:1–20...168
5:17...171
5:21–24...178
5:30, 31, 33...179
5:33–43...179
6:3...6, 6n, 20, 23, 72
6:8, 9...177
6:11...180
6:14–29...61
6:15...151
6:17–29...62

6:29...63
6:30–44...186
6:47–51...195
6:53–56...178
6:56...179n
7:15...87, 136, 177
7:24–30...181
7:28...181
7:31–37...130
8:1–10...187n
8:22–26...130
8:27–30...190
8:28...151
8:31–33...276
8:34–38...242
8:35...70
8:35–38...277
9:1–13...191
9:5–6...192, 296
9:8...191
9:33–37...278
9:47–48...163–64
10:13–16...278
10:13–31...242
10:14...180
10:35–45...129
10:51... 296
11:1–10...226
11:10...227
11:11...228
11:16...229
11:17...228, 231
11:20–24...180, 296
11:27–33...118–19
12:13–17...238
12:17...238
12:18–27...237, 308
12:24–27...275
12:28–34...243
13:1–2...256
14:2...248
14:3–9...249
14:9...250
14:10–11...255
14:12–16...249n
14:13–15...255
14:18–25...257
14:22, 24...254
14:27–31...262
14:32–42...258
14:43–52...259, 296
14:48–49...259
14:53–72...260

Sources Index

14:56–59...260
14:61–64...261
14:66–72...262
15:1–15...263n
15:2–5...268n
15:6–15...264
15:7...228
15:6–15...264
15:16–20...265
15:21... 266
15:22–24...266
15:23...267
15:25...266
15:26...268
15:27–37...267
15:32...267
15:34...267, 281
15:37...267, 281
15:38...286
15:40...267, 269
15:42–46...269
15:44...268
15:47...269
16:1–8...273
Luke
1:5–80...49
1:35, 46–55...12n
2:41–52...16, 32
2:49...32
2:51–52...33
3:3...48
3:10-11...53
3:11...47
3:16...53
3:19–20...61, 62
3:21–22...55
3:23...33
4...300
4:1–13...194
4:16–30...98–102
4:31–37...96
4:38–39...130
4:40–41, 42...131
5:1–11...125
5:4–8...128
5:12–16...87
5:17–26...132
5:27–32, 33–39...142
6:1–4...200.
6:12–16...143
6:14–16...175
6:20–22...135
6:27–36...243

6:31–36...138
6:34–35...141
7:1–10...165
7:5...165
7:6–8...165–66
7:9...166
7:11–17...200
7:24–28...188
7:28...69
7:31–33...16
7:34...95
7:35...144
7:36–50...133
7:38...133
7:47, 48, 50...134
8:1–3...144
8:2...144
8:4–8...135
8:22–25...154–55
8:26–39...168
8:40–42...178
8:44...179n
8:49–56...179
9:3...177
9:5...180
9:7–9...61, 149
9:8...151
9:10–17...186
9:18–21...190
9:19...151
9:21–22...276
9:23–26...242, 277
9:27–36...191
9:46–48...278
9:58...124, 172
10:1...143
10:4, 8...177
10:13–15...180
10:18...176
10:19...176
10:21...118
10:25–28...243
10:30–37...40
10:40–42...236
11:2...18
11:2–4...22, 59n, 77
11:14–33...147
11:20...93, 147
11:23...147
11:37–40...85
11:49...146, 151
11:49–51...279
11:52...292

326

OTHER ANCIENT SOURCES

Sources Index